Tracking

the

Caribou

Queen

"This is a brave, unsparing story by a gifted writer with her eyes wide open to Canada's hypocrisies. Can we find the courage to look at our own hometowns with Margaret Macpherson's unflinching gaze? She insists we try."

— LINDA GOYETTE, co-author with Kathleen Steinhauser and Nellie Carlson of *Disinherited Generations: Our Struggle to Reclaim Treaty Rights for First Nations Women and Their Descendants*

"Macpherson uses a deft touch to write about the unintended racism she participated in as a child and teenager in Yellowknife, NWT. From sweetly touching to intensely honest, this memoir takes a hard look at the author's complicity in perpetuating stereotypes about Indigenous Peoples in Canada."

— RHONDA KRONYK, contributor to *In This Together* and editor of *Gather*

"Margaret Macpherson's memoir invites us all to reckon with our own stories of white privilege, entitlement, and racism, so we may participate fully in undoing the paternalism, misogyny, and patriarchy that have shaped and benefitted all colonizing peoples. You will be deeply moved as you read Macpherson's disturbingly real, honest, raw, searingly sad, and finally hopeful story."

— NAOMI MCILWRAITH, author of *kiyâm*

Margaret Macpherson

TRACKING THE CARIBOU QUEEN

Memoir of a Settler Girlhood

NeWest Press

Library and Archives Canada Cataloguing in Publication
Title: Tracking the Caribou Queen : memoir of a settler girlhood / Margaret Macpherson.
Names: Macpherson, Margaret (Margaret A.), author.
Identifiers: Canadiana (print) 20210378875 | Canadiana (ebook) 20210378999 | ISBN 9781774390610 (softcover) | ISBN 9781774390627 (EPUB)
Subjects: LCSH: Macpherson, Margaret (Margaret A.) | LCSH: Macpherson, Margaret (Margaret A.)—Childhood and youth. | LCSH: Yellowknife (N.W.T.)—Race relations—History—20th century. | LCSH: Yellowknife (N.W.T.)—Ethnic relations—History—20th century. | CSH: Authors, Canadian (English)—Biography. | LCGFT: Autobiographies.
Classification: LCC PS8625.P54 Z46 2022 | DDC C813/.6—dc23

NeWest Press wishes to acknowledge that the land on which we operate is Treaty 6 territory and a traditional meeting ground and home for many Indigenous Peoples, including Cree, Saulteaux, Niitsitapi (Blackfoot), Métis, and Nakota Sioux.

Editor for the Press: Jennifer Bowering Delisle
Cover and interior design: Natalie Olsen
Cover images © Iurii Stepanov and Gagat55 / Shutterstock.com
Author photo: Dan Hogan

NeWest Press acknowledges the support of the Canada Council for the Arts, the Alberta Foundation for the Arts, and the Edmonton Arts Council for support of our publishing program. We acknowledge the financial support of the Government of Canada through the Canada Book Fund for our publishing activities.

#201, 8540-109 Street
Edmonton, Alberta T6G 1E6
www.newestpress.com

No bison were harmed in the making of this book.
Printed and bound in Canada 22 23 24 25 5 4 3 2

In memory of JEM, luminous still,
and for Daylin, Walker and Elizabeth,
our future

CONTENTS

AUTHOR'S NOTE

Tracking the Caribou Queen has been more than a decade in the making. Begun as a personal reconciliation project to more honestly understand the role race and privilege played in my foundational thinking, the work predictably morphed into a multi-layered examination of my past, my psyche, and the insidious ways systemic racism shaped my youth in Yellowknife, Northwest Territories, during the '60s and '70s. *Tracking the Caribou Queen* was painful to write.

The language in this text, offensive now, is the language of the times. For some, the material presented may trigger painful and unprocessed memories. It is not my intention to hurt or retraumatize any community of readers, but rather to reveal how my thinking about Indigeneity in those days was warped by stereotype, prejudice, and white privilege.

Uncomfortable as it was to face my own part in Canada's colonization of Indigenous Peoples, I believed that my way forward lay in telling my own experience as truthfully as I could. All of the events in this book are recounted in varying degrees of acuity and precision. In some instances, I have shaped chronology, geography, and identity to serve the story. I have changed names; melded the lives of two or more real people into one character; and altered gender, age, and even ethnicity to protect innocent people. My early life was intertwined with others, many of whom may be profoundly uncomfortable having their lives projected on these pages though the lens of a child, and later a teenager, sorting out her own issues of personal culpability. It is these people I endeavour to protect.

The book's adolescent love story is shaped by the intense longing of a lonely teenage girl. As such, I believe it is, at its heart, true.

Public figures, including my much beloved father, who spent the majority of his educational career in the Territories, have remained relatively unaltered. The attitudes of these men (and some women) were shaped by a different time and sensibility. My intention is neither to shame nor humiliate them, but rather to illuminate the systemic racism inherent in the settler experience and illustrate the trickle-down effect on subsequent generations based on entrenched ideas of paternalism, misogyny, and patriarchy.

I am, by no means, an expert on northern colonization, assimilation policy, or federal educational initiatives. Indeed, I would encourage white readers to further their own understanding of the impact of colonization by reading accounts from an Indigenous perspective.

This writing is drawn from my lived, individual experience. I feel compelled to own my whiteness — not good, not bad, just a fact — as much as I acknowledge and hold myself accountable for the missteps and mistakes that came from my generation and the generation before mine. My hope is that readers, be they Indigenous or settler, recognize aspects of their own lives in this work.

Colonizing people cannot begin to enable justice until we understand our place and agency in past injustices. In naming our participation, in owning the actions of the past, we can begin to take responsibility for our part in it. Only then can we make way for a right and equitable future as true Treaty People.

Margaret Macpherson
Edmonton, 2021

Vision

My mother fumbled in her purse for a coin to start Brownie the mechanical horse, tethered next to the large raven-proof garbage barrels inside the first storm doors of Bromley's Hardware.

"You did well."

"I didn't like the needle."

"No, I imagine not. Two cavities. What does that tell you?"

"More brushing." It came out *mo busing,* as the sparking fake-peppermint taste shaved off half my syllables. This — mandatory vaccinations and a dental checkup — was the price to pay if I wanted to go to school. Oh, and more than anything, I wanted to go to school. We had to take advantage of the dentist's twice-yearly fly-in visits.

As I straddled Brownie's body, the nickel down the slot became spurs, and he leapt to life. With his plastic back cold between my legs, I felt his hollowness. He was not Black Beauty from the book my sister Jennifer was reading aloud. Therefore, I wasn't sweet Lady Anne, the daring heroine who saved Beauty from a cruel master. Up there, ranging and bucking, I was hardly even me with half my face, my lower lip, and part of my nose dead and fleshy at the same time. My head lolled while my tummy summersaulted.

Brownie wound down, paralyzed mid-gallop, and I slid to the ground, reeling.

Now, my shivering mother wanted her hot cup of tea at the Miners Mess. We crossed the street and, with a gust of ice fog, blew through the double doors. My mother chose two green vinyl swirly stools at the horseshoe counter.

As she ordered, I watched a woman spooning tea into a plastic baby bottle. The woman was focused, blowing on the spoon, and occasionally testing the spoon-tea with her own mouth before adding it to the bottle.

My mother saw her, too.

"At least it's formula. I've seen them use Coffee-Mate."

Them.

"What is she doing?"

"Stretching. She's making the formula go farther."

"Farther from here?" What was Coffee-Mate?

My mother's little silver pot came in the exact same space her answers should fit, so while she fussed — she didn't believe in the little pots; tea was boiling water, steeped, milk first — I continued to watch the stretching.

The mother shook the bottle and put it behind her ear, a magician doing a trick. As she stood to leave, I saw in the hood of her parka a baby with shining eyes, a face like the missing sun. She was a plump, Ookpik pop-up with cherub cheeks and a stub nose, shiny with flow. Those glowing, darting eyes fixed on mine, and the baby's mouth drew in and out as she inhaled the bottle. The mother, standing now, cinched her parka around her waist. I saw through the fabric, a snug of a child, happily sucking as she straddled the broad back of her mother who moved across the café toward the doors. I wanted a baby like that. Or did I want to be a baby like that? I longed to be *them*.

There, the truth. I wanted to be other than myself. The dental medication likely helped. It loosened my imagination. It made me otherworldly in a way I hadn't felt before. I remember that encounter being in the middle of February, my family's fourth dark winter in Yellowknife. The season was stalled at its coldest, and Franklin Avenue was deserted. Outside it was too cold for snow, but in that peeking baby, I saw the sun for the briefest moment.

I think I tried to call out to them, that mother-child unit so uniquely bonded, but the freezing in my face wouldn't let me. The hot chocolate was a lukewarm riot, escaping my mouth, so I clamped my lips and turned on the stool, trying to track the parka-mother with my eyes. The swivelling added to my woolliness, and a quick revolution later, I toppled. Brownie might stampede. I think I covered my head with both arms. I was that gone.

My mother jerked me up and back on the stool. "Margaret. Get a hold of yourself." She used my whole name. Not Margie, not Marg. I had caused a scene and she hated scenes.

My mother pushed away her tea mug.

"Let's go."

As I moved my tongue in the thickened cave of my mouth, as my mother paid the bill, I saw the poster. It was in the vestibule of the café, pinned above a photograph showing a stack of winter tires. It was a drawing of the baby, but older. There was the parka hood, her bright eyes, the beaming smile.

"Who ... will ... be ..." I sounded out the letters but there were other large unpronounceable words.

"What does it say?"

"Caribou Carnival. Who will be the 1964 Caribou Queen?" Mother snorted.

But within, something surged and lurched, Brownie starting his gallop, again. Who will be the next Caribou Queen?

As we stepped out the iced-over doors of the Mess and crossed Franklin Avenue again, I decided I would be the next Caribou Queen. I was as certain of my new identity as I was of the dawning knowledge that I would never ride Brownie again.

I now understood the reason we were living in this dark, frozen territory. It was my Queendom. I had to learn it, and then I had to rule it.

⌇

Yellowknife's Caribou Carnival was a spring gathering of dog team races, foot and hand games, a broomball tournament, fire building, and tea boiling competitions. It took place on Franklin Avenue. Dressed in snowmobile suits or long parkas, my brothers and my older sister and I always watched from the snowbank curbs as women stacked wood and lit fires. We would try to get close, to warm up, but were waved off. And we'd dodge the men who shooed us away from the rows of chained huskies that were harnessed in tassels and flash for the day of festive running.

Everything was exciting, enlivened, but each year the crowning of the Caribou Queen topped the carnival. A girl from my town would be singled out and crowned in front of everyone — Ladies and Gentlemen, boys and girls, may I present the winner of the title Miss Caribou Queen to ... and next time it would be me mukluking across the plywood platform to receive — what? A sparkling tiara of ice crystals? Or, better yet, real antlers from a real caribou? Not plastic Brownie, a real caribou, a wild female, a Queen.

As my mother ushered me down the hill towards our car, I imagined myself with that crown on my head. The antler crown was heavy. The hearts of the people — that mass of unknown other people who wanted, needed, actually, a leader — were glad.

"Stop dawdling, Margie." Each word from my mother was a command encased in ice crystals, billowing clouds. Each syllable was part of the frost fort being built on her parka fur.

"I'm still frozen." I tried to keep my words warm. They sloshed around in my hot mouth, slightly slurred.

"It will be gone soon."

She stepped off the snow path and opened the driver's-side door of our car. "Get in. It will take a while to warm."

Fake leatherette crackled beneath my bottom, and the windshield fogged immediately with the energy of our bodies. My mother turned the key and we both waited. The engine caught on the second try. Everything was sluggish in this cold, the oil, the engine, the way words felt like meat in my mouth.

I gently touched my teeth together and heard a dulled click somewhere behind my ear. It reminded me of the baby deep in the parka, almost part of the mother, but not quite.

"That thing at the Mess. I could do that."

My mother was clapping her gloved hands together as if to hasten the warming of our car. "What thing?"

17

"The contest for the Queen, you know, the girl they pick at Carnival."

My mother stopped clapping. The heater wheezed and two little peepholes appeared at the bottom of the windshield where the wipers lay frozenly submissive. The holes grew as I spoke.

"I could be the Caribou Queen. I'd like to try. Do you know what I have to do?"

"Margie, that is *not* something you would like to do. It is a contest for others. It is not for you. Don't be ridiculous. What in God's name makes you think you could be the Caribou Queen?"

I turned to my passenger-side window, got close, and blew. A hole opened from my own peppermint cocoa breath. Outside I saw the winter world. Again, I imagined the black-eyed baby in the shadow pouch of her mother's parka. It was completely the opposite of the unbreachable distance I felt between my mother and me. No matter what she said, I *would* be the Caribou Queen.

I knew things. I knew caribou ran in large herds. My sister Jennifer told me in the olden days the Indian people here didn't even live in Yellowknife; they lived in the village across the ice. Our townsite was the place the caribou gathered, so the people would go there to hunt them. There were so many caribou back then, Jennifer said, a few didn't mind feeding the people. She told me every year the caribou migrated towards the barren lands in huge herds. They walked right through town; right down Franklin Avenue, before Bromley's even existed. She told me they went to a wild place called the tundra to have their babies.

The Queen must be their leader, like the Queen bee, but with hooves instead of wings. Was the Caribou Queen the one who directed them, told them which way to go, selected some of the herd to feed the people, and which of the cows would have babies? I thought of the lead caribou's words whispered into the wind, carried across the snow to the quivering ears of the herd. Would she tell them to run towards the hunters or away from them? How would she pick the ones who had to die to feed the people?

My mother twisted the steering wheel away from the curb and we headed towards home. Outside my window, through the little breath hole, I thought I saw a large white caribou loping alongside the car. The parka baby was straddling her back, sitting up straight like someone who wasn't a baby. One chubby arm was extended, her hand grasping the massive antler. Her other arm was cocked at the elbow, and her hand rested jauntily on her hip.

Both of them winked and smiled at me as we drove by.

Or that's what I think I saw. Memory canters behind my adult eyes, across the central cortex of my brain. *Whoa, Brownie, whoa.* Beware, beware the unreliable narrator. One sees what they want to see. The machinations of the imaginative mind are powerful, particularly when fuelled by diazepam or articaine, whatever the dental pain medication of the day was.

How do I tease out truth when what is true is completely entangled with unshakeable images so profoundly real, I can only believe them? Such was the caribou. Such was her rider.

Gold Range

My family moved to the Northwest Territories more than half a century ago. My father, a teacher, guidance counsellor, and vice principal from various small towns in British Columbia, had been offered a principal's job and first drove the Mackenzie Highway in 1961. This was the year the road snaked around the southeast arm of Great Slave Lake, embraced Behchokǫ̀, then called Fort Rae, and ultimately connected Yellowknife, population 2,800, to the outside world. He took my eldest brother Paul with him. When they arrived, my mother recalled, they were coated in a thick caul of dust from the 1,500-kilometre, three-day trip from Edmonton.

My mother had arrived at the Quonset hut airport a day and a half before, with four of her five children: Jennifer, almost eight, ostensibly minding four-year-old Will and two-and-a-half-year-old me, while Mother, still nursing, managed squawking Ned.

All of us were moli, white settlers entering Indigenous territory, but we had no idea what that word meant or why our act of entry was fraught.

⌇

Our house, provided by the Canadian government, wasn't ready, so we moved into the Gold Range Hotel, a building that squatted on one of the sloping roads that ran off Franklin Avenue, one of the four or five streets draining to the Lake. Humpbacked, the hotel sat right in the middle of the town. It was the second building erected in Yellowknife's New Town. The first building was the Veteran's Café, two prefab army huts skidded up the gnarly New Town hill in '46 by a man named Jacob Glick.

The landscape of my town can only be described as Precambrian Shield, but it is different from the more benign Eastern Manitoba or Northern Ontario shield country. This was rock. Massive, bald, glacial outcrops, more rock than soil, and everywhere, everywhere, scrub bush, black spruce, mosquitoes. The tundra is not far, though far, in that part of the underpopulated world, is a relative term.

The Gold Range used to be two bunkhouses abandoned when the Negus mine shut down years before. Those bunkhouses were dragged from the shore up the steep slope of the bedrock hill and planted atop Jack Glick's root cellar. Or at least that is the legend. One thing for sure, unlike the buildings in the Old Town, the Gold Range had modern conveniences: underground water and sewage lines, flush toilets, and electricity.

It is still there, a relic, a legend in modern Yellowknife.

The different rooflines of the two bunkhouses gave the hotel its haphazard look, a patched-together façade, the hasty assembly of an untrained carpenter. Clad in both brown clapboard and grey stucco, the lumpy hotel had three entrances, one to the bar, one to the café, and the other to the lobby. There, closest to the bar, was a dingy reception area, a low countertop, and a padded vinyl chair with the yellow stuffing coming out of the seat. A small push bell which made a tiny singular *ting* sat on the counter, but even if you pushed it, no one came. I know because when we first got there, I pushed the bell and waited. *Ting.*

The bar in the Gold Range was known among locals as The Strange Range or The Zoo. In its heyday, the '70s and '80s, the bar boasted live music on the weekends. With few windows, it was completely void of natural light. The plywood floor was punctuated by small, round, terry-cloth covered tables that floated around a central dance floor. At the back was the bar and the dartboards and bathrooms with their gaping stalls.

Memory is a grab bag. I've seen photos of the Gold Range prior to our arrival. It seems, in those early '50s photographs, snazzy, with perky waitresses ready to serve. That is not my recollection. Mine is more visceral, the building and its occupants more decrepit. My memories also include a great chasm between myself and anyone else who should happen through the doors of the local watering hole.

⌒〜

"Margie, I told you to use the bathroom before we came out." We were leaving the upper rooms of the hotel building, broaching the main floor. How did my mother know I'd forgotten?

"Stay put," she called to my siblings.

She took me by the shoulder, and we walked towards the back of the bar. The dartboards were eyes, bloodshot and judging: *Why didn't you pee-pee in the toilet on your own floor?* Just beyond, crouched low, porcelain toilets, but once inside I saw there were no doors on the stalls. Anyone could come in. The bathroom walls were filled with writing and pictures of tubes and orbs and one of a scary woman with big teeth eating a hot dog. She had a string of numbers underneath her picture.

I sat while my mother waited, arms crossed, but I was paralyzed by terror. What if someone came through the door? Without the protection of walls, I could not will myself to do what felt urgent just moments before.

We left eventually, unsuccessful, but when we came back later, I watched the bar from the safety of the lobby through a crack in the door. I listened while my mother took care of one of my siblings in the lobby room. I stood silently in the doorway watching the front of the bar, both curious and afraid.

Old women smoked pipes and wore flowered kerchiefs on their heads. They looked like grandmothers out of storybooks, happy and dancing and laughing and sweating and calling out to each other in Dogrib or English: "Hey, Joe, come dance with me, eh?" And the laughter spilled out past the spaces where their front teeth used to be and spread across the bar and seemed to fuel the music and the riotous whirl of people, all kinds of people, happily dancing the jig or the two-step to piped-in twang.

The wilderness of The Strange Range was my first introduction to this new frontier town, where our front sidewalk was coated in frozen vomit and just below the doors, hundreds of cigarette butts were stomped outside the three concrete steps that lead to the lobby and then our rooms.

Upstairs in the hotel, Jennifer and I shared a room with baby Neddy and my mother. The room had yellow-green walls that smelled like smoke and a single dripping sink. The toilets were off the hallway, down near the end.

My father camped next door with the two older boys. He was the only one who got his own bed, a metal frame contraption with real springs. The blankets were army grey, and the bedspreads the same greenie-gold as the snot that constantly bubbled beneath baby Ned's nose. My mother feared croup. "Go and get us an electric kettle, Norm."

"Where?"

She just looked at him hard until he left. Then turned to fashion a makeshift tent from sheets.

"We're in the war," said Jennifer. "This is a war hospital. Let's you and me make our own tent, Margie." And we did, ignoring our brother, croaking and wheezing across the room.

The second night we were there, a Friday, while my mother attempted to wash diapers in a single, stained sink, I awoke to the Zoo releasing its patrons, a cohort of drunken inmates. The noise, a babble of unknown sounds, plus the lurch and language of a street brawl erupting outside our window, prompted me to ask, "Who lives in this house, anyway?"

An almost three-year-old in the safety of my mother's silhouette, I was already appalled and dismayed by the bad behaviour of my town's inhabitants. Who lives in this house? I demanded. Who? This ruckus didn't fit anything I had ever known. I didn't exactly stomp my foot in a fit of pique, but I may as well have: "Who lives in this house?"

In the moment, an innocent sleeper awakes. She, the childish and guileless me, renders a judgment. What allowed this critical pronouncement? From whom did I learn this? And now, how can it be unlearned?

The story, the quote, "Who lives here, anyway?" is a hand-me-down tale told and retold, embedded in the mythologies of our family's immigration to the Territories. It is only of late that I have examined the reason for the outrage, the motivation for what I voiced as a child.

No, I didn't like the ruckus of the Indian bar. Not one bit. I didn't like the people who lived with us, but I quickly learned who they were and why they were not like us.

Over one and then two and then finally three weeks of small rooms and smelly, dark hallways, I learned Mr. Krause lived with us at the Gold Range. His room was next to our rooms. I heard him because his single bed was against the wall next to the bed I shared with Jennifer. There was only that between us, that, and a secret. He cried every night.

"He suffered severe burns in a shop explosion," my father told my mother. "Some of the facial grafting didn't take."

"Poor man can hardly open his mouth."

"He can open his mouth all right. He's a permanent fixture downstairs. Whisky neat, every night."

"I'm sure any one of us would be the same, so disfigured." My mother didn't want to talk badly about Mr. Krause. She was fair that way.

I felt the tug of my own lips and jaw as I pretended it was me with a burned-skin mouth. Still, Mr. Krause was neat when he drank, not like Ned who spit up chunky sour gunk and other gross things. Adults were neat in the daytime. Not so neat at night. Not the dancing ladies, not Mr. Krause.

The burned man burbled every time I woke from the bar-closing exodus. His wheezy gurgle often lulled me back to sleep again. The quiet crying was because of his sore face, half gone. I would cry, too, if I had Mr. Krause's hurting face. Sometimes, I petted the wall, which was not him, just a wall, but it made me feel better, and once I even made the crying change into steady in-out sleep sounds. I never saw Mr. Krause's face close-up, and I never wanted to, either, even though I'd petted him to sleep.

Jimmy Pon was another person who lived with us. He was one of three friends who spoke a secret language. They worked in the Gold Range backrooms where the boilers hissed and bristled. I'm pretty sure they were the ones who cleaned our sheets once a week when they weren't working in the café kitchen. We never saw them eat the food they served, although it was a game we played — *Spot the waiters eating.* They hardly ever smiled.

The people who came to the café seemed to call them by the same name, or maybe it was something we did. I recall each of the men was Jimmy Pon with a number: Jimmy Pon One, Jimmy Pon Two, Jimmy Pon Three, until they became muddled and mixed together, like the chop suey Jennifer ordered once and then wouldn't eat because Will said it looked like worms.

Once, when Paul was babysitting, we were exploring and went to an area, it may have been an upper floor, where those same men played cards. We peeked through an open door and saw a room double the size of our room. The inside wall was gone, and the huge room was filled with cigarette smoke. Even in the hazy room, we all saw money, piles of it.

"It was stacked up, almost to the ceiling," said Jennifer.

"Was it hundreds?"

Will giggled. "Hundreds and hundreds." But later that night we heard shouting. Someone screamed and there was, again, the sound of sirens.

"They're going to get us because we sneaked. We saw the money."

Even Will looked scared, until Paul sent Jennifer to the lobby to find out what was happening.

"It's just for some drunk guys," my sister reported.

It's just some drunk guys. It's just some drunks. Nobody said the word Indians, but without consciously acknowledging it, that final identifier was always implied.

School

The bedrock, a bald, grey cranial outcrop that sloped back on itself, formed a brow and cast a dark worried shadow on the stretch of bush below. My father was there with another man, the reason for the walk behind the new school.

The day was chilly despite our calendar declaring it late August. I was wearing Will's pants, cut off below the knee to mimic the pedal pushers eight-year-old Jennifer got to wear on weekends and after school. Great Slave was visible beyond the valley. A wind blew off the lake, a darkling navy blue peppered with cresting waves. My sweater, brown with a horse head, was inadequate in the wind, and my wrists were ringed in mosquito bites. The hand-me-down sweater was likely warm enough by southern standards, but we were no longer in the south. We were in the North; on the edge of the boreal forest before it petered into barrens; on the edge of town before it transformed into rocks and trees; on the edge of a cliff looking down on nothing but a broad empty gully.

We had been in Yellowknife a full year. Except for the twisted, stunted black spruce growing between the rocks, all I could see was the glint of August sun on the forever-lasting lake.

I picked up a pebble flecked with mica and slipped it into my pocket. Its weight and the sharpened edge pressing against my thigh reminded me I was real. That, and my father's tree trunk legs in khaki, his sturdy brogues rooted on the cliff edge. His solid presence lent me the courage to look.

"There, see those four ravens? Just below, go straight down. It's a log building. The Indian school." He pointed and I squinted, following his index finger with my eyes. The ravens circled endlessly, and it all looked the same.

I wanted to see the Indian school. It was why we were in Yellowknife. It was important. This stranger was important too, although I didn't know why. The fact that I was with my father was important, too. No one else had been invited to see the school sleeping in the last days of summer, the empty Indian school, no longer useful.

I looked harder and it granted my wish by appearing, a tiny log building no bigger than our canvas camping tent. The silver-grey logs were stacked to form four blunt walls, and the rusted remains of a stovepipe was sticking out the roof.

"Yes," I said. "The Indian school." I wanted them to know I had seen it, hunched in the shadow of the valley across from us. The door looked wonky, hanging lopsided on a single hinge. I saw it clearly.

"Who goes there?"

I felt a huge hand on my head, encompassing my skull, gentle and pressing at the same time. "It's closed now, Margie. No one will ever go to school there anymore."

And because I didn't go to school yet, and because the wind had come up and the visitor was antsy with mosquitoes buzzing in our ears, an endless chorus, we turned from our bedrock perch and walked towards town, the Indian school lost to thoughts of supper and if the stranger would stay with us — I hoped not — and the magical fact I had been singled-out to go on this adventure with my father.

I thought the old log school was pathetic, broken, and shabby, not appropriate for any people. But the government (whoever they were) had built a new, better school, and now my dad was going to take charge and look after all the poor people who didn't have a good, clean place to go. It made sense. We had come, now we would set things right.

⌒

What if the Dene people had been left alone? What if the far-away Feds agreed to self-governance? What if equal education for all was viewed through a lens other than that of the standardized European model, the colonial authority?

I know most settlement schools only went to Grade Six, or Grade Nine. The Territories were vast then, Nunavut just a dream. The NWT held a smattering of people, each community culturally and linguistically different. How could secondary education have been implemented differently? How could valuable Indigenous knowledge be nurtured, passed along?

I know my father and his team discussed these things. I also know there were some visionaries; a teacher education program was established in the late '60s so young Indigenous teachers could return to communities and teach elementary education in their own language. But paternalism prevailed, and decisions were made without Indigenous consultation by self-serving bureaucrats, anxious to impose their own racist order on a frontier perceived as ungoverned.

Am I trying to answer the unanswerable? Or am I simply attempting to justify something that has no justification?

The mythology is this: In 1960, my father, a high-school teacher and guidance counsellor living in the interior of British Columbia, was offered two jobs, one in St. Vincent in the Caribbean, one in Yellowknife in the Northwest Territories. The recommendation in St. Vincent at the time was that North American children — white children — would need to be flown Stateside to guarantee a solid education. My father must have puzzled over the fact he could oversee the island school, but his own brood should be dispensed to American boarding schools. "I didn't have five children to send them away," my father is rumoured to have said, but I am also convinced he did some quick arithmetic, calculating costs. He was a true Scot.

So, to a northern rather than a tropical frontier my parents came, five children in tow. My father's job was principal, and part of his leadership role meant overseeing the two-year-old brick residence next door to the school.

His school was called Sir John Franklin, named for that foolhardy British explorer who overwintered in the area after one of his failed attempts to reach the Arctic Ocean. The separate residence, colloquially called the hostel, or by residents, the hostile, was named Akaitcho Hall, Akaitcho being the Dene guide who saved Franklin's ass, kept him warm, fed, and alive so he could hasten once again to the barrens in his quest for British glory. Akaitcho was a man who shared his knowledge with the fool, despite the fool's errand. I thought of him as the Chief of the original Copper People, the T'atsaot'ine, the Yellowknives.

In my adult mind, Sir John Franklin Territorial High School represents the settler, the hardy white colonial explorer brazening out into uncharted territories in unheard of temperatures, ill-prepared, yet fuelled by ambition. Perhaps it's how I considered my dad, and his 1961 appointment to a federally run secondary and vocational school. For me, the hostel, smaller, far less ostentatious, represented the Indigenous guide, sure-footed on the earth, knowing his way around and willing to share those ways.

Akaitcho Hall was razed in 2006, ten years after the windows were boarded up. This residential dormitory was considered one of Canada's residential schools and was one of the last in Canada to close. In the town, people say there was rejoicing beneath the wrecking ball. Three Plains Cree teepees stood briefly on the grounds where Akaitcho sat, a ridiculous, half-hearted nod to First Nations and Métis peoples delivered from their communities to that government-run residence of tile and tears. Someone from city council must have decided to erect symbolic tents. They were the wrong style of dwelling for bush people. The prairie teepees were abandoned, flaps open, after the hostel had been hauled away.

I visited the site a few years later. In one teepee were a few crumpled tissues and three cigarette butts. In another, an empty rye bottle and a child's mitten, red with a white maple leaf, unravelling at the cuff.

I now recognize how terribly damaging the residential school system has been. I didn't back then. Perhaps I was too young, or too close to the heart of it. And my father? Was the irony of his own stance against family separation lost on him when he ventured north, young and full of dreams, to pull those splintered children into some cohesive order? We who rode in his wake were not old enough to know how he felt, but the irony is not lost on me. Some parents couldn't hang onto their children, no matter how much they wanted. My dad's job, mandated from Ottawa, was to see that all were educated regardless of culture or traditional ways or the vision that pervades popular thinking, the outstretched grasping hands of heartbroken parents.

I remember the shock I received a few summers ago when my older brother, Paul, in conversation with someone else, prefaced his comment with ... *in the residential school we attended* ... and went on to talk about something that happened when we were children in the winter country of the Territories in the middle decades of the last century. It was his phrase *the residential school we attended* that struck me. Why had I never heard that before? To me, it was school, just school, entirely normal.

～

I have in my possession a prospectus on Sir John Franklin School and its student residence, Akaitcho Hall, from the Education Division of the Northern Administration Branch, Department of Northern Affairs and National Resources. This government document, undated but with reference to the year 1960 throughout, lays out the three-streamed system of its "three-million-dollar plant" in a town that "had its beginning a quarter of a century ago. Before that time there was nothing in the way of civilization there."

Students "of any race," the document claims, could come to Yellowknife and choose academic matriculation, commercial courses in typing and bookkeeping, or vocational classes (including a female-only class in housewifery).

The cultural streaming of students is blatant and explicit. Besides the matriculation program, the three-pronged vocational program in commercial, homemaking, and shop is designed for those who hope to get jobs after Grade Twelve. The final program was geared to Indigenous students: "Finally for the Indian or Eskimo or the student of mixed blood, handicapped by age, language and lack of schooling, who want to find some means whereby he or she can earn a living in the modern world, the Sir John Franklin offers a double-barreled program: a choice of general vocational courses — building construction, mechanics, operation of heavy duty equipment, homemaking course for women; and 'opportunity classes' which, while emphasizing English and Mathematics, give the young man or woman the background needed to follow and master the vocational course — and to hold down a job once the student is trained."

These people, the introduction goes on to say, "may be housed at the school hostel — the fully modern Akaitcho Hall (though some may have previously known only an igloo or shack) ..."

The prospectus, including an entrance application to both the school and the hostel, is pure propaganda, the government congratulating itself on an education solution for "the student who comes from an area where the traditional life is no longer secure or even possible."

One promotional photo for Sir John deemed "the most staggering feature of Yellowknife" shows six Indigenous girls in hoop skirts and aprons clustered around a table. At least one of them wears moccasins or mukluks. The photo bares the cutline: "Among Yellowknife homemakers-in-training, are some who not long ago heated their kettles over a kudlik flame. They adapt quickly and find class teatime — with its pretty china and dainty sandwiches — a happy occasion."

An even more disturbing black-and-white photograph shows a very young woman looking through an instruction booklet while, to the side, a manual typewriter sits unused, and seemingly demanding. Its cutline reads: "The book says, 'Follow the instructions carefully' but to a young girl whose home so recently was in an Eskimo camp or Indian village, the typewriter with it complicated parts — cylinder, carriage, key, back spacer, tabulator, ribbon — seems a bewildering puzzle." While the various specific parts of the machine are detailed, the ethnicity of the young girl seems vague, the cultures interchangeable.

I may be wrong, but I'm quite sure this prospectus would have been included in an employment incentive package for perspective educators. This is the school, and these the school's documented ideals, my father and, in turn, our family embraced.

Antler

Out of all my siblings, only my sister Jennifer understood my desire to become the Caribou Queen. We were alone in the basement of the yellow house when I revealed my secret longing. She heard me out, then tilted her head, weighing a decision.

"I want to give you something, Margie." She was solemn. She called me by name.

"Yes."

"It is not for everyone."

"No."

"It is for you, Margie."

I mouthed my name, giving it back to her.

She held my wrists, anchored me to the cement floor, freezing me in position. "I'll go get it. The gift is in my room."

"Hidden in your room."

She didn't say the word hidden. I did. But I could tell she

liked the way I was turning her words into a chant, a secret ceremony. I was making it important. Whatever *it* was.

Time stopped, and if not for the lowing furnace and the steep shadows cast from stacks of tins on the supply shelves, we could have been in a cave or a tomb. Somewhere cool. Maybe we'd time travelled to ancient Egypt, or maybe further than that. Maybe to Neanderthal time.

As she walked toward her room across from the one I shared with my brothers, I heard her footsteps above, steady, mechanical.

My sister came downstairs slowly holding her hands behind her back. With a slight flourish and that same serious intent, she showed me her gift.

"I found this."

"Wow." It did not disappoint. Cradled in Jennifer's hand was an antler, broad and fanning at the base. It tapered to two smallish nubs growing parallel at the top and another one, the one I thought of as the thumb, growing off to the side at a different angle. "It's beautiful."

Jennifer held the antler just out of reach. "It's from a caribou, a female." She put on her *World Book* voice: "Of all the deer family — reindeer, elk, moose, even antelope — caribou are the only ones where the females have antlers. Sort of like you and me."

I felt a wash of conflict, but only for a moment. "But not the boys?"

"No, they don't need the power."

"Do I need the power?"

She nodded emphatically. "Do you want it?"

We both knew I did, but her question was code. Could I love the antler enough? I nodded my head.

In my hands the small antler was heavy and cool. It was covered with the strangest softness, something between skin and fur, which I stroked.

"That's velvet," Jennifer said.

"Yes, velvet."

"I found it off Con Mine Road, on the rocks."

"When?"

"A couple of days ago."

"How come you don't want it?" I was asking the real question, now.

"It died in velvet."

"What does that mean?"

"It was young. Starved, or shot." She shrugged. "I couldn't find the rest, just this. No carcass."

"Oh. It's dead."

She nodded. "I'll find the other antler. There are always two."

"Like you and Paul?"

I felt I had turned on an electric light in a candlelit room or shouted when I was supposed to stay silent.

"No, Margie. Like you and me. Like us."

"Oh."

And she held my eyes a moment longer before turning and walking upstairs, leaving me alone to cradle her gift. *Died in velvet.* Soft but hard. Dead but alive. I touched the two parallel points. Girls. Sisters. Margaret and Jennifer.

I smiled. My right hand slid down the smooth curve to the third point, some distance from the others. Here the bone was calcified, the velvet flaked away. I didn't have a second sister but I sensed that third point was connected to Jennifer and me. A long way apart but connected.

⌣⌣

An old antler found on the Con Mine Road in the mid-sixties. A child wishing to be someone they are not. I know what connects these things now and it is what I have been trying to get to for years. There is a woman, in my mind, tenuously, tangentially, connected to the Caribou Queen.

Sophie Football was a woman from outside my community who died young, on the Con Mine Road. She died in velvet and if I really force myself to go to that uncomfortable place, I know her death was the first of many I have been able to bury because they are too painful to examine. The only thing I can do is remember how it happened, how casually we took her death.

⌣⌣

The Caribou Queen, the woman, who I later learned was infamous and who became a model, of sorts, for me, whose legacy I linked with an annual spring festival, was rumoured to live in the Gold Range on our floor. She met friends in her room, but mostly these clandestine meetings were at night when my sister and brothers and I were supposed to be out of the halls.

She beckoned for me to come into her room one afternoon, and even though I was afraid, I was also curious.

"I have one like you."

The woman's hand found a framed photograph facing the wall, and she turned it toward me. There was a boy in a black and white photo, older than me, but not by too much. The lady watched my eyes look at the little boy and then she took two fingers and traced the glass. She went around his head and down his cheek and ended on his chin. "My son," she said. "I'm going to get him soon."

I didn't say anything. The lady sat and the bed made a squeaking sound.

"Is he far away?"

She didn't answer at first, and shifted making the bed squeak again, then waited some time until the squeaking stopped.

"Very far," she said.

She sat, pulling the photograph into her chest and leaned farther back on the bed, like she might just close her eyes, take a nap. I'd seen my own mother like that. Bone weary. The picture frame was pushing into her body, but she still hugged it tighter and didn't seem to notice the sharp-cornered black frame pressing her flesh. I waited. As long as the door was open, as long as I could see the hallway, I could stay.

"I'm going to bring him home."

I nodded. "That's good. You're his mummy."

She stood then, but slowly. She was tall. She was still holding the photograph in her hands. I was afraid she would shut the door, but instead she walked my three giant steps in just two small steps to her sink, across from the bed. Her sink had a different pattern on the inside than ours did. Hers was more like a flower being watered all the time. Her tap *drip, drip, dripped* and never stopped.

She turned on the water stronger, but she didn't wait for the hot, the way my mother did. Instead, she splashed the tap water on her face fast, with the hand that didn't hold her son's photo. She didn't look into the mirror when she washed. She talked to the photograph, repeating my words, *good* and *Mummy*.

Dresses hung from a pole held up on one side by the window frame and on the other by a nail stuck into the wall.

The dresses were as tall as the lady and some had feathers and sparkles. She ran her hand across the empty dresses, and I watched as they danced for us.

I smiled at her then, wondering if she was one of the dancing grandmas of The Strange Range, but, before I could ask, she moved forward and put her head against the top part of the panel door. It was exactly like our door, except there was no hook. Ours had a hook. Just as I was about to tell her she could get one, and even hang her pajamas there like we did, she spoke.

"I'll go get him soon. He was like you when I saw him last."

"Like me, but a boy."

"Yes." She smiled and the smile was all for me, this time, not partly for the faraway son.

Her face changed fast and crumpled, and the smile fell towards her neck, and I felt awkward then, as though I should not stay.

When I ducked back into the hallway I felt a drop of water on my neck, like she hadn't dried her face enough.

"New towels come Sundays," I said to the door crack as it closed. The towels seemed more important than the hook. If you didn't share a room, maybe you wouldn't need a hook.

Even though I was alone in the hallway, I felt the presence of the loved little boy keenly. Why he was away? And would the mommy find him?

I couldn't wait to tell Paul and Will about the visit and the son, but when I went into their room and said who she was, they told me a different story.

Different men visited my lady, my brothers said. Those men carried brown paper bags into her room and when they came back into our hallway, they went down the back stairs, instead of the stairs that go to the lobby.

Paul said she was banned from the bunkhouses of the mine.

"One of the miners thought he didn't need to pay a fat old squaw," he said. He made a karate chop down, a guillotine to the crotch. I didn't know which startled me more, his words — *fat old squaw* — or the action of his hand, the blade.

His cutting words, the knife.

"How do you know?"

"I heard it out there." He thumbed the window, the world beyond our two rooms.

I couldn't believe it was the same lady with the photograph. "No. She's saving money to go far away to get her small son."

"She did it, Margie. The guy's privates? Gone." This from Will.

The lady they were talking about lived in room number 222, at the back, the same place I went where the carpet was wet and ruined at the door. It was the same lady.

"She goes to the Zoo every night wearing fancy ball gowns the Commissioner's wife doesn't want anymore," Jennifer said. "She'll dance with anyone, as long as they're not white."

"I saw the dresses. They are beautiful."

"Liar. You did not. How could you have seen those dresses?"

Two weeks after I went into her room without telling anyone, I saw her again in the hall near the stairs down to the alley. She winked and tried to touch my hair, but I ducked towards the fire escape and shrunk my tummy into my back, so it hugged my spine. I remembered her hands, quick with a knife.

"I used to be blond," she laughed, but how could that be true when I could see all her black hair? How could I believe her now, after hearing the story of the knife? What was true, what not true? Maybe the son was not real, but I saw him in the black-and-white photograph in the frame. I saw him facing the wall, and then in her hands, then pressed against her flowered blouse in a son hug. I saw the faraway son and the love and the sadness. But when I tried to tell my brothers, they didn't hear.

"She's the Caribou Queen, Margie. She plays cards with those men," said Paul. "She is the Poker Queen. She always wins." And I never guessed at anything else, except to wonder if she also played Go Fish.

I decided if she ever spoke to me again, that woman, I would invite her to play cards with just me, and the son could watch us from his photograph on the bedside table, but she never did.

The woman originally dubbed the Caribou Queen lived in a time before the Caribou Carnival took on that name for its pageant winner, when the festival was known simply as the Yellowknife Dog Derby. She may or may not have been the same woman I encountered in the Gold Range. I was very young when this first meeting happened, but the memory sticks like spring snow to wool mittens. I wish memories were infallible. I wish I could be sure about all the facts, all the people, how those early events marking the passage of time buzzed endlessly like mosquitos, sometimes loudly in my ears, sometimes from a distance, but always a constant drone. I can only tell how the events seemed to me. That's all I have.

⌇

Years after the Gold Range encounter, when I was nine or ten, I saw the Caribou Queen late one Saturday morning. If it was her, and I can't be sure, she had changed. Both of us had changed, but I had not the insight to recognize my slippage from innocence to experience in eight short years.

This woman was a fixture in front of the post office, a brawling battle-axe of a woman, roaring with anger and drink. I ran into her around the same time it was said she let go with her empty Molson Ex bottle and conked Sophie Football over the head.

Conked. It's a curious word. It's a playful word, sounding impulsive and non-injurious. The phrase, cracked across the skull, sounds a lot more serious. A woman hits another across the head with a beer bottle, and I use the word conked? Is it because the woman who was hit didn't really matter to me? She was one of a parade of people, "characters" they were called, who populated the fringes of our hardrock town.

Characters, like conked, is, again, a strange word choice. According to the *Oxford Concise* a character is a person "interesting and amusing" but somehow not quite fully human. I knew of characters in movies or had at least a passing knowledge of characters from television. Fred Flintstone was a character, as was the hapless Coyote of *The Bugs Bunny Comedy Hour* fame. Why, the coyote could get massacred a thousand different ways, yet he never seemed to get hurt or feel pain. His was a personality twice removed, once by the screen, and a second time by his limited emotions. Yet, the characters of my childhood were not animated fantasy but fully flesh and blood. Perhaps white people, including myself, found it easier and preferential not to perceive Indigenous people that way.

As kids we were always thrilled to see one of these characters ranging around the downtown in daylight hours. It was considered a rare and wondrous thing to see Jimmy-the-Wind or Crazy Tomdee in the New Town at all, but when the woman I knew as the Caribou Queen occupied the third aisle of the Rexall drugstore, I thought it pure pay dirt.

I was there and she was there, the Caribou Queen, loud and belly laughing, opening all the cheerful cartoon cards, rummaging through the comic books, snorting with pleasure. I crouched near the dispensary and watched in horror and awe as scrawny Alice Thompson, on her part-time weekends-and-afterschool job, suggested in her timid mouse voice that the Queen "move along."

"Don't mess your shorts," bellowed the Caribou Queen, and she gave the rack a final whirly-twirl before she marched out, comic books spinning and fluttering like bright butterflies in her wake. In that moment, my heart leapt with love for the Caribou Queen and her bravado. She was brave and bold, way bigger than my scrawny little life.

I picked up my dad's prescription (he had something called Aunt Gina) and followed her outside. A few steps away, Charlie Ribb panhandled outside the post office. A gentle, harmless alcoholic, he quickly withdrew his open palm as the Caribou Queen swept by. She wasn't going to spare him a dime. She might spare him a black eye, but only if he backed off, which he wisely and comically did, mugging and bowing behind her back. Now, that took guts.

I heard the first Caribou Queen got her name because she once butchered six caribou in one afternoon on the ice of Back Bay. Six caribou in one go. That was her claim to fame, that, and the fact she ruled street life. She was both feared and admired.

Sophie Football, a young woman from Rae/Edzo, seventy kilometres east of Yellowknife, was found dead shortly after I encountered the Queen in the drugstore — shortly after they said she conked Sophie with a beer bottle.

I got my information from talk on the elementary school playground Monday morning, eavesdropping. I heard that two teenagers trapping marten after church had noticed twelve ravens circling on the Con Mine Road. That's where they found Sophie, deep in a snowbank, a stone's throw from our house.

"At first they thought she was sleeping it off, you know," one of the big Grade Six boys said of the hunters. Then, he put his fist to his mouth and tilted back his head, fake guzzling, as though she poured her own fate down her throat, as though she got what she deserved.

"My dad said it was just her face peeking out," said his companion. "She was froze clean through. Froze solid."

The following weekend, in the dimming afternoon after the lunch dishes were dried and put away, I asked Jennifer why Sophie didn't knock on our door. I remember her rolling her eyes. "Yeah, right, like Dad would let her come into warm up in the middle of the night?"

"Our dad would let her in. You have to let people in, especially if it's cold."

"Well, she didn't knock, did she?" And that was that.

I guess Sophie Football chose the wrong night to come to town to go drinking at the Gold Range. Everyone knew not to tangle with the original Caribou Queen, but Sophie was out of her own territory. She was fairly young, only thirty-six, and still pretty, a princess-in-waiting, a threat to the Queen's sovereignty.

When I imagined the Caribou Queen's record slaughter out on Great Slave, those six caribou, I always pictured snow the colour of anger. Blood. But when Sophie Football was hit over the head and then found frozen to death steps from my warm bedroom, I saw her death as clean and neat and very, very white.

Now that I have filled in the lines and colours of my own pencil-sketched childhood, I know this isn't so. Sophie's death was dark and violent, and like far too many since, it remains unresolved.

She may have been killed by the Caribou Queen and that rogue beer bottle, or she may have been killed by someone else. Public alcoholism and street violence were normalized, almost condoned in my town in those early days before Yellowknife became a territorial capital. So, too, were Indigenous women with missing children. That, and the casual brutality of the terrible word squaw.

Yet, I was unable to draw a line between what seemed to be the same person, a tender mother aching for a small boy far away, and a woman negating that same pain with alcohol, lashing out at anyone who came into her orbit.

For me, Sophie Football was the first victim in what has become a horrific list of murdered and missing Indigenous women, an acronym we say by rote, MMIWG2S. Sophie's death, no matter how it came about, is heartbreaking.

At a very young age, I recognized the closed door of our family home played its own terrible part. Our closed door. All our closed doors. Half a century later, I recognize how little has changed.

Scoop

We moved out of the Gold Range into our first home in late September. It was a yellow duplex, a teacherage, government-designed and furnished.

When my mother first entered through the front door, her lips pressed together smaller and smaller until they almost disappeared. She barely glanced at the three-cushioned sofa and two single slingback chairs as she marched past.

"I just thought, as principal, we might have finer things." She sighed, pulling at the packing tape on one of the few boxes my father had brought up in the back of the Meteor.

"They're all the same, Eth. That's the beauty of this place. Every house, up and down the street, same stuff. We're no better off than the people here, or here." Dad gestured right and left, but my mother didn't look where he pointed.

She danced the tippy tops of her fingers across the broad, flat armrests of the wood-framed chairs, across the curved back of the blocky maple sofa with its three low-slung, orange cushion seats.

"Government-issue, I guess ..." Was that good or bad? I wasn't sure.

A skinny alley behind our house separated us from the Johnston's house. Mr. Johnston worked at the gold mine. Our backyards looked onto each other. My parents quickly became their friends.

Mr. Johnston was large and muscled, his eyes squinty small, his face like a split radish. He was a leader at Cominco, the Consolidated Mining and Smelting Company of Canada, Con for short, but unlike most miners, he didn't live on the mine site because, well, because Mrs. Johnston wasn't up for that.

She was, and I am only repeating here, *ill-suited to the North*.

"She's always a jangle," proclaimed my mother. "And that skin, why it even makes little Neddy look native. She's wearing her mink already; not even October and swathed in furs."

"Maybe it's because she's so skinny," Jennifer volunteered.

"We don't make those kinds of personal pronouncements in this family, Miss Jennifer Jean. Eleanor is just different."

Like a whippet in a town of huskies, Eleanor Johnston was skittish and anxious. She drank unusual brews for her nerves: a thick green tea with floating leaves, or a vaguely brown, chalky concoction that smelled of mushrooms and dishcloths that sat wet in the sink too long. Her house smelled weirdly medicinal, and while others gathered for strong perked coffee with canned milk or Red Rose brewed on the back burner,

Eleanor Johnston took to her bed and sipped her medicated herbal teas, exhausted by the idea of other robust mothers and their multiple offspring.

My mom must have known something of her private troubles because Mrs. Johnston was taken under her narrow wing. Mother was a natural nurse. Even when she wasn't working, she was looking after people, helping them whether sick or well. She gave advice on how to eat and how to look good. Nutrition was very important. It was tied up with keeping your figure. Deportment was the twin to nutrition. How you carried yourself, first impressions, good posture, proper quality clothing, these mattered to my mother. One couldn't let oneself go, she proclaimed to anyone who would listen. Go where? I wondered. Down the highway? Into the bush? Where was there to go?

Mrs. Johnston's greatest notoriety among we neighbour children, besides being sickly, was that she was a replacement mother — a foreign, scary, and slightly delicious idea. She replaced the first Mrs. Johnston, who, after having produced two perfect blond sons, quite unexpectedly drowned in a riptide on a tenth anniversary trip to Florida.

I couldn't imagine any of those things: the riptide, Florida, the notion of a trip, but I understood replacement. Ned had replaced me as the baby.

I was certain Mrs. Johnston the First must not have wanted to be sucked out to sea. But she was. In my mind I could see her small in the water, waving both hands and calling for help, until water slouched into her mouth, filled up the inside air spaces. Then, *glug, glug, glug,* down she went.

I could only imagine Mr. Johnston's sorrow. It would be as wide as Great Slave, our own inland ocean, which as far as I could tell, had no end. I imagined the water taking Mrs. Johnston the First, and then giving back Mrs. Johnston the Second. Surprise. A switcheroo.

"He raised those boys himself," our mother admonished Jennifer, who had to walk the Johnston boys to and from school every day. "Boys raised without a mother will be rough around the edges, but you must tread the higher ground and be grateful you have a mother to help you through. Those boys, poor things, they're bound to be different." And then she glared at me because I'd heard when I wasn't supposed to be listening. I was always listening, trying to make sense of things that couldn't possibly be true. If I didn't eavesdrop, I would know nothing. No one ever told me anything.

Despite having a nursing degree and a career temporarily on hold (odd, embarrassing, not something other mothers did), my mother was one of the post-war generations, complete with its attitudes and judgments. She married late in life, at the age of thirty-four. After ten years on the supply shelf, she was brought upstairs like an old seed potato that suddenly produced five healthy shoots.

"Mrs. Johnston is the second wife," Jennifer reiterated, while babysitting a few months into our stay in the duplexes. "The dad married her when the boys were already born by the drowned one." She paused, for dramatic effect. "Then ..." My sister stood on the orange chair, and I watched the bottom sag even closer to the scarred floor. She'd get in big trouble if it broke. "... When those boys were mostly grown, already in school, he met the lovely Eleanor." Jennifer wanted to be on stage. She was very good with voices. Eleanor sounded half like a bad word, a swear, and half like the most elegant word in the world. It was a name like a teacup you chipped and got spanked for, but it was worth it because you got to drink milk from it from then on, every single time. The crack didn't matter, the teacup mattered, and the fact that it was yours, once precious, newly made common, by default.

Eleanor Johnston. Much younger. Married Mr. Johnston. Fled north. I liked the word *fled*. I had just turned five, reading early, according to my mother, who approved of early readers.

Jennifer leapt off the chair when she said *fled*, and then she crouched down. Her voice dropped. Will and Ned and I leaned in.

"They can't have a baby," Jennifer whispered.

"You mean, they can't do it?" asked Will, who was really too young to know about such things but seemed to know, anyway.

"No, stupid. It doesn't work when they do it. They probably do it all the time. But. There. Is. No. Baby —" Jennifer paused, the beginning of the long dash, momentarily at a loss, before regaining her composure and continuing. "The big news is, they're getting one."

"Getting what?"

"A kid."

My little brother made a so-what face. "Want to play oil trucks?" Ned asked Will.

But my older brother's eyes narrowed. He wanted to know more. So did I, but I knew enough not to talk too much, not to ask too many questions of Jennifer. She hated questions. She didn't really like kids.

"How?"

"The Old Town."

She said it really slowly like she was splitting a gooey candy bar. *The Ooold Townnnn.* We didn't go there much, but of course, I knew where it was.

"How?" Will asked again.

"From someone who already has a kid. Someone who doesn't want it anymore." But, because this seemed impossibly wrong, even to Jennifer, she added, "Or maybe because they have too many kids already."

"Do Mum and Daddy have too many?" It came out before I could stop it.

"No, stupid. I'm talking about the little kid the Johnston's are getting. It's an Indian baby."

"Oh."

"Who cares," said Will, grabbing Ned's arm and dragging him toward the room we shared. "We'll play trucks, Neddy. I'm going to be the oil tanker. I found one of Dad's old Zippos. It still sparks." And they were gone. Jennifer looked mad. She needed a bigger audience than me, but I wanted to know more about the new kid.

"When will they get it? The Old Town kid?"

She looked at me with complete disdain, and the energy in the conversation, her reveal, collapsed. "Forget it. You're too dumb to understand."

And she was right. I was too dumb. But so were our neighbours. Mr. and Mrs. Johnston did what white people who thought themselves good and kind did in the early 1960s. They took a little girl from the area, maybe even the Old Town, a Dene or Métis child, because there was a surplus of them, wasn't there? And who but they would be able to provide a happy healthy home for a child who might not have one otherwise?

They got their first adopted child as a toddler, at thirty-one months, an almost three-year-old. Before any other real memories set in, insisted Government workers. Eleanor named the little girl Carmel, a nod to her beautiful skin.

"She was all doe eyes, peeking out from behind the social worker's leg, Ethel. She has come to us because she is ready to be loved." I was under the kitchen table when I heard Mrs. Johnston talking. I wondered why this new kid wasn't ready to be loved earlier, but I didn't want to reveal my presence by asking. I liked the way the tablecloth, which only went on at Christmas and Easter and when Eleanor came, made a secret fort in the dining room.

The girl arrived a few weeks later. "This is Carmel," said Mrs. Johnston, pushing a stout, pugnacious-looking child towards me. She was wearing a too-short dress that didn't quite fit across the shoulders, and she looked decidedly scrappy. "Can you say hi to Margie, Carmel?"

Instead of saying hi, Carmel revealed her lower teeth. It was supposed to be a smile, but I could tell it wasn't. She was making all the right muscle moves but her eyes stayed the same. She took up most of the space under the table and pushed at my mother's legs, crossed at the ankles. When they asked Carmel to come out, she grabbed the tablecloth and bolted so that the cups and saucers at the very edge crashed to the floor.

"I'm so sorry. She just isn't quite used to all this," said Eleanor, gesturing to the pictures on the wall, the orange chairs, the sofa.

I liked caramels, the candy. I wasn't sold on Carmel, the kid. Maybe Mrs. Johnston got the little girl to make her sour life sweeter. Maybe Mr. Johnston was missing the first dead wife too much and the kid would soften the pang.

For five months, Carmel Johnston was the centre of everything. It was *Carmel this, Carmel that,* and it might have gone that way forever, except suddenly Mrs. Johnston started to get fat. She stayed in bed most days. Carmel spent more and more time at our house.

"I'm going to be a big sister," she told me.

I had a big sister. They weren't that great. "Lucky you."

Ten months after her sister's adoption, Sylvan Johnston was born.

〜

Under the table again.

"Tiny. He was just over four pounds. Eleanor just couldn't gain enough weight."

Another neighbour lady snorted. "Most of us don't have that problem." Laughter. "Have you seen the baby, Ethel?"

My mother, slowly: "Yes. There's something not quite right."

Carmel insisted I come see. We went to examine the new baby brother when Mrs. Johnston was sleeping. "Don't touch," cautioned my mother, who was over at their house to help.

In the dim bedroom, through the slats of a brand-new cradle, I saw something tiny and white. It reminded me of lifting a stone and finding bug eggs underneath. The baby had a cloud of fine, curly hair and a long, thin face with a broad forehead and far apart eyes, rare, according to my mother, for an infant. Those eyes looked right into mine and I was spooked. It was like that baby knew something I didn't, like he'd just been lifted off the source of something deeply mysterious. It was the strangest feeling.

"Why doesn't he sleep?" I whispered to Carmel.

"Because he wants to look at me. I'm his big sister."

My mother said the baby's listlessness was evident right from Sylvan Johnston's very first visit to the public health unit. It was on his charts: *failure to thrive*. Meanwhile, Carmel, just a scant year younger than me, noticed the abrupt switch in parental attention. She was no longer sure the new baby hung on her every movement. She wasn't convinced Sylvan liked her anymore, and she was pretty sure she didn't like Sylvan.

I would have been older when I heard this, maybe four, maybe five.

My mother, talking on the black telephone, the party line: "She was scrubbing herself raw. Eleanor found her in the bathtub, just shredded. Poor little thing, I guess she wanted to look more like her brothers, and our Margie, too, no doubt. They're such good chums. But imagine! Little Carmel, trying to scrub the brown off like it was dirt."

And then she saw me, listening again, and turned away so that the cord wrapped around her back and I could only see in my mind, the pink bloodied bathwater and little Carmel Johnston, scrubbing, scrubbing.

⌇

Carmel and I played together more and more often. Mr. Johnston had his big mining job and his older boys from the first drowned wife. Now the second Mrs. Johnston had Sylvan, who wouldn't take fluids, who lay impassive in his crib. Even though Carmel was between Ned and me in age, we were both girls and so she became my constant companion. It was my mother's way to help. We were meant to be friends, but we weren't really. I tattled relentlessly.

"She was mean. She squashed ants on purpose."

"She pulled down her pants and stuck her bum in Ned's face."

"She ate all the jellybeans even though we were supposed to share. When I asked for mine, she threw all of them in the mud and then she laughed."

No matter what crime I reported, my mother's response was consistently clichéd. "This child has not had your advantages, Margie. If you can't say something nice about Carmel, then don't say anything at all."

I didn't say anything, unable to understand my own advantages.

Carmel did not do things in half measures. When she hit, she hit hard. When she pushed, it was not to nudge you over, it was intended to hurt. She had been hurt herself, my mother mused, somewhere in her past, and she was just demonstrating how that hurt had been enacted. Bruises bloomed on my arms and legs. Carmel called the shots.

"That's mine," she said. "Give me that. I'll be the queen and you're my worker, okay?"

I let her take my toys. I let her pick the games we played, and I usually let her win. I let her be the Cowboy and I was the Indian, even though she was the Indian, and we both knew it.

I tried. I really tried, but Carmel was filled with anger that she took out on whomever was at hand. That person, during that endless summer, happened to be me.

I admit, I also thought Carmel Johnston was dumb. You couldn't change your skin colour with soap. The stupid Johnstons had picked stupid Carmel, and now, because they couldn't take her back, and because Sylvan had become so much work, they saddled me with her.

I was too meek to protest these forced meetings. Carmel was mean. She was bad. She was dumb. I didn't want to play with her, but I had to because I was told that was the kindest way to be and I wanted to be kind. I wanted people to think I was kind, anyway.

I played with Carmel, to achieve kindness, therefore I was the better person. I was doing the right thing. God saw us all. When He saw me, He smiled. Carmel, on the other hand, made Him very, very sad. I decided poor old God cried a lot when He saw Carmel.

By the time I was ready for preschool, Carmel was impossibly irritating. I tried to avoid her any way I could, but our parents were friends and traditions, once established, were difficult to break. For the third year in a row, the joined families were embarking on a Christmas gift exchange.

"I have a good idea for Carmel," I told my mother, who was chastising Ned for putting a pebble up his nose.

"Oh, good." She sounded pleased. But distracted. Ned was wailing and she was crouched over him, holding his hands, a pair of tweezers hovering. I remembered her squatted down in the hall outside our bedroom two weeks earlier, putting her hands on my shoulders and asking me to be nicer to Carmel, to be a true friend.

Now, she looked right at me again, and I held my breath, hoping I could pull it off. "We could buy her some soap."

My mother blinked, twice, smiled absently. She'd retrieved the pebble.

"Soap," she repeated. "Yes, Margie, that might be nice gift for a little girl. Fancy soap." I'd planted the seed.

Carmel unwrapped two bars of pink soap from the drugstore at our family's joint gift exchange. *From Margie*, my mother had written on the card. The colour was perfect, almost the same pale hue as my flesh-toned crayon. The bathtub water.

Carmel liked the soap. She smelled it, smiled her appreciation.

"Rosebud," she said. "Thanks."

She didn't get it. No one did.

⌒

In my pre-school mind, Carmel, and therefore all brown-skinned children, were mean, angry, hurtful, bossy, and dumb. Education, with both a public and Catholic system, did not help the racist attitude I absorbed and then executed.

In Yellowknife, in the mid '60s, Indigenous children went mostly to the Catholic school, St. Pat's, to be educated by nuns. The public school, the destination I'd coveted all my life, was more homogeneous and likely considered less hierarchical by my United Church parents. There was a smattering of non-Catholic Indigenous children, but for the most part my potential schoolmates would be like me and my siblings: freckled, blond, Caucasian.

Jennifer went into Grade Four that third September in our yellow house. Will was in Grade One. Despite having received what I thought was a direct message from the Caribou Queen that winter after the dentist, I was denied kindergarten and made to stay back home with Ned. It was agony. School was everything, the reason we were here, the beginning of absolutely everything I needed to know.

My mother's logic for forestalling my enrollment was both a kindness and a crime. She did not want to leave Ned without a playmate. Two children at home could entertain each other, whereas one would require much more effort on the part of the adult. I'm sure she also thought I was not ready. I liked being home, I liked books, I'd already conquered rudimentary reading, and I could easily get lost in early chapter books. I preferred the imaginary world to the real one, and I think she recognized the reality of life was sometimes just too much for me. I was an inward-looking child for the most part, anxious to please, and quite sensitive, though also given to bouts of pique if I did not get what I felt was my due.

The day my siblings first trooped off to their respective classrooms, my mother tried to appease me by telling me I was "in charge," a responsibility only given to my elder sibs, Jennifer and Paul. They were often in charge.

That particular afternoon, once the others had made their way to the coveted Yellowknife Public School, or YPS One, as it was called in those early days, my mother gave Ned and me canning jars with holes punched in the lids and sent us to the grounds of the hostel, right across the road near my dad's high school, the temporary home of children who came from places that were not here. I'd been to the hostel before but never without my parents.

⌣⌣

As we clutched the empty jars and walked across the road, I recalled Christmas the year before. I was made to wear a scratchy dress, lime green, and leotards, brown and pilled. My brothers wore bow ties and white shirts. Ned didn't have a white shirt, he was too young. So his shirt was yellow, but not bright like the sun, which we had not seen for at least a week. The collared shirt was pale, to match his white-blond hair.

We were heading to Akaitcho Hall where the Indian people waited for us. We had to go to the Hostel, all of us, to sit at the head table and eat Christmas dinner in the big dining room with all the kids who weren't going home to their families. This was part of my dad's job. Our job was to help him feel like this was okay.

I hated everything about our task: the hand-me-down dress, being on display at the front of the dining room, eating at a table that sat on a little platform facing the dark sea of others. I hated the dining room itself: its limp streamers and old tinsel, trying to be festive. I hated the upturned faces of the kids gawking.

I knew they were stuck here, and the staff, too, that everyone was pretending our gathering was festive, even though it wasn't. We were all pretending.

Paul liked the pool table in the recreation room and Will liked the movie, *Ma and Pa Kettle*. Jennifer liked the boys looking at her, and Ned liked eating as much as he wanted, but I didn't like any of it. I felt awful knowing the students at the hall wouldn't see their families for Christmas. It had something to do with government money, and my dad.

We filed in, everyone stood. There must have been two hundred kids. They, too, were dressed up. The supervisor said some words about manners, Matron asked a blessing, the kids mumbled along, and then my dad said some things. He talked about Christmas, about food. He didn't say anything about families. I was glad of that. When he stopped talking, he sat and then they sat and we were encouraged to stand up again before being ushered to the front, first Dad, then Mom, and then the rest of us, in order. I went second last.

All the hostel kids watched as we traipsed to the steam table and scooped up the food. The turkey was in two trays, white meat in slabs, and dark meat, separated and stringy. It didn't look like the turkey we ate. Gravy was from powder, little lumps of the mixture floating on the thickened surface, and the cranberries were jellied, from tins. The mashed potatoes were suspiciously smooth, and the peas were grey and mushy in their watery pea juice.

There were Christmas carols playing softly over the intercom system. "Silent Night." I felt a bubble rising in my neck, and pretty sure it had tears inside it, I swallowed hard, forcing it back down to my tummy. If I ate the food, the bubble might go away.

I pretended the banquet was okay because I got to go home. I knew I could cross the road — hold on to my dad's hand if I wanted, even if there were no cars coming — and be home. I'd just have to chew the food, swallow, and smile a little bit, be grateful. After supper we'd watch the movie, then tour the recreation room again with its decorated but empty Christmas tree, and then it would be over.

Remember, I told myself, *you can go home. They can't. Be grateful.* I ate.

⌒

Now, amid foxtails and fireweed, brambles and skunk grass, my little brother and I, four and five-and-a-half years old, respectively, found lazy bumblebees in early September grasses. I captured the first one and held the cool glass to my face and felt the wings and the buzzing insistence of the bee's frustration reverberate against my untouchable skin.

The bees in our jars buzzed and bumbled. A float plane flew low over the field, pontoons flashing in the sun.

"Will they die?" Ned asked.

"No." I looked at his face, leaner now the baby fat had evaporated. "They can breathe because of the holes."

"Wouldn't they be happier if they could fly around?"

"You made a nice house." His jar had grass and a twig and two dandelions, one still in flower, the other gone to fluff along the sides of the glass.

"Your bumblebee is lucky," I said, looking at my own bee, feeble and struggling.

"Your bee doesn't have enough air. Dump him out. Dump him out."

But when I turned my jar upside down and hit it with the heel of my hand, the insect continued to cling to the thick end at the bottom of the jar.

"He doesn't want to go."

"I know," said Ned. "Let's add dirt." And we did. My brother and I pulled up clods of soil with our bare hands and pushed them into my insect jar on top of my struggling bee. Something felt wrong.

"We have to go home," I told Ned, exercising delicious power. Yet, something twinged.

I left the jar and the nearly dead bee, took my little brother's grubby hand, and we walked past the flagpole with the Canadian flag shredded, the crest broken in two, the ugly red ensign incomplete. I led Ned across the big street, gravelly and wide. There were no cars. Our house was on the other side of the gravel, right across from my dad's new school. I could get home. I knew enough to grab my brother and go. I knew how to bring him home. I kicked a small rock, split down the centre by a line of quartz, and it ricocheted off the neighbour's fence post. I pocketed the stone once we were safely across the road, in the zone of home.

Through the back door, our house smelled like cinnamon and feet.

"Could I have a tin for treasures," I asked my mother. Tins were good. They came filled with good things, Christmas cookies, licorice all-sorts, yummy snacks. Mom was drinking tea, but she went to the top shelf above the stove and found a long, rectangular cardboard box that had the strange word *Ganong* on it in fancy gold script.

"This will be perfect for treasures." She patted the top before handing it over. In that moment, I was overwhelmed. I loved my mother. I couldn't imagine not having her. The box was my mother, the stone was me, inside. I punched two holes in the top of the box, one right through each g for the antler Jennifer gave me, so the two prongs acted like a handle. It also left a word I didn't know. *Anon.* Like the kids, without their moms. Jennifer and I were the two prongs. She'd said so. The third prong, the one I had no name for, was inside the box, there, but not visible, not yet.

⌇

I finally got to go to school and get away from Carmel in 1965. I'd had my teeth, my ears and my eyes checked, government prerequisites. My scruffy hair was cut straight and flat across my forehead and straight and flat from both ears back. Will laughed, but I didn't care. I missed kindergarten and went straight into the rule-bound shock of Grade One. I was hoping school would teach me how to become the Caribou Queen.

My mother insisted we wear snow pants to school, itchy wooly things to which snow stuck. It was not until the Grade One class picture came out the following spring my mother realized I never took my snow pants off.

"Margie, what in the world?"

"I didn't want them to see my ... my ... body."

"Your body? Do you mean your legs? How in the world would they see your legs? You wear leotards, for heaven's sake, and who exactly are 'they'?"

"The kids. The other kids."

She came towards me then, large, stern. "Margaret, every day I dress you in school-appropriate clothing and every day for six, eight months, you have worn these oafish trousers? Why? What were you thinking?"

"I told you, I didn't want them to see me."

My mother squatted. Her voice became softer, cajoling. "Why do you think they will be looking at you?"

Her question made no sense. Weren't they always looking?

My mother was persistent. "What, exactly, are you worried about them seeing, Margie? What do you have to hide?"

This was tougher. "Myself?"

I hoped this was right.

The crease between my mother's eyes dug in, tire treads skidding on gravel. I needed to do better.

"Sammy Gladue took my shoes at recess. He tied the laces to the rope and ran them up the flagpole. My feet were cold."

She frowned.

"Did you get them down?"

"Will did. I told him, and he told Mr. McCarthy and Sammy got the strap and now he's going to beat up Will. When my shoes came down, they had snow inside."

"How long were you out in stocking feet?"

"Afternoon recess."

"Margie, that's twenty minutes. Are you telling me some hooligan removed your shoes and left you barefoot in the snow for twenty minutes? Why did no one call me? Why didn't Will tell me? This is very upsetting, young lady. Very, very upsetting."

"I pulled my snow pants over my feet." I smiled at my mother, tried to avert her inward gaze, tried to bring her back to the bulky snow pants, my glaring social faux pas in the school photo. "It's better not to be," I whispered.

"Better not to be, what?"

"Seen." I said it again. "It's better not to be seen."

She looked at the photograph and then looked at me. "So, you wore your snow pants in class in order not to be seen?"

She held the photo up so I could view the entire Grade One class, us, all of us, standing in three rows. Unfortunately, I was in the front row, second girl from the centre.

"See all these little girls, Margie?" She pointed to Ruth Rider, Maryanne Hebert, Sally Polinski. "They all have leotards on. See their legs? Leotards. Now look at you." She pointed to me, caught by the camera with my shoulders drawn up, my small skirt crushed at my waist. "Which girl looks different? Which is being seen?"

I studied the photograph, trying to understand. Was this still about the shoes? Maybe I shouldn't have mentioned the shoes. I shrugged, but the photograph dangled in front of me.

I pointed at Maryanne. She had darker skin than the rest of us. She was from the Old Town. Maybe she was the one who stood out.

My mother sighed and the class picture fell to her side.

"No, Margie. It's not this little soul. It's you. You are standing out because of what you're wearing. In not wanting to be seen, you're causing yourself to be much more visible than any other child. Do you understand?"

I nodded my head.

The shoes, the flagpole, the rescue by my brother, and the threat that floated between Sammy and Will drifted off, restoring the peace in our safe home.

The next day at school, I took off my snow pants. I did it carefully in the cloakroom where the cubbies were, and I waited until everyone else had gone into the classroom. My mother would be happy. My leotard legs showed, but if I understood correctly, I would show less. Sammy Gladue, my tormentor, might not recognize me without the snow pants. But he did. He looked right at my legs and laughed, and I felt less protected than ever before.

I felt I could not stick up for myself because I was advantaged. And I *was* advantaged — at least I had leotards, at least I had legs and feet, and shoes to go on those feet. My father's favourite adage resounded: *I used to cry that I had no shoes, until I saw a man who had no feet.* I had everything, but I lacked confidence. In my mind the advantaged kids were the strong kids, the ones who took things because they could, the ones with street smarts and negotiating power. They knew how the flagpole worked. They talked back, they formed packs, they said swear words out loud and had secret codes. Mostly, they frightened me.

The Indigenous kids scared me the most. They had something I didn't have, and I imagined they were fuelled by power. I kept that notion in my pocket until an incident in the late summer showed me something entirely different; the spark that lit my childhood compatriots was not power. It was anger.

◠⌣◠

Besides getting to start school, and my mother beginning her job at the hospital, two significant things happened. For some reason these events are as momentous in my recollection as the birth of Sylvan Johnston.

Our across-the-alley neighbours, Neville and Edna Brewster, fostered two new children, despite having six of their own.

"They're Indians," said Jennifer. "I think they got them to be servants. They're both boys. I said hi, but they didn't say hi back to me." Jennifer liked Wayne Brewster and was hoping he would take her to the sock hop. I was interested in the new servant boys.

"What are they like?" I asked Walter, the Brewster brother closest to me in age.

"They eat shit," he said. "They eat their own shit."

What? I imagined fresh poo on a plate, curled, still steaming. It was a terrible image. "Yikes."

Later, I imagined Edna Brewster, who I was cautioned would scream if I tried to cut through their yard, serving the Indian foster boys shit. Only in my mind I didn't think shit. I thought poo, because that's what you'd say unless, well, unless you lived in the Brewster house.

But I couldn't really think about that word either, because who would do something like that? It was unimaginable, and yet, when I thought about eating poo, it was not the fact that Mrs. Brewster made them do it that troubled me, but, rather, that they would.

The foster children didn't last long. We never found out what happened, but at the end of the summer, the Brewsters gave back their foster kids.

A few weeks before school ended but before I moved up to Grade Two, a girl with an intellectual disability was found tethered to a stake in a windowless basement in the Old Town. Her name was Fay Hillis. Her sister, Arlette, had been in my first-grade class, although not in my section.

In primary school there were four sections in our grade: The Robins were all the kids whose families were associated with higher levels of government. The Bluebirds, my group, was a tier below. Our group had respectable people, parents who ran businesses or who were bosses at the mine. The Sparrows were Métis kids and some immigrant miners' kids, and the Ravens, well, Ravens were scavengers, weren't they? These students were mostly from the Old Town, mostly Indigenous kids.

Arlette Hillis was a Sparrow.

When I told my mother Arlette slept through most of morning instruction with her head on her desk, she looked stricken. "That poor little thing. I'm sure she has never had a·regular bedtime."

The RCMP detained Fay and arrested Arlette's father, Mr. Hillis, six days after they discovered Fay was going to have a baby even though she was only fifteen.

"He kept her down there on a leash," explained Will, as we sat in the shade of the fence in the back alley across from the Johnstons. He put his thumb and forefinger around my ankle. "She was tethered to a peg, Margie, so she could only go as far as the chain. Alex Hare told me she was covered in sores when they brought her out of the basement."

I didn't think Will should be playing with Alex Hare, a St. Pat's boy, and I certainly didn't want to imagine poor Fay. I could already see Arlette, head down, her hair matted and the back of her neck ringed with dirt.

Because I was silent, Will thought I didn't believe him.

"You'd be covered in sores, too, Margie, if you had nowhere to rest that wasn't smeared with crap. Think of that, eh?"

His anger startled me. "Maybe we should find the policeman and tell them about her, over there." I nodded towards the Brewster house, those foster boys, now long gone.

"What could we say against Mrs. Brewster? Nobody would believe us."

And I knew he was right because I heard my parents talking about Mr. Hillis the next day, how he got off, how his crime was never reported, never punished. It was just swept away. Fay was swept away, too. She went somewhere to have that baby. Or not.

I imagined her with the Brewster's foster boys, all of them living together in a nice house, eating good food, looking out for each other, but I didn't tell Will because I knew he would say it was just plain dumb and not true, it could never be true.

Arlette didn't come to school during those last weeks of Grade One. When she did come back, I had graduated to chapter books and moved up to Robins. Arlette, behind by those few weeks, was moved down to Ravens for the final month. Some years later, I learned bluebirds and robins weren't often found in the North. Sparrows were ubiquitous. Only ravens, one of the smartest birds on the planet, were indigenous.

Did educators do that? Are those ornithological categories possible? Were children lumped together according to some perceived parental hierarchy? Or was it related to small reading groups? Did I dream it up as some bizarre classist categorization imposed or projected on to me?

I knew, I still know, the way one does in their secret inside spaces that no matter how well I could read, I would never be a true Robin. It was simply beyond my reach. I would have to flutter in the middle somewhere between Robin and Bluebird. I should have known I would never be a Raven either, but that lesson took me longer to learn.

Wild

My mother, working first part-time and then full-time at the hospital, was busier, but busier at things she liked doing, she explained, rather than things she didn't like doing. The list of not-liking seemed to include laundry, cooking, grocery shopping, ironing, and even, ouch, looking after small kids. She probably meant Ned, who was the only one smaller than me. Jennifer got paid to watch us and because she didn't like us around much either, we had more freedom to roam the perimeters of our town.

For Will, Ned, and me, our mother's shift work cracked opened our town in novel and expansive ways. We roamed and we learned. There was uptown, where the stores were the Hudson's Bay, Roy's Confectionery, The Gold Range, the Government building, The Capitol Theatre, The Welfare office, the Pawn Shop, the Rexall, the Coke Plant, the Pool Hall, the Yellowknife Inn with its renovated café, The Miners Mess, and Bromley's Hardware. Behind those establishments were alleys and cut throughs, burn barrels, gathering places, hangouts, and haunts.

Halfway down the hill, but still considered the New Town, was the garage, Frame & Perkins, and the newspaper office that printed *News of the North*, once a week. Beyond the printing press was Trail's End Trailer Court and, at the bottom of the hill, the Old Town divided into Peace River Flats and the Woodlot on one side of the road, and Willow Flats on the other.

Even with Mother occupied, the Old Town remained strangely out-of-bounds, a place I could only access with my parents. The Old Town, beguiling and magnetic, was not exactly forbidden, but it seemed to shimmer in my mind with deep otherness shot through with the excitement of danger. It was the split stone in my treasure box, the quartz that divided the sameness of grey.

I had been there, of course, and always leapt at the chance to go again to the Old Town. Past Willow Flats and the old Woodlot, the road wound one-way around the rocks to the Latham Island Bridge and, beyond that, to Rainbow Valley, eighteen or twenty flimsy shacks that faced the northern shore of Back Bay. These houses were identical except each wall of each house was painted a different primary colour, the more vibrant shades chipping and bleaching into pastels.

In the summer the houses in the area we called Rainbow Valley — now Ndilǫ or End of the Island, in the local Dene dialect — were surrounded by mangy dogs, some tethered to stakes, some roaming. I remember Ski-Doos sunk deep in meltwater muck and kids with long, tangled hair and hardly any clothes playing on the shore. I eyed them from the back seat of our station wagon with a mixture of fear and envy. How I would love to live in the little pink house with the western wall painted green. How I longed to run, almost naked, around the rocks, and up and down the dirt road like I owned it.

The streets of Yellowknife ended in Rainbow Valley, but there was a turnaround, so we passed the rainbow shacks twice. At the far end, when my father wheeled the Meteor in the opposite direction, I could see fish guts and flies and animal skins stretched on poles drying in the sun, and just beyond, the real bush. It was something I both desired and didn't, but it was a tantalizing vision I held in my child's mind when we climbed back up the hill.

That final look at Rainbow Valley was always a backwards glance, because by then, we were headed to our own place, the New Town, where I was allowed to walk anywhere. I knew my parents were contemplating moving to a new house away from the school. They were considering a new subdivision, an in-between place called the School Draw, a narrow strip of land that ran between Old Town and New Town. It was considered the New Town, but just barely. I wanted to stay in the yellow duplex for safety, but the little pink and green house in Rainbow Valley, on the very edge of the big lake, seemed so much more exciting.

Also, a challenge. Could I live down there? Could I get my water from the lake, live with a honeypot instead of a toilet? Could I make a fire and drive a Ski-Doo and trap animals to eat? Were the shivers running up my spine fear or excitement?

When I was a kid seeing Rainbow Valley through a car window, I didn't think of a shack as a shack. It was just another place to live. I am chagrinned to know now that our "tours" of Rainbow Valley took us past two hundred Indigenous people living in those same twenty shacks. Twenty tiny, inadequately insulated, four-hundred-square-foot buildings. Two hundred people. Why did it take me so long to do the math? Was it willful ignorance or blunted empathy? Or was it childish nonchalance? — "I guess this is the way the world works."

Secure in my own world, I had no idea of those numbers, what they implied, how they spoke to oppression, poverty, subjugation. I only saw that certain people lived differently from one another. I was plagued by my own egocentric perspective: If my parents were gone, could I survive? It was persistent, that question, and as it turned out, far, far more complex than I could begin to imagine.

～

We had been in Yellowknife almost six years when Paul went out with some other fourteen-year-old boys and came home boasting of killing a ptarmigan on Tin Can Hill. "It was just standing there, like a dupe."

We were in the kitchen of the house by the school. The kettle had just boiled, and the air was thick and steamy so everything in that warm room appeared malleable and soft around the edges. Paul, however, stood ramrod straight and shouldered an imaginary rifle. As he looked down its barrel through the sights, his cheeks puffed and collapsed, a muted explosion issuing from his mouth. "There was blood, lots of it."

He looked to my mother, who was pressing one of my father's shirts on the kitchen counter, a white towel beneath her task. "Or at least it looked like lots," he faltered, "because of the snow." We were all listening, but it was eleven-year-old

Will who was awed. His eyes sparkled. Killing something. Hunting. It was what Yellowknife boys did. And now Paul, slight, pale Paul, had killed a bird. It was radical, cool, almost as though Will had done it himself. "How much blood? Were there feathers? And guts? Did you blow it to bits, Paul? Did you? Did you?"

But before my oldest brother could answer, a strangled sound came from my mother's throat. It wasn't loud, but it stopped all other sounds in that blurry close kitchen. It was an agony we had not heard before. Ned looked scared. I was shocked. Paul was immediately silenced. Only Jennifer spoke. "Mum?"

The sound continued, a deep guttural gasp. It was not the iron hitting the countertop, or the rasp of the cord across the canister set. It was my mother imitating something in the throes of death. Her face was like Dad's shirt. "What. Did. That. Bird. Ever. Do. To. You. Paul?" The iron hung midair, hissing in space.

And before anyone could answer, she slowly and deliberately placed the hot iron down on the shirt. "What did it do to you?" she asked again, putting both hands on her hips. "What did the bird do, to make you want to kill?"

We looked at Paul, squirming. The hot weighted iron began to scorch the cloth, Dad's good work shirt. We could smell the burn. But our mother did not move. She waited.

"Nothing." Tears were heavy in that single word and I prayed for them to come, to stay the iron, cool the scorch, but there was no release.

"Say it."

Smoke or steam or a mixture of both was rising from the dress shirt. My mother ignored everything but her eldest child.

"It did nothing. It didn't do anything to me." Tears sprang to Paul's eyes, his bravado evaporated.

"That's right," said my mother, pulling the hot iron up on its haunches. "It didn't do anything to you. That bird did not deserve to die." And then she peered down at the dark spade on my dad's shirt as if she had no idea how it got there. "Blood on the snow, my word," she muttered and then, quickly, looking up, commanding, "Paul, go wash your face, the rest of you, scram. I have to get ready for work."

～～

The next weekend, my brothers and I went to Tin Can Hill together to see Paul's kill site. Jennifer would not come. She was listening to the Monkees on the radio and learning how to backcomb and style her hair. She pursed her lips at me, when I asked her to come with us, made a kissing sound in the air. I didn't know exactly what it meant, except no.

Paul had been grounded. "Are you kidding? I'm never going there again. It's not that great."

"Ah, come on Paul," Will cajoled. "It'll be fun." But in the end, we went without him.

"It's because he bawled," said Will. "That's why he doesn't want to come."

"Yeah. Can't blame him."

"He's a big bawl baby," said Ned, to win Will's favour, but a loyalty rose in me and I kicked him in the ankle, so he shut up. Paul's guilty tears were not to be mocked.

Tin Can Hill lay over the brow of the plain where the New Town was constructed, smoothed out, and separated, beyond Sir John Franklin, our usual boundary. Tin Can Hill beckoned from the narrow draw between Great Slave and the Con Mine

Road, where a few new houses were still under construction. One had a floor and a framed structure; the other was a foundation with spring meltwater gathered in the hole.

"It's a swimming pool," said Ned. "We can go swimming." I contemplated the brown water, bits of lumber and pink insulation floating on the surface. "I don't think we should swim here. It's somebody's property."

The three of us continued to lean over the concrete wall. "Leaky basement," said Will. "They're going to have a mighty wet cellar." It struck us funny at the same time, and we laughed, and trudged on chanting *leaky, leaky*. Ned changed our call to sneaky leaky, and Will dubbed the brown water streaky leaky which made us think of toilets and underwear, and we laughed harder as we trekked toward the head frame of the mine.

Tin Can Hill was situated halfway between Con Mine and the construction site. It was a different dump site, a collection of garbage from the shack town that sprang up on the shores of Great Slave in the mid 30s, but something in the volume of rusting cans — can upon can upon can — was crude music to our ears. So much so, my brothers and I clambered over the bank of the tip and pawed through the last of the slush and snow to uproot the old cans. The spring snow absorbed the rusty orange residue, and it was beautiful beneath that blue, blue sky. The air was light and smelled like sap letting go. There were willows reaching for the sun and on black spruce, a sticky ooze on the bark.

As we scrambled through winter's leavings, the knees of our snow pants and the palms of our mittens became wet and streaked with rust from the ancient, foreign materials we were liberating from the snow.

"Here's one. Here's another one," and we flung the tins up in the air, sending bits of moss and lichen spinning airborne. We dug and pawed the surface, unearthing layer upon layer of discarded cans and we threw them aloft, a mad gusto spurred by the shift in season.

"Let's pretend we're Indians, real Indians who can live off the land," cried Will, rubbing his mitten hands across his cheeks, staining his face with streaks of ochre and grime.

"You be the Chief," said Ned to my older brother, and he held his own face still as Will rubbed rust into his freckles to make him brown.

"Now we can kill ptarmigan," I yelled as I smeared the rust across my own forehead and chin, hungry to feel the transformation I saw in my brothers.

"Now we can hunt," shouted Will, and he uprooted deadfall, a slender branch, and swung it over his head, a whipping stick, a raised firearm. We fell in line, something loosened within us, and my youngest brother and I grabbed sticks and marched down Tin Can Hill blasting a flock of imaginary ptarmigan as we headed home, marked as original copper people, orange painted warriors, giddy and carefree.

⌒⌒

When we returned, Paul and Jennifer were beside themselves, a jangle of nerves, jumping foot to foot.

"Margie. Will. The hospital. It's on fire. The hospital is on fire."

"Mum?"

"She's there. She's working. We've been waiting for you. We should go."

Our dad was out of town. Will turned to our older sister. "Jenny? Please? Can we go see?"

"No, yes ... I think." My sister, in charge, wasn't sure.

We could feel it. From five blocks away, we felt the heat of the hospital fire. Maybe the rust had soaked into my skin and was scalding me from inside out. I felt like I was standing by the oven door, resolutely closed, yet my body was sizzling and cooking.

"Let's check it out from the roof, first," said Paul, anxious to go, but not wanting to betray the ultimate power bestowed upon Jennifer. One at a time, my oldest brother boosted us onto the roof of our neighbour's garage so we could watch the flames rocket into the sky.

I could see the building in my mind: three-storey, wood frame, yellow, painted pale and plain, like morning sun, mid-winter. It had a zigzag wooden fire escape on the outside wall closest to the school with a drop at the end that was higher than the tallest boy I knew. Even though I could see it, I couldn't imagine the hospital underneath that roaring mass of energy, the fire that banished night.

We straddled the peak of that garage roof with the asphalt tiles warm beneath our feet and the rust upon our faces. Our Mother was in that fire. We had disobeyed her by going to Tin Can Hill, by painting ourselves brown, by wanting to be Indians. The fire had started because we didn't listen. Perhaps she had already been burned up, not so much from the fire — although I knew enough to know no one could survive the flames — but because we were such disappointing children, she might have given up her life for others. The caribou separated from the herd, slaughtered to feed the people.

"Where's Mummy?"

Ned, just turned six, voiced what I could not bear to ask.

He was thinking as I was thinking, and his little orange face was stricken beneath the layer of iron oxide.

Jennifer was suddenly decisive. "Let's go find out. We have to find out." We hurried the five blocks downtown, our eyes on the leaping flames and choking smoke. Paul and Will danced ahead, like they were on their way to a party, but they slowed, completely sobered, as we approached the towering flames that obscured the building.

The whole town was there, standing in a large semicircle. Bits of ash and ember fell from the sky. I searched that circle of citizens for my mother's face and when I saw her at last, she looked entirely different from the mother I knew at home. She was closer to the flames than the rest of us. She was standing next to a patient, a small boy covered in a blue blanket, sitting in a wheelchair. One of his feet was covered by a dark sock, the other bare. I looked to my mother's face. Her blond hair had fallen from her nursing cap, the one she always pinned on before she left the house for work. Her face was blackened by soot except for vertical stripes of white on her neck and cheeks where sweat had run from her brow.

She saw us, parked the boy with someone else, and came over. My mother crouched down and opened her arms so we could crowd in. "We got everyone out," she said, in a low voice, almost trembling. "We got them all out." She looked past us, her eyes moving beyond the great surrounding circle of the town, and upward, toward the sparks that floated above the treetops. "Everything will be okay," she said. "We got them all out."

She examined us then, as though it were we who were in the fire. She touched my back, ran a quick hand over Paul's chest, across Jennifer's shoulder. Her index finger traced

Ned and then Will's cheeks, the lightest vertical caress. She looked at the strange powder on her fingertip and knit her brow, shook her head ever so slightly. "They should be at home," she murmured to Jennifer.

"They needed to see you, they needed to know you were safe," said my sister. And my mother stood and nodded and pulled Jennifer more deeply into her embrace. "You did exactly the right thing," she said. "Now they know."

We looked around then and saw the volunteer firemen, standing sombre and immobile. I realized that this event was beyond them. It was beyond all of us. We were stunted and helpless before the flames. There was not the manpower, nor the resources, nor the water, nor the pumper trucks, nor the hoses or helmets to go around. All we could do was watch the fire consume the building. We stayed as long as we could because our mother was needed elsewhere, and our father was out of town. He'd missed something important, and I felt his absence keenly. If he were here, surely this wouldn't have happened.

Way, way past our bedtime, I walked home beside Paul and he held my hand, a rare event. "It was my fault, Margie. If I hadn't killed the bird . . ." His voice evaporated.

I looked up and saw the same stripes on his face as on my mother's. It seemed impossible that Paul should cry again. I squeezed his hand. "You were sorry about the bird. That's why everyone was saved." Paul squeezed my hand back, but he didn't look at me. He looked away, not up to the sky, the way our mother did, but into the dark shadows that felt darker still because of the unnatural glow.

Sun Spot

My mukluks had purple and blue tassels that tied at the knee. I loved the way they smelled, the way they fit, the way my feet could feel the snow, toes spread and wiggly, with nothing getting cold. But the hide on the foot was split at the heel. I must have been seven, having finally flown on stunted and inadequate Robin wings, to Grade Two, where I could again begin to figure out my world.

"The shank is still good and there's room for a bigger insole," my mother told me, patting my leg, as first one and then the other mukluk was tied off. "We'll buy new insoles and duffles this year, Margie, but you can certainly get some more wear out of these."

I stroked the canvas toppers as I waited for Mum to dress Ned. She laced his blue tasseled mukluks, noting splits on all four seams. "You're going to get new ones, baby boy," she said, kissing him on the nose.

New ones. Imagine. If I could pick out my own mukluks, I might even get beaded ones. Suddenly mine seemed ruined, too. Ned's mukluks were hand-me-downs from Will, and before that Paul, but I still thought he was lucky. To wreck my mukluks, I decided to join more games of road hockey. Gravel poking through the tamped ice in the alley was the fastest way to my goal. I wanted those beads.

Friday evening, 1967, I think, after we were washed and brushed and put to bed, Mother came into the room I shared with the boys. "We're going to Weavers tomorrow," she announced as she stooped over to kiss each of us. She smelled of soap and lemon and cigarette smoke. Until they went up to sixty-five cents a package, she'd smoke one Cameo, menthol, just one, with my father, after supper.

She stood in the middle of the room for a moment. "Will, I expect your help with Margie and Ned tomorrow. Your father won't be coming. He has to attend to other things, and Jennifer and Paul will be staying with him. It's the four of us."

As she spoke, she yanked the frost covered window open. "I want you three to go to sleep." The cold poured in, night breath, a visible wave of iced air. It didn't matter the temperature, or from which direction the wind, every night my mother opened our bedroom window. She believed in fresh air, the same way she believed in a tablespoon of cod liver oil each night. The oil slipped down our open throats like Ski-Doo snot, the outer albumin of sunshine, a replacement potion, close but not quite as complete as the vitamins we required.

In an icy bedroom, my brothers and I would not play.

The cold would keep us in our beds, and we'd eventually fall asleep. But that night, I wanted to know more.

"What's Weavers?"

"Outfitters. Trading post," said Will, from the top bunk.

"What's that?" asked Ned.

"It's where you get stuff. Weaver & Devour. In the Old Town."

"Oh," said Ned.

"Oh," I echoed.

"It's fantastic. The stuff there is really cool. I can't wait." Suddenly, our outing felt like an adventure instead of a chore. We were going to the trading post to find cool stuff.

As the cold became too much, I burrowed beneath my arctic sleeping bag, leaving only a blowhole, a mouth space, to breathe. I was a harp seal under the ice. My brothers and our bedroom evaporated into a muffled drone as my imagination whirred. But there were also shivery expectations. Tomorrow was an adventure and even though I tried, I could not beat back sleep, which, when it came, was filled with dreams of beads. Flowers made of beads were so brilliant and sparkling and multicoloured, they floated through my sleepiness and held me enthralled through the dark anticipatory night.

⌣⌣

The afternoon of the outfitters, I watched from the window as my father tried to start the car. The Meteor station wagon was a '56. The chrome fenders on the front still bore the scars of my dad's journey north. The fender was bowed out, making the front end of the car look like it was smiling. I smiled back. Its frame was bent in the final stretch of the trip when my dad and Paul were pulled seventy miles by a Cat through a mud bog near Fort Providence on the Mackenzie River. A local mechanic declared the vehicle unsafe for highway driving.

"You can take 'er around town, for sure, but not on the gravel, not in the shape she's in." This pronouncement surprised my parents. We now had no reliable transportation out of the North, nor could we afford to fly on the DC-8s that landed every few days. We were in Yellowknife, and in Yellowknife we would stay, at least until we could afford a new car. Were we trapped? No. We had arrived by choice. My parents both had jobs. They were starting out, and opportunity abounded. What did the employment incentive packet proclaim? The expansion of Yellowknife, built so far from the end of steel, was a dynamic symbol of Canada's future progress in the North. A newer car would come. Theirs was a quiet confidence in that future.

Meanwhile, the Meteor wheezed like an old man while my father babied the hand choke and ground the starter, hoping to warm the car for his family. Eventually the engine caught. Shuddering and coughing, it pumped blue fumes into the frigid November air. My father got out and we piled in. A car ride, particularly to the Old Town, was a big deal and I was anxious and quiet in the back seat with Ned. We watched the downtown buildings — some already trimmed in Christmas lights — disappear as we started the steep descent into the most intriguing part of our compact world. Bald rock edged one side of the road; the garbage dump edged the other. The garbage from the top, where we lived, fell on the place we were going, where the others lived.

The landfill was blanketed in snow except for the fresh additions at the verge, where the hill ended. Like a scab lifted off one side of a wound, the newly dumped detritus had already been carefully excavated and useful items pilfered, a reminder that goods were scarce, that materials had to be hauled a long way. I heard my mother's *tsk* as we drove by. She didn't like the garbage dump visible like that, hard against the road.

I wondered if she knew we went sometimes, with Dad, to find things. A few months earlier he applauded a blackout blind I pulled from the dump heap. Lots of people used these thick vinyl binds to block out the insistence of all-night sunshine. He checked it for rips and rerolled it, putting it in the back of the Meteor. "This will come in handy," he'd said, but when I glanced behind me now, I noticed the new-to-us blind was gone.

The garbage dump was what separated our part of town from the Old Town. I hugged the window and looked beyond the dump to the plumes of smoke that rose from the haphazard homes spread out around the gracious bay of the lake. None of the houses were built on grids in the Old Town. They were cobbled together, random roads leading to lean-tos and tarpaper shacks, homes to the dump scavengers who lived in these patchwork flats. In the Old Town we did not travel unaccompanied because dogs were not tied up or taken out on neat leashes. They wandered the lanes and alleys, guarding the quirky Old Town from up-towners like us.

I knew this in a way I couldn't explain. It was in the set of my mother's shoulders, in the way we no longer looked down onto the lake but directly at it. Where the ice met the shore, the public works department had plowed a path through the bank to form a sloping road that disappeared onto the white expanse of lake, the Dettah ice road, a five-mile sheen that plowed its way across Great Slave to the very first Dene village, settled long before the discovery of gold, long before the influx of white people. I tried to imagine a time when the Old Town was new, when uptown people didn't exist, but that was too hard to conceive. Where would we be? We were here. How could it be otherwise? The caribou herds of my imagination had scattered.

We passed the honey wagon straining towards uptown, a big green steaming truck that picked up pails of raw sewage from people who didn't have indoor toilets. They stopped using outhouses when winter blew in.

"Pee-ew," said Will from the front. He held his nose and said it again. "Stinky." He pinched his nostrils, so the word came out in a squawking falsetto, and Ned laughed and imitated: "Pee-ew." The Old Town stunk. The people here didn't have bathrooms in their houses. How did they wash?

I saw the leaning house with a ladder nailed vertically across its roof; those stepping places leading up the steep pitch to a tangle of antennas that bristled with hoarfrost.

The road continued, wending between another huge outcrop of bedrock, the Bush Pilot's Memorial, and the water. There, the Cat Man's house, evidence of his animal family, a feral colony, vanished except for hundreds of small paw prints in the snow. Did Old Town people eat cats? There, the sinking house, with its swaybacked roof folding into the centre. Next to that, on the opposite side of the road, was the first set of docks, Ptarmigan Air, a base for float planes.

I had been to the float base last summer with Dad. We watched a man ferry people in his canoe between the mainland and Jolliffe Island, where they kept fuel oil in monstrous white tanks. "Best boat ride for two bits," my dad cajoled when I declined passage. Didn't he see the skinny huskies on the smaller island outcrops, baying at the boat, hungry and snapping at the paddlers as they rolled by? He seemed oblivious to danger.

I lowered my window a crack, hoping the good smell of woodsmoke would cool my prickling cheeks, but the aroma of the Old Town in winter was heavy deer hide, oil, and frost. We'd circled all the way around the rocks and were pulling up to the trading post, Weaver & Devour, Will blabbing in the front seat.

"Old Man Weaver died upstairs, right Mum?"

"Hush, that was a long time ago. And it's not Old Man, it's Mr. Weaver to you. Don't forget your manners."

"He slept upstairs and died in his bed. Alex Hare told me and Ned, right Neddy?"

I looked to Ned. He tightened his mouth. This was Will's second reference to Alex Hare. Were they friends?

"There's a ghost." Will's last phrase was tossed over the seat like a hand grenade. It lay unexploded in my lap.

My mother parked, herded us out of the car and up the steps of the building. There were numbers on the front. 1936. The number three was broken and hung a little bit below the other numbers.

Inside, two windows shed waning daylight on the massive cash register sitting at the front on a long counter. The machine had individual number levers sticking out like the baby spoon Ned used when he was still in the wooden highchair and I was already grown.

"One, nine, three, six," I repeated inside my head, a mantra to prevent Mr. Weaver's ghost from drifting down the stairs.

There were electric lights on and the store felt huge and unknowable. The smell of tanned animal hide was

overwhelming. Behind the counter were huge shelves starting at the steep, dangerous stairwell and disappearing into
the darkness of the back aisles. They were filled to the ceiling
with foreign things — leg-hold traps, snowshoes, and bullets.
There were stacks of dusty iron fittings and clawed imple-
ments and shiny new shells of different dimensions. These,
I decided, were bad things, dangerous and sinister in their
cylindrical sameness.

The pointy claws of the traps were open and they seemed
hungry for animal blood. But what was worse, far worse, to
me were the stacks of animals without their bodies. They had
been caught in traps and skinned. Peeled. It was horrifying.

The hides were tawny and sleek, and all of them reeked of
smoke and battery acid. There were other smells, too, foreign
smells, something that reminded me of toe jam and soot. The
bigger furs — I saw bear and elk and caribou — were stacked
on top of each other, a pile of furs still holding their animal
shapes. Smaller pelts were hung from three large hooks, the
glossy tails of fox and wolf and wolverine jumbled together
near the floor, a single intact appendage that seemed removed
from the central belly slit. The furs were splayed open and
supported on each side by dangling legs, ending in pads and
claws, the paws.

Someone my mother called Irma appeared, a lady helper,
still inside her own skin. She spoke to my mother while my
brothers and I gazed at the amazing paraphernalia tendered
by this northern post. This was no ordinary uptown store. My
brothers, made giddy and wild by the raw power of the place,
dodged and ducked back and forth, pretending to shoot each
other with imaginary guns. They were hunters. These furs
were their kill. The shelves seemed to move in unison with my

companions. They swayed in and out and swooned as though they could be brought down by the pop of an invisible gunshot.

I scampered towards the back of the store to get away from all the dead things. On a wall halfway up one of the aisles were small vials of beads. An overhead light illuminated the rainbow wall and the glass tubes winked and beckoned. The problem was another kid was there, a girl from my class, Maryanne. She was touching each of the tubes of beads in turn, trying to decide which to buy. She didn't see me.

"I like the blue."

She spun on her heel, hissed, "Don't tell."

"Don't tell what?"

She pulled up her sleeve. Three tubes of beads: red, blue, pink. "I'll give you the blue one. But not now."

"When?" It was a negotiation I slipped into easily.

"Once we're out."

"What are they for?"

"My mum."

"Can't she buy them?"

The girl scowled and sleight-of-hand passed a tube of yellow beads from the wall rack to my hand. "Stick them past the elastic. No one checks kids."

I don't know why I listened, but I did. The tube of beads up my sleeve pressed against my wrist, pulsating so rapidly I was afraid the glass might burst against my racing heart.

"Now get out of here."

As I turned, intent on obeying, I saw a boy come towards us. He walked strangely, loping down the aisle, favouring one leg. He looked at me, narrowed his eyes, but spoke only to the girl. "We're going, Maryanne."

"Give me a sec. Did you get the cable?"

"Yeah, check this out." He held up a round piece of metal with what looked like a bent washer attached. "It's called a whammy collar."

Maryanne made a choking sound, the animal in the trap, and they both snickered. I tried to sidestep the two of them, but her laughter was the snare, the beads up my sleeve, the whammy collar.

A space appeared between them and I ducked, squeezed up the aisle. I hurried back towards the counter, to the sanctuary of my brothers. Just seconds before I found the familiar, Irma's hands closed around my waist, and she hoisted me to the counter. The floor went out of focus and I was convinced I was about to be tossed behind the counter with one of the stacks of dead furs. *Thief.*

But I was not the only one lifted eye-level. Mercifully, my brothers were also scooped up and plopped down beside me. Irma was going to measure our feet. Would she make us take off our coats? The tube of yellow beads was molten, searing a hole in my wrist. It ached and throbbed to the movement of the red lipstick on Irma's teeth. She talked, but I could only hear roaring in my ears. Her words were drowned in the smell of coffee swallowed a long time ago.

I struggled up and stood on the counter. From that height I could see an old woman, stooped, almost crooked, standing nearer the back of the store. She was leaning against the same countertop talking to someone else I couldn't see for the shadows. A single light was a halo around the old lady's head. She was wearing a blue kerchief, and it framed her face in flowers, red ones. I could see she was negotiating a trade, selling handiwork, mittens and mukluks. Suddenly I knew what the beads were for. This is what the furs were for, too.

The skins from the animals were what covered our feet, my feet, the fur was trim.

It was as though this little lady, too far away to speak, was giving me a message with her haloed head, bent in negotiation. She had popped up from the darkness to tell me the animals were not sad about giving their skin and fur. She would make their deaths beautiful with beads. But where were those yellow ones, seed pearls of the sun?

Irma was suddenly back with navy felt. She outlined my foot with chalk. Other feet were just holes, I saw, just the empty spaces of the people who had come before. As Irma went to the back to cut the chalk tracings, an older man approached. When he saw no one behind the counter, he came even closer. He passed Ned, touched his head, and as I sat quickly, he paused in front of me. He looked into my eyes and moved closer still. He knew. I was sure he knew.

"Sundogs," he said, reaching for my hair. He was talking about the way, on certain days in the winter, the sun morphed into three suns because of ice crystals in the air.

He was wrinkled and grinning, swaying on his feet. He wore a slouch cap with the ear flaps down, and he had only a few front teeth, three on top and a couple visible on the bottom. "Sundogs," he said again. And a third time: "Sundogs."

He was too close, too condemning, rocking back and forth on his heels, in and out, so his road-mapped face almost touched my cheek. His small eyes, shining, were locked on mine. I started to sob. He was too near. He was too old and too knowing. Would he tell the sewing lady it was me who took her yellow light?

Irma was there, instantly grabbing the old man by the back of his coat. "Archie, leave off," she shouted, hauling the old man towards the door. He was manhandled out to the porch, and before the doors swung shut, I saw his slippery toe-rubbers fail on the store steps. He lost his balance and fell in the snow, a steaming yellow wetness rising from his middle. He had wet himself, this man, peed his pants in the snow. I cried harder.

"Did he scare you, honey? Don't worry, he's gone now," cooed Irma, wanting to comfort and placate. "He's not a nice man. He's bad. Do you want a sucker? Do you three want a sucker?"

My brothers, ecstatic, picked red suckers and seemed oblivious to what had just transpired. My mother came to pay, her arms full of insoles and mukluks. I could not bear to see the old man again and I was afraid to leave the store and venture out to the parking lot where he had fallen in the snow, leaving his pee behind.

They thought I was still afraid, but that was not it. Because I was certain he would get me into trouble, I'd acted pre-emptively. Even through my tears I was aware of his sparkly eyes melting into confusion. I saw his shoulder hunch into the shape of humiliation. I knew that feeling. But the crying had started, and I could not stop. Tables turned. Suddenly the old man was in trouble. It wasn't me.

I swept my eyes to the back of the store to see if anyone had witnessed our encounter. Maryanne was still there standing near the lady selling her sewing. She also had a sucker. The stick was in her mouth, a skinny tongue, poking out. Neither she nor the sewing woman looked at me. The sewing lady bit the edge of her lip and squinted into her handiwork, and Maryanne pretended to find something interesting on the shelf.

As the boys raced for the front seat, I fingered the tube of beads in my jacket, passed it down from my sleeve to my hot palm, and flung the thing away from me. The glass was caught once in the setting sun, a flash, and then it was blessedly swallowed by the snow.

But the boy with the wire was there, outside. Even with his strange hopping gait, he had left the store, taken the steps two at a time towards the man, Archie. Now he stood in the frozen pee snow, next to the bead hole, steadying and brushing off the old man. I closed the car door quickly.

He had seen it all.

All the way home, up from the Old Town, past the garbage dump and onto grid roads and the glowing streetlamps of the place we belonged, I held the image of the old man. Without the stolen beads, I should have felt lighter, but something very, very heavy had taken their place. And that boy at the store knew.

⌇

Who is complicit? Who is culpable? Me, certainly, a scheming child, unwilling to be caught, shifting the blame to the truly innocent. Did Archie sway and weave because he'd had a few? Was Irma justified in his removal? Why were the irrational fears of a child quelled while the needs of a senior ignored? I didn't ask any of these questions then. I ask them all now.

Civilized

During our first few years in the North, my father faithfully nurtured a swath of green behind our government houses. Despite his work, the land remained barren and refused to come to crop. Sometimes I wonder if it wasn't the same for his expectations and dreams about the job in what had initially seemed like a strange and otherworldly place.

Unlike my mother, who seemed less than enamoured by domesticity, my dad needed to nurture. His family was originally from Saskatchewan, and although not farmers themselves, his people were attuned to the yield of the land, the cycle of planting and harvest. In Yellowknife there was so much land, yet the Precambrian shield was rock with almost no soil. Growing any sort of garden was like farming the moon.

He was tenacious, however.

At the first sign of spring, mid-June, as though we'd survived something important, he celebrated by grubbing in the dirt. It was an opportunity to escape those first months settling into a new system, a new job, settling an unsettled wife and a brood of unruly children.

He dug up the backyard, that poor plot of beaten clay and gravel, with great enthusiasm. He planted corn first, closest to the neighbour's fence, and then other vegetables descending in size; peas, runner beans, zucchinis, and finally rows of carrots, and even, once, a pumpkin plant. Unlike my mother, he saw our future in the North.

Because of the lengthened days and the brightness of summer nights, my dad's garden grew like magic. Green upon green, there were cornstalks worthy of giants and zucchini bushes so large my brothers and I waded through, expecting dinosaurs. It was a Garden of Eden, but missing one thing, propagation. For all his tending and prodding and weeding and husbanding, my dad's plants did not have enough time or heat to come to maturity.

"It's the sea without salt, Ethel; an ocean of foliage without the slightest edible offshoot." He held tiny ears of corn, the size of baby fingers that budded and withered on the stalk. The tomatoes he produced were hard green marbles that quickly became playthings for Paul and Will. They shot two miniature tomatoes across the counter and erupted into laughter when they collided with a dense, fruity *thunk*.

I scooped up the green tomatoes, three of them. I slid the unripe fruit into my pocket while my father despaired.

He waved a mass of prickly leaves over the kitchen sink and two sad cukes fell and pranged in the metal bowl. "Cucumbers, nothing but vines."

The drain glowered its one-eyed disapproval. The tiny cucumbers were wizened. My brothers laughed, harder. "It's like Ned's pee-pee man, no bigger than his weenie," roared Will. He and Paul convulsed and wheezed. They were beyond annoying.

I went out to the garden to investigate. Even the raspberries, the plants my father most hoped for, sprouted only thorns. I ran my fingers just outside the canes and felt the brush of prickles against my palm. I could not touch them without the thorns piercing me, and yet I loved the sensation of almost — but not quite — being jabbed.

I looked to the rocks, thinking about my dad and his wish to tame this place. He thought he owned the ground, but I strongly sensed we were interlopers here and that the land, the rock and trees, were the bosses. I was sure, quite sure, it was the land that owned us.

My mother didn't share my father's fruitless passion for gardens, but he never stopped trying to convince her. He wanted to grow food in the Northwest Territories because of his family background, but also because he had tasted the pleasures of putting up for winter.

"Peaches in sugar syrup in February, it's like summer in the snow. You kids would love it. Imagine the crunch of pickled asparagus on the coldest day in January? Margie, Jenny-J? You can't, can you?" And we couldn't, not that we would eat pickled asparagus, even if it were available.

More than fresh food in the long days of winter, my father probably wanted food security for his family. He had taken us away from crops, away from railway tracks and livestock, the things that referenced his own childhood. Without asking permission, he'd dropped us as foreigners among people in their place of scant bush and bedrock.

He was also concerned about the spring break-up and the fall freeze-up, when food could not be trucked along the Mackenzie highway. The river crossing at Fort Providence — later I learned it was called Zhahti Koe, Mission House in Tłı̨cho — was a mile across ferry ride which ceased for six to eight weeks every spring and autumn. The Mackenzie crossing was a twice-yearly waiting game that framed the brief summers. We waited for both thaw for the ferry and freeze to support the eighteen-wheelers that rumbled staples to our town three times a week. With the ferry out, first the *John Barrens*, then, the larger *Merv Hardy*, and the ice road yet too dangerous to cross, northerners lived in a space of increased isolation and uncertainly.

⌇

"What's this?" Jennifer glared at the milk pitcher. There were flakes of powdered milk still floating on the thin, vaguely blue surface. "What happened to the real milk?"

My mother walked around the table, a tiny can of mandarin orange segments in her hand. She was spooning two into each of our cereal bowls, two soft segments of orange sweetness and one spoonful of juice pooled on the grey surface of boiled oats. "The ferry went out." She had on her thickest British voice, a voice that hinted of her own upbringing in proper, more cultured climes.

My mother was a first generation Canadian. Her parents, particularly her English father, brought with him a hierarchical system anchored in Britain's societal class structure, which he attempted to recreate in the wilds of interior British Columbia. Her paternal home had a billiards room, a smoking deck for gentlemen only, and formal nights of roll-back-the-carpet dances, complete with canapes and live music. Today, her words were the high registers of the piano, staccato. She didn't add oranges to her own breakfast bowl. Nor did my father receive any.

"You've got to be kidding. I hate this." Jennifer's complaints unleashed my mother's own resentment.

"Powdered milk, powdered eggs, canned fish, canned fruit. Get used to it, Jenny. All of you! Get used to it. Didn't I just tell you, the ferry's gone out?" Her voice was razor edged and she glared at my father. Her eyes seemed to blaze indignation: *Why have you brought me to this ridiculous place?*

"There's still a quart of tri-milk," said Jennifer, hanging on the fridge door, taking inventory. "Why not have it now, while it's still good. Why start with the powdered stuff when we still have concentrate?" She pulled out the formula in its black-and-white quart. Tri-milk was mixed one to three with water. It made the winter porridge edible, alongside brown sugar.

"I was saving it," said my mother slowly. "I was saving that for my tea." She shook her head quickly, grabbed the milk carton from Jennifer. She snapped it open and began pouring thick tri-milk, undiluted, straight onto our oats. "Yes. Let's have this now. Good idea, Jennifer. It's cream. Later, we will have nothing but water, but now, cream." My mother was tired. She had worked last night.

"Mum, I don't want . . ." but she held her hand flat in front of my face.

"You'll eat it, Margie. An eight-year-old needs cream. Think of your bones, your teeth. All of you, enjoy. I don't want another word."

I thought of the baby in the Miners Mess, the one who got real formula, stretched, but real. I wanted to ask if skim milk was the same as tri-milk but I just ate my breakfast with my sister and brothers like it was my last, and hoped for the ice to form quickly, for the season of slush to be short.

Winter brought a different scarcity.

There was one uptown grocery store in 1967, Super-A, run by a man whom I assumed was a relative of the original trio of Chinese entrepreneurs who had leased the Gold Range and turned it into a legend. I was wrong, Newton Wong, the grocer, was his own man, industrious, adventuresome, entrepreneurial. He and my father were friends.

We were shopping for food on a Saturday, my father picking up some slack as my mother's workload increased. There was snow on the ground, so it was probably October. Will was taking guitar lessons from a neighbour up the street. Ned had to stay at home because he had wet the bed again. Jennifer was with him, babysitting for twenty-five cents an hour, and Paul had left the house early, not telling anyone where he was going. I knew he'd be in trouble when he got home. My mother needed a schedule of our outings, particularly when she was at work. Our father she considered impulsive and unpredictable, a haphazard caregiver. I loved it when he was in charge.

The ferry was still out, and the shelves of the Super-A were almost empty. Talk around the supermarket was of the ice bridge. When would it be up? When would it open to transport trucks? When would we be able to resupply? Meanwhile, Mr. Wong stood at the entrance to his store wringing his hands, apologizing for the markup in the groceries. "It's air freight, it's the cost of air freight. Everyone understands," my dad assured Mr. Wong.

A large man blustered past, three paper bags of groceries occupying his cart. "These here cost me a frickin' arm and a frickin' leg," he hissed at Mr. Wong, who bowed, muttered *So sorry,* over and over. It was the angry man's final words — *Damn Chinaman* — that sent Mr. Wong hurrying to his office.

Mr. Wong reminded me of the Indian man from the trading post, the one who peed himself in public. Is that why he had to run off?

"I'm sorry you witnessed that, Margie," said my father as we loaded our groceries into the back of the Meteor. "You must never speak to others the way that man spoke. Do you understand?" I nodded my head solemnly, wondering what exactly it was about Mr. Wong that allowed people to be mean and not feel bad.

As we pulled away from the store, I turned from my dad, and stuck my tongue out at Mr. Wong and the Super-A. No one saw me, of course, but it satisfied something in me. I sat smug and safe, and while requests went out on the bush radio show Bulletin Board, I practised the word frickin', and then, because nobody would know, the phrase *Damn Chinaman* in my head.

〜〜

One night that same winter, as Grade Three let out for March break, a stranger came to our door. It was dark and my mother was not pleased with the interruption of dinner.

The man who stood outside was bundled in a sealskin coat. He had a broad flat face and gnarly, windburnt skin. He was wearing a harness across his back, and in the evening light we could see he had a sled behind him, just off the porch. It was filled with frozen fish. He stood in the doorway of our house while the inside air stirred up the winter cold and made it dance and shift. He swirled around as though he wasn't attached to the ground the way we were. He was outside, cold and perplexing; we were inside, warm and familiar. Even when he talked, soft and low, I wasn't sure he was real. Jennifer stared. Will kicked me under the table. We tried to hear what he was saying but his words were not regular English, they were so puzzling and odd. Had he come to cast a spell on us?

My father did the unthinkable.

"Come in. Warm up." He indicated the jumble of boots and coats in the entrance off the kitchen. "Of course, we want fish. We want fish, don't we, Eth?" But my mother shook her head quickly, and the man stood between inside and out, between spirit and flesh, unsure of how to proceed. My mother stepped up.

"Norm," she said. "I don't think this is a good idea. And her voice was so tight and small I wanted the stranger to leave and never come back.

But he remained, uncertain on our back step until my dad pulled him into our kitchen. Then he became solid and real; just a man selling fish. My dad pointed to my mother's chair because it was empty and there were no other spots around our supper table.

He sat, but slowly. He was like Mr. Wong, bowing to us, like we were royalty. The snow on his mukluks melted, forming a puddle on the linoleum right where my mother would surely sit. The man looked like he wanted to bolt.

"It's for human consumption, isn't it? People food? Your fish?" And then my dad turned back to the table and mimed eating. He pretended to gobble imaginary fish, hand to mouth, mouth to imaginary plate, bringing the fish up slowly, focusing, smiling, smacking his lips, swallowing, clucking, rubbing his stomach, and making a great show of how good the man's fish meal might taste.

The old man nodded. His tiny eyes disappeared in his face so only his wrinkles shone. He, too, pretended to eat and then Jennifer did and Will, as well. They scooped up imaginary fish on imaginary forks and it was a feast.

"It's so good," said Will, really getting into the game, gobbling, grabbing. "This is the best fish I've ever tasted."

And the man suddenly stopped, and his hands dropped into his lap, and we all looked. My mother was holding a bundle of clothing in her arms, my parka from last year and Ned's too small Ski-Doo suit. "Take these," she said.

The man looked at the coats. And then he shook his head. He wasn't smiling anymore, and nobody was eating anything.

"No fish?"

My mother shook her head. "No. No, thank you."

He stood and turned towards us, still seated at the table. He smiled again, but this time he forgot to use his eyes. He pulled his shoulders forward and shook his entire upper body at my mother. A low sound came from his throat.

It sounded like a word. Muskox.

Was he selling muskox? Muskox lived on the tundra, way, way north of here. No, he was imitating my mother, lowing and shaking his shoulders ever so slightly. It was her stance, guarded, protective. The man was mimicking her. I wished he wouldn't.

My father pushed back his chair. "I'm sorry," he said. "Perhaps another time." The man stood straight again and put out his hand. He looked at all of us, but I felt his eyes on me.

He said the word again and shook his head and upper body at the same time he shook my father's hand and turned his back. The door opened and he was swallowed by the shock of winter air.

My mother sat down. I saw her stocking foot touch the mukluk water. She recoiled. She tucked her legs behind her and curled her feet around the rungs of the kitchen chair. Her ankles remained locked, her knees pressed together, and when she turned to my father she spoke very quietly. "We don't know where that fish came from, Norm. These mines are spewing arsenic into the lakes. We won't be eating that fish. We won't." And then she uncurled and left the kitchen. She didn't even notice what the man was showing her. She didn't see she was a muskox mother. She just didn't see.

The next morning, a Saturday, Will and I found the tracks of our visitor's sled in the snow. The footsteps led to our door and then turned back towards the lake. The sled must have been heavy as the tracks gouged the surface deeply. I tried to imagine the man with the harness around his hips, trudging away into darkness.

"Do you think he'll come back?"

"No," said Will. "He won't come back. Why would he? But that was the best fish, eh? That was the best fish I ever tasted."

I nodded, knowing that my mother would always prefer the uniformity of fish sticks, the safety of packaging. It was her way of keeping us civilized. Muskoxen stand in a circle, guarding their young. My father didn't stand with my mother. He was the rogue bull, the unpredictable one. No wonder my mother was mad.

That night she made Polynesian Spork with Peas, a casserole conjured from tin cans. She manipulated the small key to roll back the metal top of the tinned meat. The key, on its perforated edges, revealed the dubious pink glob resting in gelled glory. Salty, emulsified, with the consistency of playdough, I balanced each spoonful in my mouth, not allowing the cubes of meat to contact my taste buds before swallowing the congealed mush. What was wrong with frozen fish? How bad would it taste? It couldn't be worse than what we were eating that night.

We drank Tang and ate tinned tomato soup, and when my mother was busy with Mrs. Johnston's care, or helping with Sylvan, my father would open a can of pineapple and we'd each get a ring, floating like a life preserver in a sea of brown beans.

We did not get wild food: no caribou, no rabbit, no white-fish, no hunted game. It may have had something to do with maintaining standards, it may have had something to do with my parent's particular social circle and their lack of access to hunting, trapping, and fishing. Yet still, as though the town would claim its due, the wild roared within us. How could it not? It was everywhere.

⌇

My father got a new job in 1968 or 1969, I can't remember exactly. I'm pretty sure I was in Grade Five and was asked to spell *superintendent* by my homeroom teachers. My face was hot and burning as I stood, singled out to stumble through so many syllables.

"Sit down," Mrs. Valdese commanded, shaking her head. She called on another girl, who sounded out my father's job first and then spelled it.

"What does it mean to have an intention, class?" prompted Mrs. Valdese, but this time her eyes floated over me like my mother's did when I asked questions about dreams and magic and the secret energy of stones.

My father's new job came with a lot of travel. He was often gone. It also came with a new government house.

"There is a little house I like," I told my mother as she banged through the pots and pans drawer, collecting items we now had to move.

"Oh?"

"I only saw it a few times, but maybe we could have that house."

"Margie," she said, looking up from her sorting. "We don't have a choice. What little house?"

"It's pink like the rocks around Long Lake."

"Long Lake."

"No. It's in Rainbow Valley, mostly pink but with a green wall, too."

My mother snorted. "Rainbow Valley? What on earth makes you think we should live in Rainbow Valley?"

Maybe it was not such a good idea. "The house is pretty, and the kids play outside all day long."

"They're truant. Those children are exactly the ones your father is attempting to educate. Rainbow Valley, my word!" And she told me to find an empty box from the back porch to start the packing.

Truant. I decided I would ask Jennifer. The word *true* means honest and good. Maybe truant meant honest and good but without table manners. It was how I wanted to be, and the pink house shimmered behind my eyes when I closed them lightly and looked at the sky. I carried the empty cardboard box into the kitchen, balancing it on my head, and the little house shifted into the square shadows of moving chaos.

In the school draw, our new house was all green. There was no pink. Three days after my mother got the curtains up, our new next-door neighbour, Mr. Crenshaw, threw his son, Don, into the snowbank after one or both drank too much whisky.

Don took our snow shovel and smashed it through the windshield of his father's brand new '68 Chevy. Then he walked away into thirty-five below. The glass took a slice out of Ned's foot the following spring, but Mr. Crenshaw wasn't around to see the blood. In fact, we didn't see him much after that.

"Did the son ever come back?" Ned asked me, as I recounted last winter's drama a third time, explaining what caused the nasty scar on his foot.

"Would you?" I countered. "Would you come back if our dad did that to you?"

He shook his head solemnly. "Our dad wouldn't."

I raised my eyebrows. "You never know." Then, just because I could, "Quick, Neddy, run! Here comes Mr. Crenshaw!" And, like a skinny rabbit on top of the snow, he skittered towards the safety of our side door.

~~

One night, just after Remembrance Day, an old Indigenous man wandering the newly built School Draw lowlands between Old Town and New Town saw my sister Jennifer through her basement room window, a square of golden light on a dark winter road. He came into the house, a split-level, went downstairs, and found her in her room.

"I was just sitting on my bed, listening to Steppenwolf, but I had these things on." She twisted the cord of her brand-new headphones. "I actually smelled him, Margie, I smelled him, just before he put his arms around me. It was so scary."

I thought of campfires. "Did he smell good?"

She shuddered, reliving the drama for my sake. "No, stupid. He shouldn't have been anywhere near me. Thank God, Dad was here."

And I comforted her and slept in her basement room that night, even though when I saw my dad and that old man swaying on the stairs together, I was totally confused. As they swung back and forth, as my dad muscled the old man towards the side door, I thought they were dancing. Not fighting, dancing.

Royals

"But when will I ever get to meet a real queen again?"

I was pleading with my parents to let me go by myself to McNiven Beach. Royalty was there. Her Royal Highness, Elizabeth II, had brought her two eldest children, Charles and Anne, to Yellowknife. It was 1970. Charles was only a year or two older than my sister. He might be looking for a princess. I had to go. I was almost a teenager, firmly in double digits.

Yellowknife became the capital of the Northwest Territories at Canada's centennial. Fort Smith wanted this honour, but was too near the Alberta border. It was deemed not northern enough. Yellowknife fit the bill better, and it seemed even the Queen of England agreed. She came to celebrate, bringing her children so they could see the great barren reaches of her outer colonies. Our town had obliged by preparing a

BBQ and a dance. I was planning on going with a girl from school, Alice, who'd contacted me out of the blue, but she'd been grounded for swearing at her mum.

"I called her a bitch because she is one. And now I can't go. Bitch."

My parents were dubious. My mother, a true monarchist, was working night shift and wouldn't be able to partake in that part of the Royal visit, while my father, more socialist by nature and politics, remained entirely unexcited. "Why don't you go with Jennifer? Or the boys?"

Was he insane? Jennifer and her friends had been fussing with their hair all day, seeing who could design the highest beehive. She misted my face with hairspray when I had gone to see what she was doing.

My brothers would be there, true, but they would pretend to have accidentally stumbled onto the dance. *Oh, what's going on? We just happened to be walking when we heard the music.* They were too cool to want to meet the Queen and her children. I was not.

"Please. I'll know people once I get there. The whole town is going." And it was true. But what I really wanted was to be able to go alone. I was secretly happy Alice was grounded. I wanted to see the Prince and I wanted the Prince to see me. I was eleven years old, still the Caribou Queen-in-waiting. Would he recognize this northern brand of royalty?

"It's just McNiven. I go there alone for swimming lessons all the time."

"Not at night, you don't."

"What night?" We'd entered the five days in June when the sky retained her red-and-pink dressing gown the entire night. As soon as the sun dipped below the horizon, it began to rise again. Northerners were that close to the top of the world. We were kings and queens of the castle, and my parents, the dirty rascals. I looked beseechingly at my father.

"Let her go, Eth. Margie is completely competent to go out in the daylight, and she's right, this is a fairly special event. I've heard they want young people at the beach to dance so the teenage Royals can participate as much as possible in teen culture."

I rolled my eyes. My father, the bureaucrat, knew zero about teen culture. My mother still looked dubious. "She's not a teenager." To me: "As long as you're back by ten, and I'll have your lenient father keeping his eye on that clock, Margie. I mean it."

McNiven was a ragged strip of sand on the edge of Frame Lake, about a half-hour from downtown. By the time I arrived, Prince Charles and his sister, Princess Anne, were standing in the sand, wearing stiff denim jeans, seams pressed in straight lines. I watched them dance in the beach sand to the strains of a hastily assembled legion group playing some brand of bad rock and roll. From my spot in front of the change shack, the Royals were deeply disappointing.

The Queen held a stiff purse in both hands. Her dress, with a matching coat of zigzag geometric design, looked like a costume a clown might wear in a parade. I'd seen the sort of bold geometrics on Twiggy in Jenny's fashion magazines, but they looked ridiculous on a middle-aged woman. The Queen's perma-smile was tighter than her zigzag dress, and both the Prince and Princess looked terribly uncomfortable, pretending to be normal teenagers doing normal teenager-type things. The midnight sun was a spotlight on their robotic sand dance, and I could see they were rigid with the effort of not batting at clouds of swamp mosquitoes that were thick in the evening air. The prince was wearing a blue sweater. You could see a skinny necktie knotted at the collar of his white dress shirt. He had a long nose and ears like fly swatters, jutting from below his painfully perfect haircut. The mosquitoes were flying up his royal nostrils and into his Jughead ears.

Despite the crowd, I was aware of a little circle of distance separating them. The only people filling that space were security men, obvious in their black windbreakers.

Poor Prince. Poor Princess. They would never be allowed to come to the shoreline of any lake to walk alone. There was no way I would be able to get near them. Even if I were closer, we would not be able to bridge the gap that existed between us. And yet they were the rulers of this place. Not just Yellowknife, the whole country.

Why them? What did they know about fireweed or ice fog or mining, or the Old Town? Who made the Royal family in charge?

I was about to go when I spotted Will up on the rocks behind the beach. He was sitting with a girl from my class, Maryanne, the one who knew I was a thief. They were close together, and his hand rested casually on the top of her leg where her skin met the fray of her cut-offs. Their heads were bent towards each other, and they were laughing. I felt another circle draw itself around them. Was she telling my brother about my crime? What was going on? Their intimacy excluded me. I was as separate from my brother and Maryanne as I was from the performance of the dancing Royals.

Heading home, the McNiven Trail crossed a broad muskeg bog. Usually, I loved to walk across the spongy land, but that night I felt hollowed out, like an ant-infested log. The loam was springy beneath my running shoes, and I could feel it running deep into the earth. I thought of old bones buried beneath my feet, the skeletons of caribou that used to gather here before the Royals called the land their own.

I scampered across the unstable surface, feeling the wobble and sway of this jellied earth. It reminded me of my dad's neck when he laughed, or the horrible, moulded salads, aspics, of church potlucks.

What did the Royals think, looking out at our lake, pretending to be like us, pretending to like us? And the thought morphed into something else. What did the Indigenous Peoples think of us white people coming? As I hurried across the trail, I realized I could be sucked into this quicksand, and the Prince and Princess would just keep on dancing. I was other to them. I was other to Maryanne, too, and that shook me.

My insignificance was sobering. But could it be something we shared? Did Anne and Charles feel lonely and disconnected out there, dancing for the people, pretending it mattered that our little town was now the capital city? Capital city of what? Muskeg? Bush? Bugs? I tried to imagine England but all I could conjure were images I'd seen in books: castles, fields of nettles, a rough seascape, a man in a ridiculous Q-tip hat guarding a gate.

Could those royal teenagers even imagine this pliable earth beneath my feet? Did they know anything about this land? About the lakes and trees and people who lived here? Maybe being a royal wouldn't be so great. Maybe it was like living on the surface, always walking on top of a bog, never really being anchored, never having any place to call home.

Were we white people also on the surface, stealing space from original people who lived on the land for hundreds of generations before?

Did Will lean over and whisper something to Maryanne, or did he kiss her behind her ear, on her neck?

Nothing about my adventure felt right, and I arrived home forty-five minutes before my curfew.

Makeover

Carr's Drugstore was a place we were allowed to go on Saturdays to spend our twenty-five-cent allowance. Will and Ned were with me the day I discovered Gloria. Jennifer was off on her own, or more correctly, with a group of girls from St. Pat's, girls who had not won my mother's full approval. They smoked, for one, and Darlene, the ringleader, swore like a sailor. I didn't know any sailors, but I figured, in my mother's mind, sailors were coarse.

Gloria was the exact opposite of coarse. She was refined, a doll, an exquisitely crafted porcelain doll, a foot tall, wearing a ruby-red dress trimmed in dark lace. She held a parasol, a tiny perfect parasol in her tiny, perfect china hand. She wasn't a doll for a child. She was a doll for someone like me, someone eleven-and-a-half years old who could look after her properly.

"Wow, look!"

"Big deal," said Ned when he saw her in the window. He puffed out his cheek, made a puffing fart sound with his mouth. "Who'd want that?"

"Do you think that parasol opens?"

"Parasol," scoffed Will, suddenly affecting a fake French accent. *"A parasol for a Paris doll."* He grinned at Ned. "Why would Margie want a stupid Paris doll? Are you French? *Ooo-la-la, Mademoiselle."* He was swinging his skinny butt side to side, ridiculous in frayed cut-offs. My brothers cracked up and Ned held the drugstore screen door open for Will, then swung it closed just before he stepped into the store. I hung back on the sidewalk, looking in at the doll in the window. It was not for sale. This doll was a raffle prize.

I looked more closely. Perhaps the design on the parasol would match the black lace on her dress. It was exquisite, this first prize beauty. The doll had real glass eyes, liquid brown, that seemed to look deeply into my own eyes. Her perfect hair fell into dark ringlets behind her beautifully moulded face. The dimple in her blushed cheeks and the lips that curved upwards seemed to be speaking directly to me. *Take me home,* the porcelain doll was urging. *Take me home.*

Mr. Carr was also encouraging.

"Every time you buy something, you can fill out a ballot," he explained. "You put it in this little box here, through the slot, see, and we draw the winner at the end of the week. You know your phone number, don't you?"

And because I did, and because each of my brothers and I spent a dime, we got three ballots, three chances on winning Gloria, front and centre of the confectionery.

"If we win that thing, you'll owe us all your allowances forever," said Will, but he wrote my name instead of his own, and even said the first line of the Our Father before stuffing it in the box on the counter. I wanted the porcelain doll more than anything I'd ever wanted before.

Somehow the doll had knowledge. She held secrets. She needed a person like me to share those secrets with. Gloria. I spoke her name that night in bed and conjured up the turn of the cheek, the bright eyes, no, the understanding in the eyes, until the doll became fused with my dreams and danced madly across my wildly covetous nights.

Three days later, when I picked up the phone there was an unknown female voice. "Is this the home of Margaret Macpherson?"

I knew it was about Gloria. I knew what had travelled between me and that doll was real. I knew I would have her, but a sudden shyness overcame me, and I passed the receiver to my mother and listened to her puzzled, "Yes?"

"What doll?" And then: "No, oh, no. I don't think that will be necessary. It's for the hospital auxiliary, isn't it? Well, I'm a member and I don't think the optics… Go ahead and pick another. Yes, perhaps a less privileged child, someone in the Old Town, perhaps, a more appropriate winner."

I stood, slack mouthed, as my mother continued. "Yes, they would be a good choice." Pause. "The mother told me he was gone when she brought the child in. Lacerations." Another pause. "No, there's an older girl, a twelve-year-old? Margie's age, I think."

The conversation continued, but I was sick, heartsick, belly sick, sick with this new knowledge I was somehow too good for the glorious Gloria. I made my way out of the instantly hot kitchen into the cool tiled bathroom where I sat on the toilet, gutted.

"Margie, what's wrong? Are you sick?" Jennifer pounded on the door. She probably wanted to look at herself in the mirror again. I *was* sick. Sick and silenced. I turned on the sink tap, hoping the gush of water would release pent up tears, but nothing happened.

"What are you doing in there?" demanded Jennifer, bursting in. "Selfish twerp," was lost in the slamming of the toilet lid. Those two words repeated and echoed after she crashed out, but I still couldn't cry. How could I cry when I was rich, not poor? Not having Gloria didn't mean I had nothing. I had books and other, smaller dolls. I was allowed to choose a bedspread and matching curtains out of the Eaton's catalogue. I was not from the Old Town.

∼

Something switched inside me after Gloria disappeared down the hill to a more deserving kid. If I was unworthy of Gloria, being too privileged, maybe that sort of prize was unworthy of me. I convinced myself I didn't really want a doll made from porcelain. What were you supposed to do, crawl into bed with a glass doll? How ridiculous. She'd be a lump of ice in the winter, and if that cold white face broke, you'd be hugging shards of sharp edges, a sack of blades.

"Crack." I said aloud, imagining Gloria's face splitting open on the first frosty night. Maybe she'd already taken a chunk out of the kid who'd got her. Wouldn't that be sweet revenge? I was, after all, eleven-and-three-quarters, about to start Grade Seven, and nobody in those higher grades had dolls. Dolls were for babies. I was done with dolls, and I pitied the unknown kid saddled with Gloria, the ice maiden.

If I was going to be considered richer and better, I'd best

learn to use that to my advantage. I knew what power looked like because it walked the hallways of public school, a cabal of mean girls who patrolled, seeking signs of weakness in anyone who didn't fit their mould. It meant becoming friends with the Grade Seven leader, Suzanne Koutsopoulos, Suz Kout, for short.

To get into Suz's good graces, I needed to find someone weaker and more needy than me, and my victim was the girl who got Gloria, the one my mother singled out for my doll. Maryanne Hebert, the girl who incited me to steal and then never said a word later. She still owed me a vial of blue glass beads.

I'd seen Maryanne on the rocks with my older brother. Since our encounter at the trading post I'd steered clear of her. I certainly didn't want to meet the older boy with the wire.

I did know Maryanne by reputation. She had an attitude. She often came to school late, if at all. She'd slouch in with barely a glance at the teacher and creep to her seat as though there should be no pause in the lesson. She was like a muskrat: shy, skittish, lurking in the shadows. If she missed the Old Town bus, she'd have to walk up the mile-long hill to the New Town, her constant excuse for tardiness. "No one woke me up."

Once, in Grade Three, late as usual, Maryanne rode up that hill clinging to the hitch on the back of the bus. The driver, oblivious to his passenger, later told a disciplinary committee he had no idea a child was clutching the back bumper, becoming more and more splattered in slush as the mud flaps failed and the wheels kicked up melting snow and muck. Maryanne was only seven or eight when she made her name as that fearless hitchhiker. It was the second autumn after our meeting at Weaver & Devour, the fall of unfinished business.

She was a fighter. She was a thief. The best thing I could do was reform her, especially if she was going to hang out with my brother. If she was just a little more like the rest of us, a little more compliant, a little more presentable, a little less Indian, she could fit in. I was, it turned out, my mother's daughter, and I thought a transformation was in order. Why shouldn't it be steady, practical, amenable me who showed her the way? It had to start with her appearance.

Maryanne had black hair, a regular rat's nest, but I sat in class casting surreptitious glances her way. I silently contemplated her skin tone, dark but not so dark she couldn't be fixed up.

If Maryanne was the sly rodent in the classroom, Suz Kout was the predatory wolf. She was junior high leader and her word was law. She ruled by choosing who to deputize, who to exclude, who to mock, and, mostly, how to look. Suz set the fashion standard to which all others aspired.

One day, after home bell, I saw Suz slouched in the hallway leafing through a brand-new *Tiger Beat* magazine, a glossy edition with Bobby Sherman on the front cover. It was a perfect opportunity.

"Hi." I stopped just in front of her and leaned against the wall. Our lockers were four apart, so it wasn't entirely strange we should speak. Suz looked up, made a small coughing sound, as though something unpleasant was caught in her throat, and flipped the page.

I slumped down next to her. "Where did you get that?" I already knew Suz shoplifted from the Hudson's Bay at least twice a week. She'd shown the whole locker row her booty. At first it was just nail polish and lipsticks, but her items were getting larger and more daring. A full glossy fashion magazine had to be shoved under a shirt or shifted to the small of the back, tucked into the waistband of a skirt in order to get it out the door.

She didn't answer.

"Someone told me you were going to be a beautician. I think you'll make a good one."

Suz lifted her eyes from the magazine. "Aesthetician." Her tone was flat, bored. She flipped the page of the magazine.

"My big brother Paul can get those magazines free from the drugstore, but they have the covers ripped off and they're always a month behind."

"Humph." Suddenly, "Are you related to Will?"

"Yeah, he's one of my brothers. The others are Paul and Neddy."

"Will. The one who plays guitar?"

"Yeah. Do you know him?"

"No, but I'd like too. He looks a bit like this guy, eh?" She pointed to the Bobby Sherman cover photo. "What's your name again?"

"I'm Margie."

She turned another page, scanned an advertisement for pimple cream.

"I was wondering if you wanted to help me with a little project?" I thrust my jaw towards the Pond's Fresh Start advertisement. "You know that kid, Maryanne? The one from the Old Town? She could use that Fresh Start. I was thinking we could, you know, fix her up, make her decent looking, so she wouldn't have to skulk around the hallways. What do you think?"

Suz's eyes shifted to mine. "Why would I want to do that?"

"Oh, I just thought it would be nice to have someone to practise on, being an aesthetician-in-training. You know, making someone scruffy into someone pretty? Sort of what they do in these magazines. A do-over. We could give Maryanne a makeover."

She closed the magazine. "Fix her up?"

"Yeah, make her look more ..." I paused, "... like us."

Suz didn't bat an eye. "You think your brother might be around?"

"He usually is," and just like that, we were on the same team, and better yet, our project was my idea.

I needed to keep the conversation moving forward. "With a little cover stick or some foundation, I think Maryanne could look okay. What shade of foundation would work, her being an Indian?" And we started flipping through the magazines as the hallway emptied out and the dust motes floated and fell to the clanging of the janitor emptying the trash bins.

For the next week, Suz and I talked about Maryanne, speculating on her background.

"That narrow face, pure Indian. Those slanty eyes, same thing." She looked me up and down appraisingly. "She probably gets her clothes at the charity thrift shop my mum runs." Suz's mother was a member of Daughters of the Midnight Sun, a clutch of white women, who ran the second-hand clothing business out behind Welfare just down from the Pawn Shop. I wished my mother had those sorts of volunteer jobs instead of her shift work. I missed having her home.

It was true, Maryanne wore stripes and flowers at the same time, as though it didn't matter. Her horrible striped pants made her look shrunken-in, skinny beyond comprehension.

"She's like one of the Brides of Dracula," said Suz. I wasn't allowed to see *The Brides of Dracula* when it came to the

Capitol cinema, but I nodded anyway. If there were a candidate to be married to a vampire, it would be Maryanne.

"We need to dress her better and at least try to match things up. She looks like she shops out of a ragbag instead of the Bay, like every other normal person." And, miracle of miracles, Suz laughed. Not at me. With me. We were that close.

A plan was hatched. We'd fix up Maryanne and we'd do it just because she needed it. We'd invite Maryanne for a sleepover in my backyard. I'd set up the tent; we'd get all the stuff, and just like that, boom, a makeover.

"How do you know she doesn't have fleas?"

"Not enough scratching. Besides, it's my tent."

"I'm not going in it if there are body bugs." Suz made a face. "Every time you'd go camping, it would be fumigation city, an infestation of Fleabert bugs all through the summer holiday."

Fumigation. Infestation. Suz was smart. But I was counting on her wanting to be more than just smart and popular and pretty. I was counting on her wanting to be good. I'd make sure Will saw her being good.

At recess the next day, we spotted Maryanne lurking in the schoolyard, near three scrawny pines, their bark stripped by knives. She was sitting there by herself, smoking, on the edge of the rock. We sidled over. Suz did the talking.

"Hey, so Maryanne, Margie's mum is going to let her set up the tent in the backyard this weekend and me and her thought you'd like to have a sleepover."

Maryanne narrowed her eyes. I tried to imagine how they'd look with a little eyeliner, maybe some colour on the lids, blue or purple to make her look less angry.

"What?"

"Yeah, we were thinking we could set the tent up, talk a bit, read a few fashion mags, have a pajama party, you know? What do you think? Do you want to come?"

"I've got an extra sleeping bag," I volunteered, realizing our classmate might not have one. We had a spare bag at home, an old one that had Ned peed in more than once, but I figured Mom washed it and even if she didn't, would Maryanne care?

She still looked suspicious. I became increasingly aware of my own face, au naturel, not even a hint of makeup. What might sway her to the surprise makeover party?

"My brother Will might lend us his portable eight-track player so we can listen to music." She perked up and I got a good look at her teeth, crooked, and really small, rat teeth, for sure, slightly yellow. Still, with a little lip gloss, maybe an orangey colour to play down her skin tone, those teeth could look whiter.

"You're Will Macpherson's sister?" Sheesh, same as Suz, all about the brothers.

Suz elbowed me in my ribs.

"Oh, yeah, Will. I doubt if he'll be around. Just us. You, me, and Suz. And maybe my brother Ned."

"He traps with my cousin Lawrence."

Will traps? I didn't think so, but I nodded, making a note to read up on colours. Jennifer told me how colours were seasons and we all had our own special set of colours that made us look our best. I was winter, which is good, because that's the long season. Most white people were winter. Maryanne's season was probably those short three weeks between fall and frostbite. What did they call it? Indian summer.

I almost told Maryanne she was an autumn — the burnt campfire hair and those yellowish teeth like fallen leaves —

when the bell rang and reminded me to shut up because the fixing-up was the secret part of the party.

Maryanne went into school right away, without waiting for us, but over her shoulder she said she'd decide after school. There was a note in Suz Kout's locker that afternoon.

"I'll come Friday." There was no signature, but we knew it was from Maryanne, even though all the words were spelled right. The printing was really small and sort of squished together and scratchy. Suz and I started gathering all the beauty magazines we could get our hands on to prepare for the next day.

I didn't have a lot of makeup because my parents didn't believe in it, but I had a small stash of things I'd bought with babysitting money, stuff they didn't know about. I had an eyelash curler, something my mother mistook for Will's guitar tuner when she came upon it by accident changing my sheets. I also had mascara, black, and something called Apple cheek blush. Oh, and the end of Jennifer's pearl shimmer lipstick, enough to feel sophisticated when I remembered to put it on after leaving the house.

Suz Kout had lots of stuff and we smuggled some extras from Jennifer's top drawer. She would be gone on a band trip to Hay River, around the Lake, so we swiped lip gloss and brown mascara. "We need all the help we can get," said Suz, when I noticed her pocketing a new eyeliner. "It's a big job, fixing up the Fleabert."

That night I was anxious and couldn't sleep. I thought about how we were going to make over Maryanne and maybe cause her to be so pretty she'd get crowned Caribou Queen. Not only was I projecting my own fantasy onto her, but somewhere in the back of my sleepless brain I think I was also hoping she'd be grateful to me, so much so that my childhood theft would be obliterated by blinding gratitude.

I thought of transformation, a caterpillar changed into a glorious butterfly; Maryanne transformed from a regular Indian girl into a beautiful butterfly with jewelled wings, all because Suz and I cared or wanted to make it look like we cared. I was determined we'd save Maryanne from herself.

On Friday, school seemed endless. Suz and I met at first recess, but Maryanne either didn't come out, or was up on the rocks, smoking, away from the cruel playground. Maybe she hadn't arrived at all. We finally saw her at the noon break after second bell, but we didn't wave her over or anything. We didn't want her to think we'd be friends on the playground. People at school were surprised enough that Suz Kout was hanging out with uncool me. I couldn't wait to see their faces when the madeover Maryanne reappeared.

We made a plan for getting Maryanne to my house without a lot of people seeing. I decided it was because Suz didn't want people to know she had a good, soft heart. At final recess she slipped over to Maryanne.

"Margie got a detention for looking at someone's spelling test, so you can meet us outside the detention room twenty minutes after bell, okay?"

I was good at spelling, I'd never cheated, and I didn't even know which room was detention hall, but Maryanne nodded and muttered something about missing the last bus. She was clutching a lumpy plastic bag.

The rendezvous worked, the schoolyard was empty, and no one saw the three of us cross the rocks. At my house we set up the tent. Maryanne definitely knew what she was doing.

"Looks like you've gone camping before," said Suz.

"Every summer, on the land," she nodded.

"What do you mean? Like, up the highway? To Prelude Lake or Sammy's Beach or something?"

"No, we got a summer camp. My dad runs traps. Up the East Arm."

The East Arm was real wilderness, not more than a couple of people lived up that way. Plus, I didn't remember Maryanne having a dad.

"How the hell do you get way up there?" Suz asked.

"We got a freighter canoe. We paddle, motor, paddle some more."

Suz frowned. She looked mean and uppity, and I froze in the middle of connecting the big frame poles that held up the canvas roof.

"When you say traps, do you mean like Indian traps? Like a trapline?"

Maryanne stopped fiddling with the bar on her side and looked over at Suz.

"Yeah. My mum's Dogrib." She poked out her pointy little chin. "You got a problem with that?"

There was a split second of silence, then both of us shook our heads.

"I'm mixed. My dad, he married Dogrib."

"He's a Frenchie, right?" It sounded like a challenge coming from Suz's mouth. Or a slur.

Maryanne shook her head. "More white."

"You mean like a voyageur?" We'd been studying the fur trade in social studies.

Maryanne frowned. "Scottish, maybe, way back."

"Yeah, right," said Suz. "And my grandfather was a Negro," except she said it long and drawn out. *Knee-grow*.

Maryanne dropped her corner and the tent collapsed in a big puff of air. "I could go home."

"Nah," said Suz. "I was just kidding. Jeez. We want you to stay. We don't care if you're an Indian or a Mate-ee or whatever," and she looked darts at me, like I'd better say the right thing or the whole makeover was going to go tits up.

"Nope, we don't care. I used to play with a girl like you, all the time. Carmel. She lived across the alley. She was even more Indian than you. Why, you'd look super white beside that kid, way more Scottish. You know how to play bagpipes?" I held my nose and karate-chopped my throat, so a weird moaning came from my mouth. Maryanne frowned but she picked up the tent corner again.

I cast a good look at her as she worked. I could see the Indian parts. She looked like Carmel, minus the fat. It was in the shape of her eyes and her cheekbones, high and pronounced. Jennifer told me high-end fashion models pulled out their back teeth to get that look. Maybe Maryanne was already beautiful.

We eventually got the tent up, got the bags unrolled, and because we didn't want to scare her, we didn't tell her right off what we were planning to do. We had the skincare kit, deep moisturizing facial wash, an exfoliating grapefruit mask, toner, all the products. We had the little brushes and enough eyeliner and eye shadow and lipstick to paint the whole Goddamn Dogrib Nation, but first we had to put Maryanne at ease. We decided to get into our pajamas and just hang out.

Maryanne was suddenly shy: "Could you wait outside when I change?' Even though Suz rolled her eyes at me, we did. I was thankful I didn't have to see her half-naked, all ribs and skin.

There was some rustling, a crackling sound, and when she called us back in, she was wearing these cheapo pajamas, straight out of the package. They still had the cardboard creases in them, and those starchy pink pajamas had little white horses on them, looking so new and big on scrawny Maryanne, it made my throat tight. Neither of us said a thing, but I wondered if she bought them because she didn't have any, or because this was her first sleepover.

Maryanne crawled quickly into Ned's sleeping bag. Me and Suz sat on top of the bags, pretending everything was normal. The air was hot and still inside the tent.

"What do you do at that camp all summer?" asked Suz, pretending she really wanted to know.

"I don't know. We fish. Hunt. You know. Regular stuff."

"For Indians. Regular for Indians."

"I guess." Maryanne propped herself up on her elbows. "It's probably not much different than what you do when you go camping."

I thought about our tent trailer; the propane stove, and the cool little compartments where you stored things. We'd bought it a few years ago once Mother refused to drive the Mackenzie anymore. "Just take the lot of them camping," she'd tell my father. "Lord knows, five days alone would be holiday enough." I knew Mum was after Dad to get one of those portable toilets, too, so we didn't have to use creepy outhouses with their germy, lime smell.

"We fish," I volunteered. "My brother Paul once caught a jackfish so big it fed the whole family."

"We don't eat jackfish. We feed pike to the dogs." I thought of Muskox man and his sled full of food, our refusal to buy.

Suz spoke. "What else do you do in that camp? What does

your mum do? Does she ever dance around the campfire or talk to the northern lights?"

"No, that's stupid."

Nobody called Suz Kout stupid to her face. I didn't dare breathe.

"At least I read," Suz countered. "Lots of dumb Indians don't even know how to read."

"That's because our language isn't written down," said Maryanne, quietly, maybe sorry for calling Suz stupid. "It's oral, you know, telling stories and stuff. It's from the ancestors, even the ones who have died."

"Cool."

"Weird," said Suz.

I could only hear the sound of the others breathing and the buzz of a lone mosquito at the top of the tent. I tried to see the bug in the dimness, but all I could make out were the makeup bags me and Suz had collected stashed against the back canvas wall, waiting to do their work.

"Say something," challenged Suz.

"In Dogrib?"

"Yeah. Tell us one of the stories."

And then Maryanne scrunched down in Ned's sleeping bag, closed her eyes, and started speaking in this other language, so deep and strange it seemed to come from inside her skinny little belly instead of from her mouth.

In the semi-dark of the tent, with the words rich and different, I got the strange feeling she knew stuff me and Suz would never know. Even though she tried to fool us with the pink pajamas, I knew Maryanne was going to paddle her voyageur canoe up the East Arm every summer with her family to pick berries and fish and live on the land. She was going to keep on speaking her language and tell stories about her mother and her mother's mother, and all the ancestor's voices would be in those stories, so much so that she'd never have to write them down.

All the makeup in the world wasn't going to change Maryanne. Her hair would be just as messy as ever, and she'd still be skinny and the pink pajamas wouldn't be pink anymore, they'd be faded and dirty, but you know what? It wouldn't matter at all, because Maryanne wouldn't care. She'd just hop in that old canoe every summer and point it up into the wind. Then she'd paddle hard, all elbow joints and wiry arms, and head up the East Arm of Great Slave until she was clean out of sight.

"I don't want to do it anymore," I told Suz, as the story wound down. She knew what I meant, because she started packing up right after Maryanne's voice trailed off.

"You can stay here, Margie, but, me, I'm going home. You and her can talk Indian until your tongues fall out of your faces, see if I give a shit. You're the one who needs a make-over." And with that she rolled up her sleeping bag, grabbed her makeup bags, and walked out of my yard.

"What's her problem?" asked Maryanne. "What makeover?" But I didn't want to say, because it just seemed so small and stupid all of a sudden, and Maryanne probably wouldn't get it, anyway.

I am rightfully ashamed of my part in this story. I cannot begin to imagine how Maryanne felt, understanding our pathetic intentions to transform her. And that's the thing. I didn't think of her feelings, whether or not she was aware how half-hearted was my offer of friendship. Charity offered out of pity is a poor excuse for bonding. What I wanted was to be admired by Suz. What I got was a small glimpse into the uniqueness of Maryanne's world. I didn't deserve her generosity, and yet, somehow, it was offered.

～～

Things were different between Suz and me after the night of the failed makeover. She no longer spoke to me in the halls when we moved up to Grade Eight, and sometimes when I walked past a group of girls, I'd see Suz in the middle. She'd say something and all of them would laugh.

Something had shifted with Maryanne and me, too. It was almost the end of summer holidays when I saw her again. This time I was invited to her thirteenth birthday party in Willow Flats. Although I didn't consider myself a true friend, something of what happened that night stuck, making me a candidate for the party.

Maryanne was a still a fighter. I'd seen her walking down Franklin Avenue or outside the post office, her hands curled into quick fists, her feet flat and bare. We pretended we didn't know each other, that she hadn't come to sleep in my tent and hadn't spoken in the deep resonate language of her grandmother.

The birthday invitation was delivered in a lumbering mumble. "Come to my place, a party, on Friday. I'm thirteen. Ask your mum. We got stew." It was more a command then an invitation, but partially from shock, partially from curiosity, I nodded. My mother gave me permission when I told her I was going to another friend's house. She trusted me more than she trusted Jennifer, who, in her adolescence, was challenging boundaries and acting out. I felt bad about the lying, but not so bad that I'd admit to my solo sojourn to the Old Town.

My mother, understanding the obligation of a birthday, purchased a gift from the Hudson's Bay, a hand mirror with a bevelled edge and a matching brush with soft, useless bristles. It was an old-fashioned present and embarrassing to me, mostly because it reminded me of the makeover and my mother's persistent comments about Maryanne's untidy hair. I knew I could not give her the gift selected by my mother. I also knew my mother would never understand why I felt it inappropriate. I stashed the brush set in the garage, substituting one of my own treasures — a real geologist's rock pick — in its place. When I tucked the stout pick into the back of my jeans to smuggle it out of the neighbourhood, one thought prevailed; I might need it for protection.

I walked to the Old Town with the late afternoon sky still filled with light and I found her house not so much by description or address, but by the sound of the gathering within.

The house Maryanne lived in was small by any standard. It was set along the lakeshore, one of the original cabins built, then abandoned once prospectors deemed the Gold Rush legitimate and the New Town was erected. Maryanne's house was far from the main road, far from basic amenities: sewer, water, and electricity. But from her yard I could hear the big lake nuzzling the shore. I could smell the spruce-gum wind and feel the press of night upon my body, the softness of the flats spread about, and the glow of the New Town above, barely illuminated behind guardian rocks.

I didn't recognize anyone as I edged into the front storm porch. None of the people gathered were from our school. They may not even have been from our town.

The house had only two rooms that I could see, the first open and the second hung with old floral curtains floor to ceiling, dividing the back portion into bedrooms. Maryanne, with two brothers on either side, had an interior room, all trembling cloth walls and, of course, no windows.

It was into this space I was led, after the relatives in the front room checked me out. The curtain walls were a patchwork of thinned fabrics, now faded. They were knit together with tiny, perfect stitches. I recalled the mukluk seller at the trading post. I could almost imagine her at home in one of the Old Town dwellings, needle flashing, her face backlit, as she concentrated on the task at hand, steadily sewing beads onto hide. Someone here had handsewn the drapes. The tiny, even stitching seemed incongruous with the general hubbub of the house, but I noticed it and for some reason, it steadied me. I was totally out of my element.

Maryanne's single bed occupied almost all of the curtained room, and we sat there while the different coloured curtains swung and dipped, emitting snatches of conversation, the strong, wild smell of game from the oil stove, and odd drafts of fresh air as the front door opened and closed to people coming and going amid animated chatter.

There was laughter and conversation beyond the drapes, and Maryanne and I perched inside, unsure of what to say to each other. I felt strange with her. It was certainly not like it was at school. We had no context. Her bed was unmade, and, nervous, I plucked at her nubby sheets. Maryanne's pillow was a flattened piece of foam rubber shedding bits of yellow stuffing. It looked crumbly, as though it had been gnawed.

A poster of Little Joe Cartwright from *Bonanza* was safety pinned to the curtain above where Maryanne sat, and because it was the only thing familiar, I latched onto his ruggedly handsome face, a life preserver tossed to a drowning swimmer.

"I have that poster." I smiled up at the white teeth and coiffed hair of the lean cowboy. "He's so good-looking."

Maryanne followed my eyes and frowned. "He's stupid," she said. "Stupid." And, as though to prove her point, she reached up and behind, dragging the poster from its place. She balled it up, a sound louder than any conversation in the house; although, slowly, slowly, other noises came back, sharper and more intense.

I heard the burble of the promised stew, the murmur of relatives, a small whining voice repeating *I want it now* over and over again.

"Holy crow, Maryanne. Why'd you do that?"

"Bullshit."

"What?"

"All them boys living together with no mum, like they're all so special. Stupid. Just bull."

"You saw them?"

"On TV. Twice."

"I never saw them, but I got my poster from Rexall."

Maryanne narrowed her eyes. "You know what's best about *Bonanza?*"

"What?"

"The beginning, when they burn the map." She starts humming the theme song from the TV show, a tune that immediately suggested galloping horses.

"The map?"

"Yeah, the land. Bullshit cowboys burn up the land." She pitched the crunched-up poster across the room where it fell to the floor. There was a pair of shorts there, underwear still inside. They embarrassed me, so I didn't say anything about the map or the poster or the television show.

139

Instead, I sat back on the bed. There was something partially hidden, partially sticking out of Maryanne's sheets. I shifted my weight so as not to squish the lump near the top of the bed. Maryanne saw me squirm and pulled at the bulge. It was the raffled doll, Gloria. It had been almost two years since I'd seen her in Carr's Drugstore, but I had this strange sense that although she was forced to live away from me, she was — in some bizarre way — still mine. I thought of the Brewster boys, the foster children taken and then given back. I thought of the hostel. I thought of Carmel.

I took Gloria from Maryanne and turned her over in my hands. The doll looked totally different. One brown eye was missing, and her curls had been cut jagged around the face, blunt and uneven on the sides. A long crack ran up one leg and came out at her neck. I couldn't tell how much more damage was done, because the ruby dress, now in tatters, still covered Gloria's ceramic body. Someone had written a word that began with the letter s on her arm in ballpoint pen, but I couldn't make out the lettering. The parasol was long gone, but I was convinced it was the same doll.

"Where did you get this?"

"That old thing?" She shrugged.

"I think it's the same doll I won. My mum made me give it away."

"You didn't like it, either?" And she smiled.

"I thought I liked it. But it's not really very nice." Even in my own ears, my voice rang with judgment. "I mean, who would make a doll with a clay face? Who wants old Clayface?" I tried running the words together hoping Maryanne would laugh, but at the same moment I realized it was true. The doll no longer mattered. I looked more closely at Gloria.

"I tried to make her more, real, you know? Like you and that other kid wanted to do to me." Maryanne laughed. "Who wants something that looks all fancy-pants? Not me. She got a fix-down. My brother, though, he shouldn't have wrote on her arm like that. He's just eight."

"But how did you get it?'

She blushed.

"I got her because I was the best volunteer at the hospital. I worked there, you know, last summer. My cousin was in the hospital all the time. He had polio when he was little but he's good now. I used to help him. I was a volunteer."

"My mum works at the hospital."

"Oh. Well, we probably didn't work the same time."

"My mum does shift work. She's there all the time." I'd caught her in a lie and I didn't want to let go.

She took the maimed Gloria out of my hands. "I think we need to put it in the ground."

"What?"

"Well, it was yours, but wasn't. And then it was mine, but not really mine, either. Let's bury her or, I know," her face brightened, "lets float her out on the lake, let her be her own self in the water."

Float her on the lake? Let her be her own self? I didn't know what Maryanne was talking about.

"Be her own self?"

"Yeah, in the water. See what happens."

Confused, I simply nodded.

A male voice broke our silence. "Come and eat!" and Maryanne leapt up. "We'll do it after supper." She parted the curtain at the exact place and the other room opened around us.

Eight or nine friends, neighbours, relatives, had assembled in the larger space. Each held a bowl and they lined up behind the central cooker, an oil stove that bore no resemblance to my mother's enamel Moffat with the four gas rings. This was something totally different. On the blackened cast-iron surface, an even more blackened pot simmered. The soup-stew was ladled into each bowl in turn by Maryanne's tiny dark-haired mother.

There was little formality, no birthday song, just food and a hot, close room full of faces gathered in a circle to eat in celebration of Maryanne's presence in the world. There were lots of aunties and a smattering of uncles. Among them, I was the only stranger.

I took a chipped blue bowl and held it, ready to eat whatever was served at my first Old Town party. The boy in front of me stepped aside. "You go first," he said. It was the same boy from Weavers, the one who saw me pitch the stolen beads towards the old man.

I moved in front of him quickly, hoping he wouldn't recognize me, and waited while Maryanne's mother ladled up a large portion of meaty gravy and potatoes. It smelled delicious. "Take bread," she said, and then to the boy behind me: "Show her the fry bread, Lawrence. We got tea, too. You're welcome." And I really did feel welcome, welcomed and warmed at the same time. Maryanne and I ate together. The big chunks of meat in the rich thick sauce were delicious, sweet and gamey at the same time, and the bread soaked up the gravy.

After we'd finished, we headed down to the lakeshore with Gloria.

"I thought we could put her out on a little boat, maybe light it on fire, but I don't see nothing here that would float."

She picked up a rock and skipped it across the surface of the lake. The skims sounded in ricochet, a sweet *thwap, thwap, thwap* and I suddenly remembered the pickaxe in my backpack. "Hey, we could bury her. You know, let her be her own self?" I was mirroring Maryanne's words back at her, trying them on for size, but she seemed to understand.

"Yeah, buried. We'll make a cairn. That's what you do." She looked at the geologist's pick I hastily unpacked. "That's neat. We'll use it to dig a hole."

"It's for you. Happy Birthday."

"Oh, okay." She looked at the pick and then at me. "Cool."

Maryanne started moving rocks aside with her foot. Once we got to the shale and sand, I began to dig. Neither of us spoke of why, but just as I was about to put the doll in the hole, Maryanne held up her hands.

"She wasn't right, for me, or for you. This is right."

And, it felt right. I nodded.

Maryanne took the battered doll from me and placed it gently, almost lovingly, in the pit now filled with water. We started to pile rocks on top. I didn't know if she meant it was right that we were burying her, or if she and I were right together, but either way, I loved her saying it. Our act of disposal felt like a ceremony, like I also received a gift, even though it wasn't my birthday.

I picked up a small white bone from the beach. It was so much better than Clayface with her matching parasol. I slipped the bone in my pocket. I wanted to remember this day. Maryanne had the key to what I needed to know. I wanted her toughness, her ability to do whatever she wanted. I thought of the Caribou Queen, not pulling knives and beating up people with beer bottles, but the way she was before the porcelain people came with their stupid useless parasols, when she was in her place, out on the barren lands, north-east of the lake.

I think in that moment I realized that the Caribou Queen, the concept, not the person who bullied and belittled people outside the post office, lived far away from things in town. She had the power to direct the herd to death or life. I imagined she could transform herself into one of them and run and run and run. It was caribou that fed us tonight. Was the stew a gift from the Queen? Did she butcher that animal herself or just send it to Maryanne's mother to feed me? Maybe the food and the gift were the same. Maybe Maryanne could be the one to teach me to become the Caribou Queen, but I also knew enough not to ask.

I'm not sure if Maryanne would even remember me now, or that important thirteenth birthday: my first independent foray to the Old Town, the doll, the burial, the way we stood together on the edge of the lake, on the edge of our adolescence.

Have I invented those feelings of respect, extrapolated, imposed them upon someone who may or may not ever know she mattered to me? Was that overwhelming feeling of belonging false? Or was it simply something I needed so badly I invented it, made it real by dint of desire? I don't know and I may never know, but I still believe to this day something special passed between us.

Corrals

At the new green house we made friends with neighbourhood kids. Jennifer was mostly gone, running with that new crowd of cool girls, so Will became our leader.

In late September, Ned and Will and I went picking cranberries on the old Negus mine site. We invited Dick and Joe Thurber from up the street, mostly because I liked the Thurber brother's dog. Spike discovered the old mine shaft. He barked and barked and wouldn't stop until we came to see. The mine shaft had grown over but not so much that it wouldn't swallow each of us, an open throat.

"I don't think we should," I cautioned, but the boys were beyond listening.

"Let's see how deep it goes," said Will, gathering rocks.

It was his idea, so we let him drop the first stone down the shaft, and we listened to it tumble through the darkness until, what seemed like an age later, the plunk of water echoed below.

The boys twitched and wiggled, elbowing to get more rocks, insisting they would fill the shaft, but the mouth of the mine consumed our stones, and we quickly became bored, distracted by old assaying core samples and broken bits of metal and equipment that lay on the surface of the mine site. The core samples were smooth and round and weighty, and we filled our pockets with them, imagining they were laden with gold.

Further from the open shaft was a rock cut filled with water. My brothers and their friends stripped down to their underpants and pushed each other until all of them were paddling around in the quarry. It was shallow enough to stand up at the edges, over their heads in the middle.

"Come on, Margie, don't be a chicken," they called, but I was shy with the neighbour boys and I watched, wishing I could shed my clothes so quickly.

Arsenic was a dangerous biproduct of gold mining, so I comforted myself with the knowledge the water might be laden with it. My brothers and their friends splashed in the sun-warmed rock bath while I petted Spike, speaking to him softly about what a good dog he was.

Joe Thurber was the first out. He stretched out on the rocks, his briefs clinging. "Aren't you hot in all those clothes?" he asked and then, turning to the boys still in the water, "Have you guys ever played Stuff the Duck?"

My brothers were puzzled, but Joe's brother understood. He snorted: "They're not going to play that game with their own sister."

"What is it?" asked Will, clambering out and drawing up his knees to his shoulders. Gooseflesh stood on his skinny arms, rounded in warming.

The Thurber boys exchanged glances. "It's a game you have to be bare naked to play. You put grass and stuff inside a girl, inside her panties and up her hoo-ha. Like stuffing a duck."

I felt my face burning.

"Why would you?" asked Ned.

"Some girls like it."

"Who?" I shook my head.

"We've done it with some of your friends, Margie," said Joe. "They like it."

"Like who?"

"Indian girls."

"I don't believe you."

"We didn't want to do it to you, Margie. I'm just telling you. It was your sicko brother who asked."

I felt a tingling in my crotch. I was hollow yet filled with sticks and grass, stuffed before them. I choked out my rage.

"You're swimming in poison. Why do you think I didn't go in?" I saw four scrawny boys shivering around a trough of toxic water. "No wonder you wanted to play stupid, dirty, sex games, your minds have rotted from arsenic."

I wished Jennifer were there. She'd spring at Dick and Joe, smash their ugly heads together.

I was equally glad she wasn't there.

"Come, Spike." I was embarrassed by what my brothers had heard and deeply afraid this ugliness would remain between us.

⌇

That same summer, a few months before I turned thirteen, a man brought horses to town. I don't know how it was arranged, but I do know the horses were trucked up an endless highway to get there. Once the news was out, I longed to see them. I imagine those poor horses now, shaking and sneezing in that dusty transport, ears laid horizontal, restless and worrying in those makeshift stalls, not knowing that the highway north was well and truly a three-day road.

The ranch — what the man called his operation — was set up at the Bristol, a monument to Arctic aviation at the intersection of the Yellowknife Highway and Old Airport Road. The Bristol was an ancient Wardair craft, the first wheeled freighter to land at the North Pole, purchased by the town and mounted on massive steel pillars. It was a place for teenagers to go and make out. Paul had been there, and Jennifer, many times. Will, almost fourteen, claimed he wasn't interested.

"Yuck. I never want to go to the Bristol. I think Paul just wants people to think he's a big deal."

But I wanted to go to the Bristol. I wanted to go for the horses. I loved horses. I read everything I could about horses, about racetracks and steeplechase and ranchers, about cowboys and girl detectives who rode horses. *Black Beauty* was still my favourite book.

For Christmas four or five years earlier, the Christmas after I gave Carmel Johnston the pink soap, Will and Ned and I received plastic play figurines, real horse people, Johnny and Jane West and Chief Cherokee. Will was Johnny West, I was Jane, and Ned ended up being Chief Cherokee. Being a Chief almost made up for not being one of the West family, so it felt more or less fair.

"Are we married?" I asked Will.

"No, way. Yuck. We're brother and sister."

Our plastic riders came with their own horses. Mounts, Will called them. My mount was a palomino; Johnny rode a bay he claimed was fifteen hands high, even though all the plastic horses were the same size, just different colours. We pretended Chief's pony was a stolen pinto. He rode bareback because there were only two saddles, two bridles.

"I should have one. If I stole your horse, I probably stole your saddle, too," said Ned.

"All Indians ride bareback," I consoled as the perpetual peacemaker in our younger sibling consortium. "Look at Jane." I swaggered my cowgirl figurine across the cement floor. "Even when she's walking around, she's got bowlegs."

Ned flicked off Jane's plastic red cowboy hat with his middle finger. "Shouldn't wear that in the house." He was jealous because Chief Cherokee's headdress was fully moulded to his head and the feathers were made from blue plastic instead of real feathers. Jane West had blond braids and a red vest and chaps I could take on and off.

The boys played horses with me for a few days during that Christmas break, but ultimately, I had to recruit Carmel Johnston to gallop around the furnace where I'd established a corral and an imaginary ranch house. It was where the West siblings lived when they were not fighting the Chief and his roving band of horse thieves.

Melly — I'd decided the name Carmel was just too dumb — would only play if she could be Jane and Johnny West simultaneously, and under her control the plastic people spent a lot of time kissing in their bedroom. Because they were moulded to be on horseback, Melly saw their spread legs as an opportunity.

"Let's pretend Chief wants to scalp Jane, but, you know, down there," she said coyly, eyes lusty and sharp.

"But isn't scalping about hair?"

"What are you, some sort of retard?"

⌣⌣

Unlike my make-believe assembly of straw and stable in the basement, the real corrals at the Bristol were fashioned out of old pallets. The horse operation was just outside the town limits, and it was in full swing by the time I finally talked my dad into driving me out.

"It's truly the end of the road," he said, shaking his head sorrowfully as we drove past the signs that advertised Trail Rides, five dollars each. "Anywhere beyond here, and you've got to fly or ride one of those poor, mangy beasts."

He was referring to the six horses now tethered in the shadow of the Bristol. I begged him to stop — the horses were a true novelty in a place unable to grow feed to sustain live-stock — but he drove on, intent on some other Saturday task.

"Can I go riding? Please Dad? Please Dad? Please?"

"It doesn't look like this hobby farm is going anywhere soon, Margie," he noted. "A fin is a little steep, but I'm pretty sure we can swing it."

The next morning, I flocked with half the other town kids to the Bristol site. We were hoping for jobs, offering our services for free, just for the pleasure of leading those thin ponies over the punishment of granite. I hugged the makeshift corral and became quickly smitten watching the six horses mill about, whinnying and nickering in their dung-filled enclosure.

Within days all the baby birch on the grounds were stripped of leaves, and by the second week the horses were pulling at spruce boughs and rose bushes.

The day I finally got to ride, the horses looked thin, scabby, and sway-backed, but I refused to see. I chose a chestnut mare, the least sickly of the lot.

"This one is about ready for the glue factory," said the man who ran the operation. He was short and round and had a patchy beard. He talked with a cigarette in his lips, so his words came out only one side of his mouth.

"All of them. No sense in spending a dime on this lot." He tipped over an old wooden milk carton, indicated I should stand on it to get my foot into the stirrup. As I stood on the box, he hauled back his right leg and released it hard, a cross kick to my horse's belly. She drew herself up, and as she did, he cinched the saddle strap around her girth.

"See how the bitch puffs herself up? Got to show them we're on to them, we know their tricks. Got to show them who's in charge. You be the boss, kid. Horses are smart. You wouldn't want to fall off a horse 'cause the saddle slips, would you?" I thought of the Caribou Queen, not human but still in charge.

He guided my foot into the stirrup, and I heaved myself onto the broad haunches of the horse, mindful of my weight upon her back.

"Git up, windbag," he muttered, and walloped my pony on her fly-infested flank.

Off we went, me and five other kids, clattering up the thin gravel paths between the jutting bedrock. The horse's heads hung down, and they marched, nose to tail, while I carried my weight in my knees and held to my image of a defiant Jane West, tall in the saddle, thundering across the plains, ready to battle redskins, ready to meet danger head on.

The girl behind the trail leader, dressed in a red-and-white blouse with denim cut-offs, squealed every time her horse tried to grab a mouthful of foliage from the trees. "He's bucking. He's bucking." But the horses weren't bucking at all. Theirs was a resigned plod and the ride was over before I could muster the courage to tell the girl to shut up.

"That was so much fun," said gingham girl. She pushed one of her braids behind her back and tugged at a navy polka-dotted kerchief knotted at her neck. "I'm going to call my horse Dewdrop because he was covered in dew when I first saw him."

"He was covered in sweat," I countered.

The horses got no breaks between riders. They were lathered and dripping as a second and a third lot of children took to the trails. I felt terrible after the ride, but I couldn't say why when my dad came to pick me up, except that the horses worked too hard.

"They're made for that, sweetheart. Didn't you like riding?" And because it cost five dollars, I nodded, affirming my own dubious control.

～～

The snow came early that fall, and one day the horse operation was gone. When it warmed up again, as it inevitably did before winter, Ned and I walked cross-country to the Bristol and sat in its open cockpit to look down at the empty corrals and the mounds of frozen horse plop. A swarm of blackflies, enlivened by the sun, was the only evidence it had been there. The horses and the trail-riding captain had vanished.

I turned inward that season, the first winter of my long adolescence. I loved to get away from the house, away from squabbling brothers, away from the long list of chores that had to be accomplished so my mother was not too tired to do her job at the hospital. I wandered alone, perfectly happy in the bush.

I kept on with my collection — leaves and flowers that I pressed between pages of books. I looked for shapes in the clouds, ways to read the sky, as my legs carried me farther and farther from town. I'd steel myself against the cold, endure frost-tipped eyelashes to witness footprints of hares and voles and top-crust walking creatures. I loved the winter-haloed sun, the ice fog shortening the light, lengthening the shadows. It felt as if there was a secret in the bush I was just beginning to know. It was like learning a new language, and I wandered through the trees on old snowmobile tracks or animal trails, following nothing but an urge to be away from the confines of the house.

The winter landscape comforted me with its sameness, the drifts of unmarked snow, disturbed only by my footprints. I loved that they, too, would disappear. I followed scrub trees that gave way to frozen lakes, great pans of ice, and then more land, steep at the shore, but always covered in a soft robe of snow, smoothing out the unseen gullies and dips. I followed ridges, sculpted by the wind. Sometimes they collapsed beneath me, and I was suddenly thigh deep in snow, floundering, but mostly it was easy walking once away from the street lights. Then the sky became a better map and I wandered towards dim stars just blinking on in the afternoon twilight. Unconsciously, I was practising what it might be like to be my latest version of the Caribou Queen.

I know part of me wanted to be discovered. The romantic notion of a nomad, the hunter/gatherer of past generations inspired my walks, but that could only be made real by the eyes of another.

I imagined myself Dene, the Caribou Queen, fighting my way back to the tribe from which I'd been kidnapped — no doubt because of my exotic beauty and abilities upon the land — but there were no friendly fires burning at my destinations, no welcoming feast or reunion, just a decision to return, a backtracking through the bush, following my own footsteps towards the dusky lights of town.

One weekend in late November, though, I discovered someone *was* watching me. A young man approached from behind a screen of trees. He startled me. "What are you doing?" he demanded.

It was Maryanne's cousin, Lawrence.

"What are you doing?" Lawrence asked again.

"I'm walking."

I stepped back because he was so close. I could smell his body and the grease in his hair, male and potent. He was wearing Ski-Doo boots. He leaned in. "Where? Where are you walking?"

"I like to follow the tracks." I decided I might as well tell the truth. I indicated the marks in the snow, the prints of rabbit and evidence of the claw and wing brush of a bird. "I think something got caught by an owl. Or a raven. See how the tracks end?"

He didn't even glance at the snow. He narrowed his eyes. "What are you, some kind of trapper girl?"

I liked that, but I kept my eyes downcast. "I like the way you can see stories in the snow."

He still didn't say anything, so I risked a look.

His bulky cloth coat was partially undone. His Adam's

apple bobbed on his slim neck beneath a sharp chin and angled face. He might have been Jennifer's age. Fourteen. Maybe older. Fifteen. His coat was missing a button and there was a huge grease mark on the right pocket where his hands disappeared except for two wrists, their knob bones exposed to the chilled air.

"Aren't you cold?"

"Nah," he replied. "I'm used to it."

"I have a good parka from the Bay. And I always keep moving." Why was I giving him information?

"How old are you?"

"Thirteen. Just turned." A lie, I was still twelve.

He grunted. "I'll come with you," He walked just in front, down the narrow trail. "Maybe I'll even show you something."

We walked a short distance, single file. I wasn't sure I wanted him with me, but I didn't know how to tell him. I was uneasy, concerned about what those hands thrust deep in his coat might conceal. I was also uncomfortable with the way he rubbed his nose with the back of his sleeve, leaving the frozen evidence of snot smeared on his coat. It wasn't polite.

Still, I liked his eyes, the way they took everything in, including me. He was silent yet strangely animated, a full presence I could not avoid, and before I could stop him, Lawrence grabbed my mittened hand in his bare one and stuffed it into the pocket of his coat. I was now pinned to him, my hand between his hand and his side, just above his thigh. The grip was strong and possessive but not insistent. I knew I could pull away if I wanted to.

"My name is Lawrence."

"I met you before. At Maryanne's birthday."

"Yeah. I remember. You could be my girl."

His girl. Just like that. He didn't ask my name and I didn't offer. I saw an edge of recklessness in his face that frightened and compelled me. I *could* be his girl.

He pulled me toward a stand of trees and then to a patch of willows, whose long fingers seemed to claw me back as Lawrence led on. He walked as if he were alone, as though we weren't connected. I felt helpless to do anything but follow. He pulled me towards another patch of dense brush that opened up onto a lake. Which one? Where were we? Jackfish? Long Lake? Frame? I only felt the pressure of my hand in his.

We made our way towards the ice.

Once out of the shelter of the trees, the wind dispelled the strong oily smell from Lawrence's coat. I felt better in the open air, and when I stumbled, his arm tensed to hold me up. At least we were not touching. I was glad about that. My mitten kept my hand from his flesh even though it was squeezed inside the pocket of his coat.

We breached the bank of the lake and I saw a stump, poking up from the ice, a few hundred feet offshore. It was lichen-covered, brown and white, and strangely regular, considering the frozen landscape. It wasn't until Lawrence led me closer that the stump morphed into a frozen horse head reaching out of the snow, much of the flesh ripped from its skull.

"Fell through the ice. It must have been looking for water and with the weight ..." his voice trailed off. He looked at me, wanting a reaction.

The neck of the horse pointed towards the sky. I shut my eyes, but I still saw it scrambling, straining away from the shock of water and the constant cold as the early ice gave way beneath its thirst. It drowned. It couldn't get out of the freezing lake.

"It happened at least a month ago. Look how the ravens have picked it clean."

His words forced me to open my eyes. I looked. The neck and muzzle of the horse was virtually stripped of flesh. There was only gristle and bone and the skull glaring white against patches of skin and hair. The ears were just tufts, the eye sockets empty and staring. It was almost unrecognizable. It seemed impossible that a few short months ago I'd swung up on a horse just like this, maybe even this same one, hyper aware of my weight upon her back.

"Ever seen anything like it?"

I wrenched my hand from his as my whole body contracted. I needed to be away, but I couldn't take my eyes off the frozen head.

"It's hard," he said. "But it's nature. Nature's way."

"We have to tell someone."

"Why?" he shot back. "There's not much we can do now. Besides, it didn't belong here. This is caribou country. Horses can't survive. The climate is too hard. Winters, impossible."

I looked at him, and then beyond, past the horror of the frozen horse head to the comfort of the clean ice. "You're right. The horse shouldn't have come here. It was wrong. My dad said that, too."

"Maybe it's the same thing for people. Certain people don't belong."

"What do you mean?"

He shrugged, dismissing me as easily as he'd taken up with me minutes before.

I feigned nonchalance. "You're right. What's to tell?"

I acted like none of it mattered. "I'm going home." I turned quickly and walked back along the trail we'd made. I was fighting stupid, angry tears for the horse and for my own inability to say what I wanted.

When I was far enough away, I turned back.

"Oh, thanks, by the way, thanks for nothing. If you really want a girlfriend maybe you should show her something beautiful instead of something nasty." And then I ran.

⌇

I clearly wanted a boyfriend. I was at that age when the idea of a boyfriend was more appealing than actually having one. I wanted a movie version of a boyfriend, not the real flesh and blood of shared experience this Indigenous boy offered and which I appeared to reject so totally.

Yet, that was our first real connection, a mixed encounter. I thought about it for days and days afterwards. I'd never considered being anyone's girl before, except in *Tiger Beat* fantasies, with Donny Osmond suddenly realizing it was me he pined for in "Go Away Little Girl." But the movie star faces of Donny or David Cassidy always morphed into the plain face of Lawrence, and at night I'd hold one of my hands in the other, trying to relive the moment he and I almost touched.

Lawrence didn't see me do it, but I snatched something from the snow that day of frozen horse flesh. It was a fragment, maybe a tooth or a piece of a tooth but more likely something from the neck or spine of the horse where the ravens did their work. For some reason I felt my stolen bone had fallen from a great distance, the thing leftover, the fragment of the horse the birds couldn't consume. I imagined claws opening and a horse piece falling right down to me, right in front of my escape. It was the pocket bone that gave me the power to go home and tell my parents about the frozen horse head and the horrible thing Lawrence took me to, made me see.

The bone chip, hard in my palm, was about the size of a marble but it was not round. Instead, the outside was rounded, and the inside was divided into segments, like sections on a leaf. It could have been a vertebra or a piece of cartilage from the horse's nose, but when I thought about the nose, I thought of muzzle and muzzle was too close to nuzzle and it made me too sad. I held the horse bone tightly in my palm, surrounded by my own fist, a keeper.

In my top dresser drawer, I found the flat Ganong-turned-anon box. I opened the lid and carefully placed the bone with my other keepers: the spruce needles in a tiny mustard jar, the rocks, so many rocks. But I knew each of their stories and why I had them, so much so that they felt like old friends. This new thing, the bone bit, was not as good as my caribou antler, but it was close.

I took the horse bone and placed it near the antler, between the fluff from the ptarmigan nest and the cone from the family of Jack pines that lived near Lakeview cemetery. The trees had allowed me to take their seeds. I connected the cone husk to the horse bone to the feathers and finally to the antler, so all my talismans were touching.

That night, I dreamed of horses, but it was not a dream composed of the daytime reality of Lawrence and the poor dead-in-the-water pony. This was a good dream, because all my horses were alive. They had become north wind horses and they galloped and loped and cantered across my unconscious mind as sleep unfurled. Their nostrils weren't picked to bits by birds, but rather flared, snorting again, the wind from the bellows of their lungs was warm and the north wind horses were freer than they'd ever been on the trail rides above the Bristol. There was no clatter of broken hooves on bedrock. There were no worn-out shoes, splintered feet, and unyielding stone. Instead, the sky was their biggest pasture, and the horses ran between the constellations with manes and tails turning into stars that fell down around me and lit a path where I was walking beside someone, holding their hand.

As the dream receded, I felt I had witnessed a transformation and even the frozen horse was now in that place where the Caribou Queen oversaw all creatures, even me.

Because it was Saturday morning, my older siblings slept on, but in the kitchen, I could hear first Ned and then my mother fussing about breakfast. I knew I should go and rescue Ned — my mother had just come off a night shift — but first I stole a few minutes with the box hidden at the back of the drawer, behind my underwear. There it was, the horse bone fragment that had reassembled itself last night while I slept. It made me wonder, which was real, the thing I saw out there on the lake, or my night world that had everything to do with knowing what is terrible can be made better?

I picked new underwear. I didn't want old underwear, the ones with the tiny strawberry bow at the belly. I was too old for bows and strawberries now. I had seen a real horse dead. And, I had dreamed it back to life.

Catching my reflection in the mirror, I wiggled my hips. I was practically someone's girlfriend. Sexy, but flat-chested and covered in gooseflesh. I reluctantly shrugged on an undershirt, because it might snow, and my favourite shirt with the secret pocket sewn on the inside, and ordinary brown pants because it was, at last, the weekend, and I didn't have to wear a dress.

My dad would stay home and make fried eggs and hash browns from last night's boiled potatoes. Maybe, if I could bring my vision back, I would explain the north wind horses to Ned, who was the only one young enough to believe in their magic.

〜〜

My father and Paul tracked down the dead horse a week and a half after I spilled my story. I didn't tell my parents I was not alone.

They lit a fire on the ice, but I didn't know if the fire melted the ice to release the horse into the lake or if its head was burned off. Either way, it was gruesome.

"A bonfire of broken flesh," my dad reported, shaking his head. "I heard in town that fellow abandoned those horses in an old gravel mine once the trail riding season ended. I guess the cost of hauling them out was beyond his means. Poor things. A gravel pit, of all places, that's just about the farthest thing from a pasture I can imagine." He continued to shake his head. "If it's true, he should have been arrested. What a terrible thing to do."

"They shouldn't have come in the first place," said Paul. "That guy was a horse's ass."

My brother said exactly what Lawrence had said. Maybe I could be his girlfriend, after all. Here was Paul talking to my folks like an adult, saying a swear word right in front of them, and they didn't seem to mind.

That night, I went down into our basement and did my own secret purge. I found the old West figurines, the Jane and Johnny dolls, the ridiculous Chief. I imagined one of the plastic horses kicking the head off Jane or stomping Johnny West to a pulp, but the figurines were seamless plastic and there was no way I could mutilate the riders. Instead, I packed them inside a shoebox, the three horses on top of the dolls, and carefully closed the lid. I swore I would get rid of the box in the spring, maybe with Maryanne, but Christmas came and I forgot about the shoebox and my noble intentions to try to make things rights by the gravel-pit pony.

～

The encounter with Lawrence out on Long Lake in November 1971 was my first real contact with someone outside my safe circle of family and friends. He didn't belong in the circle. I knew that, but what I didn't recognize was his not-belonging was based on race.

He was different, the fantasy noble Indian of my imagination. He became like the north wind horses, roaming across the starry sky of my dreaming, because the reality of human cruelty was too much to bear. If I couldn't abide some fact of life, I remade it in my own mind. If I couldn't bear the idea of a starved, drowned, frozen horse, I made it into the flash and canter of northern lights across the sky. If I couldn't bear the thought of loss and confusion on the faces of some of the Indigenous kids in my community, I imbued them with power.

It wasn't something I did consciously, these perpetual falsehoods I invented and then chose to believe, it was simply a way to make the reality of that harsh landscape softer, more palatable.

When I remember those continuous days of night and the unavoidable paralysis of cold, I realize I plumbed my inner landscapes and entered a world inside myself, because the temperatures and the scant hazy hours of blue sunlight bookended by blackness was not a place I could dwell in for long. Without the sun, we lacked vitamin D and were given cod liver oil every evening to compensate and keep us healthy. This trembling tablespoon of prevention, plus an orange or grapefruit every second morning, was used to offset our daily oatmeal. Porridge was fuel in the furnace of our bellies, and it hugged us from the inside, dispensing enough energy to transport us those three long blocks to the safety of the Hudson's Bay store, where most school children cut through to thaw.

Plunging out of those warm Bay doors into the frigid cold made the last three or four blocks to school a treacherous pound. Could you reach the skin-snatching metal school doors before all feeling was gone from your legs, before the hot of frostbite burned off your feet at the stubbed ankles and shed your toes like splinters in an icebox boot? And my Indigenous classmates? Were they watched more than me, were they made to feel like interlopers in that warm, northern store? Likely.

We children burrowed inside in the long night of winter, so our patterns resembled those of all hibernating creatures. Sleep and daydreaming were an antidote to the great ponderous weight of winter — the blank slate of January and February and March, where the thermometer stuck between minus thirty and forty degrees below without a hint of even feeble light. What did we think?

I thought of horses and fresh grass, fantasized of places that didn't kill the living, places that lent themselves to words like *thrive* and *flourish*, words like *blossom* and *nurture*. In my internal pasture there was always sun and fresh feed and warmth, even though it was the farthest thing from real.

I was lucky for the daily morning dose of vitamin D, my own oats and oranges. Many didn't have these things. But mostly I was lucky for my imagination, that my inward winter voyaging always took me to kinder climates. Some, not born with the same nature, not nurtured by books and close family, ended up like that survival-seeking pony, trapped and ultimately dead.

Seven students from my school, some Indigenous, some settler, killed themselves in my junior high years. A half-century later I can only name the ones I knew personally: Bill, shot himself; John, hanged; Duncan, also hanged. A couple of girls, one named Nancy, took too many pills, and another girl, the saddest suicide and the most talked about among teenagers, suffocated herself with a bread bag. A bread bag! Why didn't she do what most kids did, drink, drink a lot, and then just lay down in the snow and wait?

I believed if you wanted to survive, you had to find a way to make sense of things. I kept darkness at bay by constantly adding light. My writing was my flashlight on the small, dark space near the top of the planet. It was a place I occupied, and it saved me. Even if it wasn't all true or, conversely, was too good to be true, it was better than the noose, the pills, the gun, or the bottle. It was better than the face press of the plastic bread bag. Telling stories, embellished stories, even overheard stories that did not belong to me, was my antidote to despair.

Appropriation

I was in Mr. Swan's English class contemplating my Grade Eight creative writing assignment. I needed to write a composition for a national writing competition sponsored by a bank. For the first time I could recall, the Northwest Territories had been included with the rest of Canada. This in itself was a rare thing, according to my language arts teacher.

Mr. Swan told us to write about what we knew. Winter was what I knew. My early life was that snowy field upon which I witnessed only after-the-fact dramas, the ones I'd revealed to Lawrence — the small hare taken by a bird, just the tracks ending, and the wing swoop brushed though the snow, a tiny spill of blood or nothing at all. I had to imagine everything that happened in between. Or, even more difficult, admit that nothing happened, or ever would happen in my little life on the fringes of the boreal forest. I sighed, discouraged, and continued to gaze at the world of white. I thought of the student residence, Akaitcho Hall.

I could write about that owl, I decided, and about that little furry snow creature being taken. I could write about the kids in my class plucked out of the bush, brought to school.

I invented a Dene boy. Subconsciously my character may have been based on Lawrence, but not really, not intentionally. I conjured the exact moment a bush plane landed on an unknown lake, north of my imagination, to take him away from his parents. The float plane was the owl, the predatory white man. The boy, his prey.

I knew this. I knew it from those first Christmas dinners we suffered through when we arrived in Yellowknife. I knew it as I got older, as I became aware of students arriving in town to begin or complete high school.

What would it be like to be taken from the bush and landed in a small town with two traffic lights on our main street? What would an elevator be for someone who had only lived among trees or tundra?

Jennifer and I had ridden an elevator when we visited The High Rise, the only building in town above three storeys, to drop off a book to one of Mother's single nursing friends. It was strange for me, that sense of leaving my stomach behind as I rose in the air, but I considered myself worldly. I'd been on a plane. I'd been to Edmonton, 1,500 kilometres south, where we rode an escalator to get to the shoe department in the Hudson's Bay. What would an elevator ride be like for my abducted Indian boy?

And, how sad would he be?

I envisioned my character's parents. In my mind's eye

they were old and weathered. I looked around Mr. Swan's classroom. In the garbage were discarded lunch bags. The parent's faces, I thought, might look like those crumpled lunch bags, wrinkled and brown. It wasn't a huge creative stretch.

In our school, most of our teachers were white, with the exception of our science teacher, a real upper-caste Indian from Goa, schooled in London, and our math instructor, a Mr. Chei, from mainland China. There may have been others, but many teachers only stayed a short time.

As a townie I didn't think of privilege. I didn't think of oppression. I didn't think of entitlement. I didn't think.

I was doing what the 1972 language arts curriculum taught me to do — name colour, name race, but in a not-*so*-racist way. It never dawned on me that I was equating Indians with garbage. How could a lunch bag be racist?

In my composition, I entertained the deliciously wicked idea of not having parents. *Let's pretend we're orphans and our parents are dead.* My friend Carmel and I used to play orphans. Countless childhood games started with that phrase. It wasn't a big step to imagine the confusion of my fellow classmates who had actually left their homes and their parents behind.

I poured my heart into that short story, literally putting myself in that imagined boy's moccasins. What did he feel when the float plane landed to take him away? What would I feel? What did he think when he looked into the face of his mother, the woman who didn't want him to leave their camp with its fish drying in front of a smoky fire? It was suspiciously like the camp Maryanne conjured in the makeover tent, the romantic East Arm Indian camp of my imagination. But I knew what I'd feel: the fear, the excitement, not to mention the anguish of my parents. I became embroiled in the fictive capture and removal of the young boy.

When I wrote the story, I felt the same bubble I'd swallowed years earlier at the Akaitcho Hall Christmas dinners. I felt as a creative writer I was simply recreating what actually happened. Not to me, of course, but I was determined to show how stoic and proud and difficult it would be, to be thrust into the controlling hands of an anonymous government. I adopted my character's surroundings, his culture, his emotions, his voice. I transcribed my understanding onto one of Mr. Swan's scribblers.

I titled my story "The Pride of my People." Yes, *my* people. I wrote of Indigenous Peoples as though they were mine. I wanted them to be my people because I found them intriguing. I liked Lawrence. I liked Maryanne. I envisioned all Indigenous Peoples as freedom seekers, in tune with the land.

My characters in the short story were not the Indigenous folk who lived with us in town. No, not the ones who had moved to town in exchange for electricity and running water. Those weren't my people. My people lived in log cabins and communed with wildlife in a way I never could. My people lived off highbush cranberries and creatures of the trapline, animals that gave their lives, practically put their own heads in the snare in order to feed my people.

The Caribou Queen led my people. They had secret ceremonies and told long, meandering stories. When the northern lights appeared in the sky, my people talked to their ancestors, something we white people didn't have a clue about, mostly because we didn't seem to have ancestors. If we did, they were called relatives and they lived in faraway places with barely pronounceable names, Sas-ka-toon, Sas-kat-che-wan.

The Indigenous Peoples of my teenage imagination were superior in every way, as they worked their way into story. I made them exotic, untouchable, pure in a way white people could never be. These were not noble savages; they were the noblest. It was the garbage bags in reverse, an elevated stereotype, impossibly wrong-headed, equally racist.

White people, my real people, were scoundrels, kidnappers of children. Imagine, taking a kid out of the bush where fire building and fish smoking is exchanged for algebra and cursive writing?

This was my father's realm, the territory of the Federal Government. Yet, for the life of me I could not reconcile my gentle, well-respected father with the Indian Agent, that terrible person who ripped Indigenous children from the protection of their parents. But nor could I pretend he wasn't the federally appointed Superintendent of Schools for the Northwest Territories.

I gave my story to Mr. Swan after class, just one day before the deadline. If he read it, he never said, but he did submit it to the competition on my behalf. Four months later, my Grade Eight short story won me three hundred dollars, second place only to brainiac, Russell Rosen, who won five hundred for a faux *Encyclopedia Brown* mystery story about robots.

I wrote "The Pride of my People" more than fifty years ago. I have called it my first fiction, but I realize now, it could also be called my first appropriation.

As a witness to the out-of-placeness of my schoolmates, I felt I had the right to reimagine and reconstruct their experience on the page. My arrogance, my own ignorance, is astonishing. But I was still convinced very little happened in my hometown.

I was wrong on both counts. Things did happen. And unlike the innocent bystander, I am called to confess to being a full and culpable participant.

Prey

The next spring, I found myself back on those old pony trails behind the Bristol. I was walking, idling along, feeling grateful the snow was mostly gone.

The grey granite held the early heat, and I liked nothing better than to stretch out in a quiet place, letting my shoulder blades settle on stone, stretch my spine to feel the warmed rocks beneath my body. I was in trouble at home. I'd brought home a math mark, sixty-six percent, and while I marvelled at the symmetry of those curved numbers, my mother did not share my sense of wonder. She didn't see them as newly hatched eggs with little arms curled over, reaching to the sky. She saw the percentage as my indolence, my lack of interest in numbers.

"These are marks, Missy. And marks matter. How can you be satisfied with mediocrity? Jennifer was always on the honour roll at your age. She not only won the senior mathematics award, but also the music and social studies award. You're going to have to pull up your socks, Margie, if you ever want to amount to anything."

I'd curled my lip. "I like the way I am. And I don't like math. Why do I need to learn math, anyway?"

The backtalk earned me an extra hour of fractions, but once I'd sulked enough, the formulas returned, sorted themselves out on the page enough so that I could discern a pattern and connection, and I was able to finish my task.

"I'm done. Can I go out now? Just for a little walk?" And my mother relented, satisfied she'd taught me an important lesson in applying myself.

As I got farther and farther away from the house, I decided the rocks were my real mother and they could hold me in a way she couldn't, no matter how she tried. I trusted the rocks beyond reason. They were eternal, like the sky and my days beneath the sky. I thought of them the same way I thought of summer.

That afternoon, I found birch bark with its centre rotted out, a perfect ring, and a rock so covered in orange lichen I thought at first it was food. I loved the poetry of a soft rock, the fuzzy inflexibility of contradiction, and I carried those words in my head as I walked.

Suddenly, before me were some men: Arty Beaulieau, Rocky Gladue, my Grade One tormentor's older brother, and one of the Ripley boys, although which one, I couldn't say. They were a few kilometres out on the land, inland from Great Slave, beyond the headframe of the Con Mine. They were lounging on the rocks, sharing a bottle amid the brown and green bits of glass that suggested other bottles.

They saw me before I saw them, I suspect, because I was practising my sure-footed pony routine, imagining myself not on horseback exactly, but more as a herd animal, agile and leaping expertly from outcrop to outcrop.

These three were older than me. Will once warned me to steer clear of all the Ripley boys, even though I'd caught him at the rink casting longing glances at the only Ripley girl, Joanie, figure skates flying, tiny skirt twirling atop massive, shapely thighs. "Bad business, those Ripley brothers," he'd said, so when they called to me across the uneven landscape, I was wary.

"Whose kid are you?" Arty asked.

I said nothing.

"You're the old principal's kid, aren't you? Your dad is with Sir John, right?"

"The big man with the big strap."

It was the Beaulieu boy who spoke, a Grade Twelver specializing in auto mechanics and street fighting. He took a swig of amber liquid, passed the bottle to his companions. "Your old man ever take that strap to your back end?"

He glowered as I shook my head. Something moved between us, some energy, and I recalled the Thurber boys and their game.

"Only on the hand," I squeaked. "And only once. Because I lied."

There seemed no option but to tell, and in telling I might be spared something terrible I couldn't begin to imagine.

"Sounds like this one's got a lily-white ass, guys," snorted the Gladue boy to the others. "You think we might need to take a look, boys?"

It was enough to make me run, leaping across sloughs and crevasses, hightailing it in the direction that had to be home. I was nimble on the bedrock and swift, and the men did not follow. Only their laughter pursued me as I galloped towards town, a new fear fixed within. I felt for the first time these men could hurt me, could humiliate me. I thought I was safe walking alone, but as I picked my way across the rocks towards our house, I realized for the first time, as a girl, I would never really be safe.

⌇

Single men came north to make fast money. They lived in the bunkhouses, six long, single-storey buildings constructed near the mines and joined by above-ground pipe boxes. The miners could shower at the site and walk to their single rooms above the snow on the wooden utility corridor that connected the bunkhouses, to the cook shack and the dining hall and the rec centre. The bunkhouses, the first buildings visible from the road as you came into the mine site, could hold almost three hundred men.

"I won't have any daughters of mine going anywhere near those bunkhouses. Jennifer? Margaret? Do you understand? Both mines are off limits, strictly off limits. Do I make myself clear?" This, after my mother learned some of Jennifer's friends had gone to the mess hall to play pool and flirt with out-of-town boys, who had recently arrived at Giant Mine for their long, underground summer shift.

My mother could forbid us to go, but she could not silence the rumours of wild bunkhouse parties or the quick exchange of flesh and coin. The mines were a place where people did not stay long. Miners, we were told, were not to be trusted. Yet to us, the mines represented the only excitement that ever shook our wilderness of rock and raven. It was normal men should become interested in girls budding into adolescents, but because the only hint of attention I'd received was from Lawrence — *you could be my girl* — and the threat of those men on the rocks, I was oblivious.

～

One of my father's colleagues, who had just moved north to work for the government, had a daughter a year younger than me, Annie. By way of introduction, my parents gave me enough money to invite Annie to the Capitol Theatre one Saturday afternoon in winter to see a matinee of Disney's *Bedknobs and Broomsticks*. I would have been thirteen, maybe older, Annie still twelve.

We didn't know each other, so there was an awkward, saw-tooth formality to our outing.

"Where do you like to sit?"

"Wherever you like to sit."

The theatre was darkened and mostly empty, but we settled in a middle row, shedding our parkas and mittens and storing them on an extra seat next to Annie. Although I hadn't been to many movies, and certainly not without my older sister or the safety of my brother, I did have a sense of what would happen: newsreel, cartoon, and then the feature film.

It was during the cartoon that a man plunked down in the empty seat next to me. I shifted closer to Annie and allowed myself to become reabsorbed in an animated cat and mouse chase on screen. The man also shifted, and the limb that occupied our shared armrest suddenly crossed my body, his hand resting on my upper thigh. I froze, tense and barely breathing, yet unable to react. I didn't say anything, and the hand began to creep towards the crotch of my pants, lightly, but with increasing insistence. I was the bedknob; he was the broomstick. I was momentarily paralyzed.

I pretended to drop something on the theatre floor, and as I reached for this imaginary thing, I thrust my opposite leg forward and connected my boot to his shin.

"Oops, sorry."

I wasn't sorry at all, but he got my message, despite its indirect delivery, and shifted back to his own seat. Why couldn't I act or speak? Why had I disguised my defence as an accident? I stopped the molesting man with a kick to his shin, and before the feature began, he moved to another area of the theatre. I'd pretended my foot accidently flipped up and connected with his leg, but perhaps he was pretending, too, and in his mind, his hand had accidently fallen towards me.

I didn't tell the new girl what happened that afternoon because I didn't know Annie and I was embarrassed. The next time my father encouraged me to invite her out, I claimed she had lots of friends, most of whom were not my type.

He did not challenge me, and every time I saw her, I felt shame, as though, somehow, I was to blame.

⌒

That winter, the Gerry Murphy Arena was packed with people, the whole town out to celebrate the finale of the dogsled races, our frigid spring festival. The final day of the Caribou Carnival was moved inside for the first time in known memory because the temperature had dipped to thirty-three below and a north wind blew in deadly horizontal sheets across the ice.

I was happy for the change of venue, because once the

dog mushers were off, there was not much to do but wait. Now, inside the arena, there were broomball games and finger tug competitions and one-footed high-kicking. They would continue all day until the brave bundled up and headed back out into the deep freeze to cheer the ice encrusted mushers through the home stretch.

I had babysitting money, three dollars, in my pocket saved for this very event. The concession was selling bannock and brown beans for $2.50. Or, for a full three bucks you could get sliced wieners floating in the bean broth.

Ned and Will and I came together, Jennifer and Paul separately. Normally we'd be instructed to stay together, but inside the arena we were contained enough to scatter, each seeking our own friends. Gone were my mother's rules: *Do this. Do that. Remember your manners. Remember your station, but don't get on your high horse.* Good riddance.

I saw Will standing across the large canvas drop cloth that covered most of the ice. Three small rinks remained open for the ice games and the broomball tourney, a nod to the natural rinks usually cleared on Back Bay. Two boys were competing in high kick, and Will stood watching, his hands sly, his eyes following every move. He was wearing Paul's leather coat, big on him, but strangely appropriate. He looked older than his fourteen-and-a-half years, and for a brief second, I was able to appraise him as though we weren't siblings. A flash of handsome, and then he was just Will again, Will in Paul's coat.

Paul had ordered the coat from the Eaton's catalogue the summer before last, paid for it with the money he got stocking shelves at the drugstore.

"You look like a hooligan," said my mother as he modelled the bomber jacket, a fresh thrill from a foreign brown box.

I didn't agree. "Whoa, you look like someone from a city."

In one of the rings, a competitor jumped with both feet and stretched his right leg high above his head at an uncanny angle. The target, a little bone on a string, rocked back and forth. A hit. The bone was ratcheted up a notch.

I watched Will while I waited for the next kick. How did he know the Carnival was going to be moved inside? Paul's coat wouldn't have worked at thirty-three below. In fact, everyone looks the same at thirty-three below. Men and women were indistinguishable except by the cut of their parkas. Even then, with hoods drawn tight across chin and forehead, and scarves masking all but frost-tipped eyelashes you could pass a winter walker and never discern friend or foe.

But here was Will, busting with boyish confidence. Maryanne and two other girls were also pretending to watch the high kick. From where I stood, I could see they were watching Will. Each time I took my eyes from the dangling bone and the thrust of muscled thighs, those Old Town girls pressed in closer and closer to my brother.

I was about to call out to Maryanne, when Will suddenly turned to her and opened his arms. Their hug was quick, but their intimacy unmistakable. Looking around to see who had noticed, I saw there weren't a lot of Indian people in the crowd. It seemed suddenly strange to me that both big events, the Hand Games and the crowning of the Caribou Queen, were demonstrated by Indians, yet watched by whites.

I felt uneasy. Something felt off-centre, not quite right.

The presentation stage was set up as it should be, just past the blue line. On the stage was a podium and a stretch of orange shag carpet marching up the plywood steps. What was bugging me? I thought back to last week.

Caribou Queen. I'd revealed my lifelong yearning to Jennifer a week before Carnival. Mistake. She was no longer the compassionate, antler-giving sister of our childhood. This was a sneering seventeen-year-old.

"You? Caribou Queen? You've got to be kidding. No matter how much you want it, you'll never get to be Caribou Queen. Everything about you is wrong, so just get it out of your head, okay? Caribou Margie, that's too funny. Have you been out hawking tickets door to door, trying to get folks out to the Fair? Is that what you're doing when you're supposed to be doing homework? Not likely. I've got to remember to tell Mum. She'd have an absolute shit fit!"

Jennifer's version of the Caribou Queen's qualifications baffled me, and I stood, trying to digest what she'd revealed. I thought the Caribou Queen had to skin a muskrat, gut a fish, and make tea on an open fire within a certain time limit. I'd imagined she'd have to do beadwork on hide and repeat some of the old stories to the Elders without ever asking why. Those were things I thought a Caribou Queen might need to do. I was too embarrassed to ask my sister but needed to know. "What do you mean, tickets?" I stumbled. "Isn't the crown made of antlers?"

Jennifer hooted. "You're living in la-la land, Margie," she wheezed between great gulps of laughter. "Maybe back in Dog Derby days there was some of that shit, but now it's all about who can sell the most tickets to the Carnival. Antlers? Oh my God, get a life."

I looked around the arena again. Could Jennifer be right? The only Indian people in the whole place were the ones demonstrating the old games. It was stupid. Like the Royal teenagers, the Caribou Queen was a position without power.

She didn't commandeer herds with her voice. She probably couldn't even use her status to get to the front of the bingo lineup at the Elks Hall.

I felt as though the bottom of my belly had let go, so real was my disappointment, but anger flared to reseal the wound. What did Jennifer know, so busy with her stupid piled-up hairdos and sooty eyeholes? She was the farthest thing from the Caribou Queen I could imagine. I'd watch anyway. I'd see who'd won the distinction.

But first, I wanted French fries.

I pushed through the gate at the rink boards and passed the penalty box where a little knot of two- and three-year-olds were playing unattended like pups in a wooden box. As I stood in the concession line trying to decide between fries with or without gravy, I heard the blare of the intercom. "Judges, the winner of the Miss Caribou Queen 1973 will be announced in six minutes. Six minutes." The announcer, loud and insistent, sounded like Mr. Oliver, our shop teacher.

I was finally at the front counter when someone cut in front of me. It was Rocky Gladue, the man I saw drinking on the rocks.

"She was here first," said the lady behind the counter. She was flushed from the heat of the deep fryer and wearing a hairnet.

"Well, I'm here now," said Rocky. "I want a burger and a Coke."

The woman blinked once, twice, and raised her hand, holding a spatula. "I don't serve bullies," and she slapped the flat end of the flipper onto the counter. Tiny beads of oil flew up, and Rocky stepped backwards. "Get behind her," said the little woman.

It was an incantation, an exorcism happening in broad daylight. I was speechless. Without changing her posture, the fry cook turned to me and smiled. "What can I get you, my dear?" Her voice was lilting, Irish.

"Fries. Just fries."

The crowd behind me had moved onto the ice, but Rocky didn't move with them. He stood behind me, too close. "Don't think I don't remember," he hissed into the back of my neck as I took the greasy container from the fry cook. "I know exactly who you are."

As I poured three quarters into the palm of the Irish lady, I caught her eye. She winked. All the anger and resentment I felt towards Maryanne and Will and the Prince, too distracted to see what was in front of his royal nozzle, surfaced. "Fuck off," I hissed to Rocky, and he sloped away, muttering. It was the first time I'd ever said the F-word to a human being.

"Thanks," I said to the concession lady.

She held my eyes for a moment. "Don't give them bastards an inch. Hold the good ground," she added. "Those you need will come into your seeing."

Who were the bastards? What was she saying? It sounded like a riddle. "What do you mean?"

She held the spatula up again, but this time it was a lance or a flag. "What's your name, girlie."

"Margie Macpherson."

"Well, Margie Macpherson, you're a pretty thing and the young men will be coming around before you know. But you have to know what you want. *Do you?* Do you know what it is you're after?"

It was such a hard question. "I know what I used to want."

She bent low over the counter. "What was that then?"

"I wanted to be the girl out there being crowned." My voice dropped. "I wanted to be the Caribou Queen."

The woman paused. "Aye, a queen, above the others." Her voice changed. "It's a servant you want to be, not a queen."

Before I could ask what she meant, she was back at the griddle scraping bits of fried onions and stray morsels of meat into an oily trough. A servant. Another puzzle.

I scampered back onto the ice, arriving just in time to see someone who looked a lot like a grown-up Carmel Johnston walk across the stage towards the podium. The girl lowered her chin to her chest and one of the judges placed a plastic tiara on her head.

Could my old neighbour be the Caribou Queen? It looked like Carmel but I couldn't be sure. This person was a lot bigger now, yet even with her head bowed, she commanded space. The girl straightened. She was beaming. Her face was lit with something I couldn't really describe. Why did I think there was no power in this position? Carmel — it was her, it had to be — tilted her jaw up towards the rafters and glowed with pride.

Carmel Johnston was the Caribou Queen. Was she a Queen because she was a servant? The contestant at the podium seemed confident in her role. If this really was Carmel, she knew who she was and what she wanted.

No one clapped louder or longer than me.

⌇

The crowning of the Caribou Queen is still scrambled in my thinking. Did it start off as an Indigenous position? I've seen pictures of five pageant queens from the '60s, and they were all white. Was it usurped by white girls wanting glamour?

I thought I couldn't be Caribou Queen because I was white. Or maybe it was because white people didn't know how to be servants. Maybe I was just plain wrong. Maybe everything I ever thought about the Caribou Queen was wrong.

Soul

Another reminder of Carmel and our childhood relationship surfaced in an encounter with her brother not long after the Caribou Queen crowning. Sylvan Johnston drifted back into my life a few months into Grade Nine. I was almost fourteen. Sylvan was four years younger than me, still in elementary school. My only real memory of him was ages ago, when my mother invited his mother over to play daytime bridge. Mrs. Johnston — Eleanor — became so agitated that little Sylvan was left in the care of his older half-brothers, she had to leave halfway through a six-no-trump contract. It wrecked everything; the bridge game, my mother's social standing, even the tea party, which was one of my mother's many attempts to include Eleanor in with Yellowknife's social elite. Excepting that episode and its ensuing drama, Melly's pale and unlikely brother meant little to me.

Everything I knew about him was by word of mouth. According to all, he was the perfect son, given in exchange for the second Mrs. Johnston's adoptive charity. He was a natural pianist, playing for the Mission Sunday School and finally the congregation from the time he was eight; he was an honours student, winning top marks and a certificate in Grade Four; he was a Cub Scout, lending a hand, and a teacher's helper, running attendance rosters to the office. Sylvan was a public speaker, beating older Grade Seven classmates with his speech about travel: *Imagine yourself on a fanciful, far-off tropical isle* ... began wispy Sylvan, and a hundred winter-weary auditorium kids were with him, imagining Sylvan's sunny sojourns.

A meeting of the Mission's Young Peoples Group once fell on the same day Anne Murray — Canada's songbird — came to town. Except for Stompin' Tom, who sold out the Emily Murphy Arena and wowed us with his plywood plank, beaten thin, and his foot-stomping ballads, our Anne was only the second star to ascend to our north of 60 skies. And the whole town went to see her.

I went. Jennifer and Will went. Even Paul, who blabbed on and on about the Woodstock experience as an antidote to Anne's pulpy folk-pop, went. Mary Baptiste went. Angela Warniuk, who took voice lessons and once sang the second verse of "How Great Thou Art" in an unaccompanied Sunday school solo at the United Church, went in her new lemon-coloured dress, bought especially for the Anne-occasion.

All the kids in my class, including Carmel Johnston, went to that Anne Murray concert. All, except Sylvan. His commitment to the Mission's Friday Young Peoples Group took precedence, and I imagined him sitting in a circle of empty chairs whispering *thou shall love thy God* while the rest of us sat three blocks away in the arena, loving Anne.

I saw him after a volleyball game in the junior high gym, Anne Murray come and gone. It was strange to see an elementary kid out of their range, their separate wing of the school, but Sylvan was no ordinary child, and he approached me as though age and station meant nothing to him.

"Hello, Margie."

"Oh, hi. What's up?" I cast my eyes around the empty gym.

"I want to give this to you." He handed me a pamphlet twice folded. On the front in large bold text were the words *What profits a man to gain the whole world and lose his own soul?* I stopped dead, dropped the volleyball to the gym floor, the religious tract hovering between, in those long, pale fingers. "What does that have to do with me?"

He flushed and I was glad.

"I just thought you might want to look at it," said Sylvan in his strange, wispy, singsong voice. "You're a good person, Margie. I've watched you. But is that enough?"

I took the pamphlet, flipped through it quickly. "For your information, Sylvan, my soul is just fine, thank you very much." I feigned a deeper offence than I felt, but the pamphlet burned, and I quickly tucked it into the back pocket of my jeans. I figured I could give Sylvan a little lesson on the evils in current events. "The people heading for hell are those crazy terrorists in Montreal, the ones blowing up mailboxes and scratching their FLQ logo all over the bellies of babies with safety pins. You think that's me? You think that's what I do?"

He didn't respond, but I felt completely defensive.

"Maybe you should try to save the soul of your own sister instead of mine. Melly smokes." It didn't seem like enough.

My own parents smoked. I reached back and pulled from my memory something nasty, something unresolved. "She really *is* the Caribou Queen. She's just like that old hooker who lived at the Gold Range."

Sylvan looked at me in his vague way. "Melly? Oh, my sister, Carmel." And with that feeble acknowledgement, he drifted out of the gym. I went to the door and watched him float like a skinny ghost down the hall towards the music room. Even then he seemed detached or at least connected to the material world in a completely different way.

Sylvan Johnston's single-minded commitment to saving souls made him an easy target for bullies. He refused to fight back. His goodness reflected on the rest of us, and we retaliated. Sylvan's hair, which fell into natural blond ringlets, was tugged and mussed up, his glasses stolen, his homework scattered, and his religious beliefs mocked. "Goody-goody two-shoes" was polite. "Goddamn Jesus freak," more common.

I regularly watched a group of ten-year-old boys taunting and teasing, poking and prodding in the playground, chanting:

"Sylvan, Sylvan, quack and quiver,
Saw him eating snot and liver."

After each round of that awful verse, one of the circling boys would dive towards Sylvan and pull at his hair or prod him in the chest or back. I witnessed his torment from the steps of the junior high area, but I did nothing, only felt glad it wasn't me. As a fourth round of the song began, I saw someone streak past, straight across the playground towards the circle of elementary boys. It was Carmel, running head down, like a quarterback toward her fragile sibling. There was shouting and the vicious circle of bullies scattered just as the bell rang.

Melly suffered none of her brother's torment. She fended off bullies easily with a tongue as sharp as her eyes. She was tough and much more resilient than her spiritually stricken little brother. While Carmel was earth-born and natural, Sylvan was a delicate transplant, a hybrid being, struggling to survive.

And he didn't.

He was delivering something to our Grade Nine classroom when it happened.

"I can't see," he cried in the biology lab as we sat writing up the dissection of the earthworm. "I can't hear. What? What?" He sank down in a chair near the doorway, a table away from me.

There was rising panic in his voice, a frantic look around, to me, to others, and then his head hit the floor. There was an eruption inside his unnaturally large brain. Mr. Cogswell called the ambulance immediately and they came and took Sylvan away. Although I told myself my mother, working at the hospital that day, would fix Sylvan up, his attack left the rest of us biology-bound students stewing in our own meanness.

I went home and found that graphic tract he gave me, what, five, six days before? I read the story of a man who had everything but died suddenly and alone. The text seemed prophetic, and I read it again and again, pondering Sylvan's final question to me: *What profits a man if he gains the whole world but loses his own soul?* I thought about the Irish woman at the rink, the one who told me to be a Queen you had to be a servant. I thought about Rocky Gladue and how I'd stood up to him at last, but also how I'd humiliated him publicly. Jumbled up in my mind were ideas of profit and servant, giving and taking, and even more mixed up, the idea of a soul. What was a soul and where was Sylvan's right now? More importantly, what was the state of mine?

We waited for news on Sylvan, astounded such drama could occur to someone we knew in ordinary daylight. My mother, who was on a different ward that day, made a few discreet phone calls in her best nursing voice. *Aneurism, implosion* were the words that drifted into the dining room where I sat, continuing my biology project.

The words in my textbook, propagation and the complex evolution of species, seemed to deepen the puzzle. Will once told me told me erroneously that if cut in two, earthworms became two separate creatures. Earthworms multiplied by division. If a spade in the garden severed one, suddenly two worms tilled the earth, making good the ground for my father's garden. It wasn't true, of course, you couldn't cut something in half and make two new beings, but it did cause me to question what happened when someone's life was cut short.

I thought of winter with the land hard packed under six inches of snow, the earthworms beneath, long and narrow, their holding pattern predetermined, waiting to wriggle up towards the sun when the time was right.

I thought of Sylvan, his long, pale piano fingers, his strange evangelical offerings, and I imagined me being gracious and polite. I saw myself bringing him homework in the hospital, Mrs. Johnston hovering over those cool, white sheets. *I'll leave you two to talk.*

In the privacy of that sterile place, without the pack of other kids chiding and teasing, I'd ask Sylvan his thoughts on regeneration and reincarnation. We'd talk about a soul, what it was, what it really meant. Most of all I'd ask, why me? Why had he singled me out in the gym, just days before? What made him so certain of my damnation? And what did the message of servitude and soul mean, coming, as it did, on the heels of Carmel's Caribou Queen victory?

I babysat every Thursday for the Maples, and despite the daytime drama, I walked to my job that night. The sidewalks seemed tilted. Two street lights in the School Draw were burned out. They made a strange buzzing sound. The tips of foxtails were still poking through the spring snow in the yard of one of the empty government houses up the road. They cast strange shadows on the snow. I noticed someone had nailed a piece of plywood over the space where the door should have been.

Half an hour after I got Roger Maple to bed, my mother arrived on the front porch. I could see it in her face, through the screen, but I asked anyway. "Is he okay?"

My mother shook her head. "No, Margie, he died on the emergency flight to Edmonton. I'm so sorry, sweetie. I know you two were friends."

"Not really. It was more Melly, Carmel." But the tears came anyway, prompted mostly by the word *sweetie*, and my mother gathered me into her arms on the Maples' plaid couch. "Airborne," she mused aloud, holding me while inexplicable sadness washed over both of us, "already halfway home."

What profits a man if he gains the whole world but loses his own soul?

I thought about that when Mrs. Johnston called the next evening and asked if I would sit with the family. "Carmel needs someone, and you were always my children's special friend, Margie. Sylvan loves — loved — you," her voice breaking on the tense shift.

I did not want that honour and would have told her so, except for my inability to speak.

I gathered my resolve but croaked: "Sure. Yeah, I guess," and replaced the black telephone on the hook. If I were a special friend, Sylvan Johnston must have had fewer friends than I thought.

I'd been one of two people at his seventh or eighth birthday party more than a few years ago, probably invited to keep Carmel company. "Someone closer to her own age. Someone to help Carmel celebrate her brother," was the way my mother phrased it.

"Just go, Margie. It won't hurt you to offer a little support to that poor older child. It hasn't been easy for her, you know. Carmel — ridiculous name, what was Eleanor thinking? — Melly, has had her difficulties. Not knowing her parents, where she belongs ..." until there was no room for argument.

At the party, Melly and I had pretended not to notice the twelve plates Mrs. Johnston stacked beside the frothy, chocolate birthday cake shaped like an airplane. I thought of Maryanne's birthday, the stew, the wordless celebration of her, and how, in that impossibly white room, three voices made a reedy song.

"I'm sure something just held them up," insisted Mrs. Johnston, as their terrible clock ticked away from the proposed party start time. I knew in my heart those horrible playground kids had boycotted Sylvan's birthday party. "I'm sure Sam and Allan and Mark and Andy are coming. Why, I've spoken to their mothers." Mrs. Johnston's moth hands fluttered at her side, helpless to hold back the emptiness in that room.

In the end, Sylvan smiled and pretended the party was a great success as we sang our three-voice rendition of the happy birthday chorus a second time and tried to ignore the table laid for twelve.

Those same kids, the ones who collectively boycotted his birthday, wept at his funeral.

Both classes, the Grade Fives and the Five/Six split, sat in the balcony of the United Church, lent for the service because it was larger than Sylvan's own Mission church. I wasn't with them, of course. Nor was I with my own classmates. I was down in the front pew with the Johnston family.

Halfway through the service there was a ruckus from the balcony. As the guitar played a muted eulogy, one of the worst offenders in the bully Sylvan campaign squealed, "His hair. A ringlet. Look, it's caught in the hinge. His hair. Oh no, no."

Two girls started to cry, one started to scream. I looked at the coffin. There was nothing to see except lacquered white wood and brass handles, the box emitting a terrible stillness, more pronounced because of the din in the balcony. There was no ringlet, no sense that a person, a little boy I'd known my whole life, lay dead inside.

Mr. Johnston bowed his head more deeply. Mrs. Johnston closed her eyes and the trembling in her shoulders spread to her back and neck, until the whole pew vibrated. The older stepbrothers hunched like their father, trying to make themselves disappear. I sat shoulder to shoulder with Melly, as she kept repeating under her breathe: "It should have been me. It should have been me. It would have been better if it had been me. It should have been me."

As I gazed at the white flowers on the white coffin and heard the music and thought about my own guilty soul — the one I may or may not have — I was overcome with remorse. I silently nodded, thinking it might have been better if Carmel, the darker, sturdier, less desired child, had died, and sweet, little Sylvan had survived.

And Melly saw me nod.

She froze, blank face registering something entirely new, something beyond pain and sorrow. She flinched, and shrunk, and then rallied, all in a split second. "Goddamn you," she hissed under her breath. "You can burn in hell."

I must have felt the tongues of fire at my feet, because I remember lifting them off the floor, looking at my good shoes, feeling the way they pinched. The pain of the too-small shoes allowed me to ignore the extent of my cruelty. Wasn't I simply agreeing with something Melly said about herself?

The shoes, the feet, the fire, the scorch of those words shocked me. It was not so much what Carmel said, which seemed only to affirm my destiny according to Sylvan's tract, but that she'd say those words in church. At her own brother's funeral. No wonder we couldn't be real friends. My smug superiority would not allow it.

⌒〜

After the death of Sylvan, I wandered around town, or more often, out on the rocks to the deeply private places that only I knew, contemplating Sylvan's final message to me, whether I had a soul, what would happen to my body after death, and if there was a God? I chose to ignore Sylvan's sister's more pressing warning, that I was damned already. What could Carmel tell me? Despite possibly being Caribou Queen, I didn't think she had any answers to my pervasive and largely philosophical questions.

Could there be answers inside Sylvan's place, the small church building called the Mission? It was halfway down the hill, a building with pink asphalt shingles on the exterior. I'd gone to meetings in that building exactly twice, gathered with other neighbourhood children around a painting of a blond-haired, blue-eyed, totally white Jesus. He looked like a modern rock star. He had long hair, haunting eyes, and a tender smile that seemed to quiver on his lips as he shared secrets with the littlest ones nestled on his lap. Most of the kids in the painting were black or brown but the rock star Jesus didn't seem to mind.

I went back to the Mission four weeks after Sylvan's funeral. It was a Tuesday afternoon, towards the end of June. The building was open, but there was no one around. I followed a hallway that led to an office. There was a colourful crayon sketch of what looked like a giant vine reaching to the edge of the paper and a small stick figure in the corner holding either a cross or a lopsided candlestick. The word Padre was written in rainbow, complete with a purple accent backwards over the last letter. I knocked.

Father Bridges, or Padre, as he'd asked his congregation to call him, was a conscientious objector (his words), known throughout our community as a draft dodger (Jennifer's words).

"They came from Africa. They're missionaries," Will corrected.

Jennifer scoffed: "No, stupid, they're Americans going to Africa. This is just a pit stop. You watch, the Padre and his pretty wife will be out of here before school starts." Jennifer loved to prove herself smarter than Will. She had skipped a year and was in Grade Eleven, moved into my dad's high school, and was treading with confidence all over Paul's turf.

"How would you know what they're doing?" my brother shot back. "When is the last time you even darkened the door of a church, Jennifer? Hypocrite."

She turned to me then, looking for an ally. "I was there a couple of years ago, wasn't I, Margie? We went to the rummage sale. But that's not the point, Will. The point is those Bridges consider this town just like Africa. It's a different kind of mission. They're getting their feet wet here — chilling out — so the Congo won't seem so bloody hot."

She turned to leave. But not before adding: "You watch, once she has that baby, it's *see you later* for those two. They'll take their kids and pack it in before you can say Jesus Christ Almighty."

"Jennifer. If you can't say anything ..."

"Get lost, Margie. Since when did you become smitten by that hippy Padre Father? Father to whom? Will just likes him because he's got long hair and plays the guitar. Maybe he's Christ himself, come back to save the poor old Indians from shooting themselves in the foot."

⌇

Again, up against my sister's dismissive pronouncements, I felt compelled to seek my own answers.

"Come in," came a voice from behind the door. What did I need to ask? I stood tongue-tied and rooted in the hallway until the Padre himself pulled the door to his inner office open and gestured I enter.

The office was filled with books and a desk overflowing with papers. On a bookcase on the left wall of the room, a black-and white-photograph showed Mrs. Padre heavily pregnant and glowingly fecund, with flowers in her hair.

"What can I do for you?" His voice was kind and pitched low, like someone coaxing a cat from a precarious perch. He extended his hand: "Father Tom Bridges."

"Padre," I repeated, thinking that would please him. "I saw the sign."

"And, what's your name?"

"Margie. Margie Macpherson."

He seemed to consider for a moment, and I felt I should offer some explanation for my arrival.

"I was a friend of Sylvan Johnston. Sort of a friend. You know? The boy who died."

He leaned back in his chair then, indicating I should sit. He placed his fingers together as though playing the kid's game — *here's the church, here's the steeple* — "Sylvan, yes. Poor Sylvan," he murmured, contemplating what?

I didn't know where to sit, as all the surfaces of the chairs were covered with papers, so I remained standing, waiting for him to speak again. His name between us rang like a small bell. *Ting.* Sylvan.

"God wanted him back, Margie. It is not for us to question God's will. It was the will of our Heavenly Father. Who are we to say otherwise?"

He asked the question as though he expected an answer. "Nobody?"

"Nobody, indeed, Margie. Nobody indeed." He smiled at me then, and I knew I had pleased him. "From dust we came, to dust we shall return. Sylvan's physical being may be gone, but his spirit is soaring with the angels. How old are you?

"I'm fourteen," I told him. "I want to know about this." I reached into my back pocket and pulled out the dog-eared tract. He took it, read, flipped through the pages. "Fourteen," he mused aloud. "An age full of transitions. Where did you get this?"

"From him, from Sylvan. It doesn't sound like dust or even angels to me."

Padre leaned backwards in his chair, linked his fingers, and put his hands behind his head.

"No, this is about sin. It's designed to make you afraid." He tossed the tract onto his desk, casually, dismissively, daring me to pick it up again. "Be good, listen to your parents, and tell the truth. Do you do those things, Margie?"

I mostly did, so I nodded.

His voice dropped. "Do you have a boyfriend? Are you doing things with your boyfriend, things you aren't proud of?"

I took a step back. "No."

I thought about Lawrence and almost being his girl. "There is someone who wanted ..." What? What did he want? To implicate me in the death of that frozen horse? To teach me something?

Padre leaned across his desk. "You need to keep yourself pure. God can enter a pure heart. Dark hearts are troubled hearts. The sins of the flesh are all around us. Do you understand?"

"Flesh. Like, living people?"

"Flesh. Desire. Here." He reached towards me. "Give me your hand."

I stepped back. "I'm not allowed. And I've got to go. My dad is waiting just outside."

Because he was still behind his desk, I was able to excuse myself and leave, but I practically ran down the hallway. He had offered me nothing. There was no talk of souls, whether we had them or not, how I'd fare if Sylvan's sudden fate became my own.

I would have stopped my questioning heart right there, too, if it weren't for something that happened as another summer froze over and I entered my first year of high school.

⌒

While my friends were experimenting with smoking, eye shadow, and nail polish, while my brothers and my sister were singing about yellow submarines and strawberry fields, while my face became a mess of pimples and I only had to look in the mirror to know I wouldn't be the subject of any hit parade songs, I sought solace in the bush.

My cells called out for cold. I craved the secret intersections of grey rocks and deep clean water. It made me happy in a way I couldn't explain. I witnessed the finality of flies in frost and was puzzled and elated by the mystery of their reawakening. I had no one to talk to about these things, but I knew what I felt was somehow linked to dead Sylvan with his pale face and questioning eyes.

Later, as summer wound down, I was walking past the top trailers of Trail's End, where they were building the new hotel, when I heard the engines of a float plane purring in the sky, heading towards Back Bay. The hotel — with its concrete and steel-girder frame, torn fibreglass insulation, and construction detritus — had ruined the rocks, as far as I was concerned. I thought of the water beyond the rocks, the air inside the floats on the plane, the expansive liquid runway the pilot was headed to, unhampered by human engineering. I'd heard on rough days, when the lake kicked up whitecaps, float planes could flip, turn turtle, in a split second. I'd also heard a man from town was decapitated by the blades of his propeller plane at one of the float bases the previous summer.

Since Sylvan's dramatic death, I'd became obsessed by the idea of being ready to die at a moment's notice. I knew readiness was important, but I still wasn't sure what it was I was preparing for. Sudden death seemed everywhere, inevitable. *What profit a man if he gains the whole world?*

As I headed for home, I walked by the hostel and saw two boys smoking near the main entrance. I was pretty sure one of them was Lawrence. It would make sense that he was back. Grade Ten was about to begin and I was pretty sure no senior school classrooms existed in his community. He was talking to a boy with ginger hair, a show-off boy who, according to Suz Kout, had come to town last year from Inuvik because he got the boot from Grollier Hall, another hostel up north. His parents may have moved here. Ever since the visit of the Royals and the capital city designation, Yellowknife had grown.

The float plane sounded just behind my ears. It was the buzz of the stolen children. The hostel kids, alone together, their families far away.

I felt Lawrence tracking me as I walked by, and when I looked up to catch him, he flashed his eyes down, nudging a cigarette butt with his foot. The brief angle of his face was enticing, those lovely, narrow eyes. I knew he didn't live in town full-time, only visited occasionally from somewhere up north.

As the mosquitoes and horseflies lit and fed on my flesh, I thought about Maryanne and the fun we had when we were together at her tiny house. I thought of moosehide, skin on skin. Something comfortable. I glanced down at my polyester top, some failed Home Ec. smock Jennifer had sewed and then abandoned when the seams went wonky. It looked garish now, an outdated hand-me-down, so far removed from the subtle shading of bark and bracken.

As I walked away from the Hostel and Lawrence, I remembered Gloria, the buried doll, her ringlets ruined, and now Sylvan, the buried boy. After we'd piled the rocks on Gloria, we went back to Maryanne's. Lawrence was gone, but we had tea with a skim of fat on its surface because Maryanne's mothers stirred it with the same spoon she had used to ladle lard into a cast-iron cook pot. The tea was delicious, and I could take as much sugar as I wanted.

We'd sat behind the house on the bench of an old Ski-Doo enjoying the last long legs of late-night light while watching a man work near the lake. He stuck his hand right inside a fish and didn't seem to mind the guts or the greenish slime sack that slipped between his fingers and fell to the shore. Did fish have souls? Did the ravens who came to eat the fish guts? Did I?

At home, I crept in the side door, certainly wanting no one to know I'd visited the Mission people, but more importantly, not wanting anyone to question my innermost ruminations.

My mother, the mood detector, saw me and frowned.

"You're sullen and withdrawn, Margie. Go do something for someone else. Stop mooning about." Before we could escape, Ned, Will, and I were issued a job, cutting wood for Mrs. Anderson in the Old Town.

"At least, we get to go somewhere interesting," I said, trying to placate them. "She's in the Woodlot, the two-room shack with the plastic windows."

"We were playing splits," said Will, quickly pocketing the jackknife he'd been throwing just beyond the reach of Ned's feet. "If you weren't mooning around, Margie, we wouldn't have to do this. Jeez, what's with you, anyway?"

"Mrs. Anderson is a widow. How would you like to be a widow, Will?"

"Since when did you care about widows?"

"Yeah, Margie, since when?" echoed Ned, and then, with his face screwed up: "What *is* a widow?"

"It's a spider who kills her mates."

"No, don't listen to him, Ned. A widow is someone whose husband died. Mr. Anderson's Ski-Doo went through the ice on Jackfish Lake after they put the generator in." I was the one who knew. I was also going to be the one who decided what Ned should know.

"What? Man, it took two years to build that power plant," Will scoffed. "How could he not have known the ice would be candled?"

"He was old, I guess. Forgot."

"Yeah, but he should have known, Margie. Crossing Jackfish on a Ski-Doo with a loaded sled? Come on. He may have been old, but also pretty dumb. You've got to admit."

"The town killed him," said Neddy.

I looked at my younger brother, eleven, trudging down the hill beside me, hoping for a chance to carry the axe. He was willing to toss and stack firewood for the opportunity to be with Will, to do something manly with his popular older brother. But what he said seemed right.

As far as I knew, the town built the generator, but Mr. Anderson had to be over ninety when it slowly heated the water in Jackfish Lake. What he thought his whole life was sound and certain became soft and unpredictable in two short seasons. His sled was the thing that broke through, but I imagine it carried the Ski-Doo in after it. I always wondered why he didn't jump. Maybe he did. The marks in the ice and the way it was broken proved he tried to haul himself up before the cold took him. That's what I'd heard.

"Why doesn't Mrs. Anderson go to the old folks' home up-town? You know, the Mountain Haven Lodge or whatever it's called."

"Mountain Aven," I corrected. "It's the official flower of the Northwest Territories."

Will snorted. "See any flowers, 'round here? Any mountains? Those stupid little flowers are white and puny," he muttered. "Why can't someone from the town just force her out? She's too old to live by herself in the Old Town."

My older brother couldn't seem to walk off his resentment. Jennifer, now two grades ahead, was studying for her calculus exam, a big one. Dad was talking about law school, about Jennifer's bright future. I was pretty sure Will was more pissed off about that than about having to do charity work.

"Ask her yourself," I replied because we were almost at the house.

I pushed Ned towards the door with the flaking blue paint. His knock was small, but she came after a while, a person old beyond reason, a soft slouch of a woman.

Mrs. Anderson seemed held together by a rope at her waist. She wore baggy industrial overalls rolled up at the leg to reveal long johns, moth punctured and grey. Her face was deeply weathered. I couldn't tell if she was Indigenous or just tanned from so much outdoor living.

She didn't seem happy or surprised to see us. More like we were expected, like it was our duty to help an old woman. "Stack the wood there," she pointed. "Less wind come winter. There." And the peeled-paint door closed firmly in our faces. We obeyed because we were raised to obey.

"She's a crooked old bird," said Will, out of earshot, behind the shack. "Look at this place. It's not much more than two upside-down shipping crates." My brother's indignation gave Ned licence to gripe, and as the maul split a crisp cord of spruce and birch in the wood-smoked air, words raged between them.

"She doesn't know our mum made us come," said Ned. "And look," he pointed beyond the woodpile, "she still poops in an outhouse."

"Icehouse, more like it," replied Will, hot with sweat. "If it weren't for us — for people like us — she'd be a goner. Winter coming on. If it weren't for us ..."

And I thought of old Mr. Anderson, those claw marks by the fresh hole in the ice. *If it weren't for us.*

Each log I stacked became a meditation: If it weren't for us the Indians wouldn't need charity. If it weren't for us the caribou would still be plentiful. If it weren't for us people would be hunting and trapping the way they used to. If it weren't for us maybe the kids wouldn't have to be separated from their families, leave their communities, and come to town to go to school. Maybe Carmel could have grown up with her own mom and dad instead of the Johnstons. *If it weren't for us.*

Mission

My second encounter with Padre and my complicity in evangelical conversion occurred quite by accident a few months later in November. It was 1974, and I had moved to Sir John Franklin, joined my elder brother and sister in what I still thought of as my father's school. Paul had left home that year, moved south to go to university, a parental expectation I was not sure I would be able to fulfill, judging from my marks. I was in Grade Ten, fifteen years old, and more attuned to the idea that good work might save me from Melly's fearful lake of fire than I was to my teachers' efforts to educate me.

Kallik Makoktok lived in Akaitcho Hall, and I befriended her because I wanted her to lead me to Lawrence. Maryanne was no longer available. She'd been held back, made to repeat Grade Nine.

By the time Kallik and I met, a few weeks after she landed in Yellowknife from Coppermine or Cambridge Bay, one of the settlements of the eastern Arctic, she chose a new name for herself. Distanced from her family, she discarded Kallik Makoktok, her Inuktitut name, to become English-sounding Kathy Mist. Her new name was the spray, the misty meltwater hovering above the solidity of her given name. A new town, a modern town, and she wanted a new and modern name.

Akaitcho Hall was packed with teenagers, some first-timers, others newly returned to town. With the exception of July and August, there was no time in my memory when the Akaitcho kids weren't there. They had always been coming to Yellowknife. Each season, September through June, kids had been flown from their communities to be educated in the territorial school, but now, perhaps being among them, I finally saw them.

Sir John Franklin had long been a full-fledged high school operating on the Alberta curriculum and offering full matriculation to any student who could meet the requirements. My father, increasingly consumed by educating entirely different cultural communities under one curriculum, was never home. He wasn't the principal of the school anymore. He now walked up the hill twice a day to the Laing building downtown, a bureaucrat in the department of education. My mother, too, was consumed with creating mental health initiatives, working towards her dreams of a healthier society. The decidedly slackened rules around home life gave me more freedom to explore. It didn't hurt, either, that both parents were convinced I was on a spiritual quest.

I had a lot of freedom, a large and expanding range. And Kallik, though keen to get her diploma, wanted that same freedom for herself. She loved being in the larger community, but she didn't love having to abide by the rules of the residence.

She was out well past the 9:30 p.m. curfew when I ran into her in the Gold Range Hotel Café, drinking coffee and sitting with the Mission minister, Padre. Kathy's head was cocked to one side, a broad cheek laid against her hand, supported by her elbow, and she seemed to be listening intently as Padre questioned her about an uncle or grandfather, some Medicine Man from her home community.

"But he's a shaman. He knows all about ceremony. He works in spirit, but it's all connected to here." She put her opposite hand on her heart, and as she did her dark hair fell across the open canvas of her face. "Why would you call him an instrument of Satan?"

Padre was silent as Kallik clucked and murmured her a slow denial, the most contrary sound imaginable, the antithesis to Satan's stronghold. Clenching of jaw, yes; howls of pain and angry denial, okay, but surely not this sound issued from the intensity of love and memory.

Padre saw me hovering and pushed out a chair with his foot: *Watch. Sit. Listen,* he implied. Or at least that's what I heard.

"The Devil has many forms. Sometimes the Evil One enters people who worship false idols, someone like your uncle, or even someone like you, little one." Padre reached across the table and pushed Kathy's hair away from her face, looked into her eyes.

She recoiled, slightly.

"I understand your people have worshiped animal spirits and ancestors. This is simple ignorance."

Kallik shook her head. "My uncle uses scrimshaw and ivory tusks in ceremony. He blessed all the people, even when everyone got sick. Lots of people, they died. Lots of children. But he tried to help. My uncle is a good man."

"And could he save them with black magic?"

"They went to the sanitarium down south, even my auntie, his wife. She never came back. Many didn't come back."

"You see? Lighting lamps, calling on ancient spirits. Nothing works without the Power of the Holy Blood. Scrimshaw?" He cleared his throat, reducing Kallik's uncle's ceremonies to phlegm.

I couldn't stay silent. "But epidemics in the Arctic were brought by white people. That doesn't have anything to do with religion or ..."

Padre cut me off, glared. "We are here to help. *'When two or three are gathered in His name ...'*"

He was wanting my collaboration, my endorsement. Kathy looked confused. Was she evil? No more than I. No more than Padre. I could see his sanctimonious testimony, his quick judgments, but I couldn't see my own. His voice was a command: "Both of you, come with me."

He paid the bill, and we followed.

"We need to pray with you," said Padre, his hand on the small of Kathy's back, as he steered her towards the pink-sided Mission House along Franklin Avenue. I followed, unwilling to let Kathy go alone. Was this about the state of the soul? Why didn't he see the Devil in me? Why Kathy?

"We can't remove one Power without replacing it," Padre explained. "We can't send her out into the world as an empty vessel. The past is powerful. The Devil is within. I can feel Him, but even the Prince of Darkness can't stand the power of the Almighty. We have the authority. We are He."

We? He?

We entered the dim church lit only by the Pawn Shop yard lamp. I heard Kathy whimper, so I rested my hand on her arm to let her know I was there. Padre lit three candles on the altar. He prayed out loud: "I call out the Satan of this child's ancestors. Oh, Powerful, Holy God, be gone, Devil. Behold Jesus Christ. Enter into this lost soul and direct her henceforth and evermore. As your child ..."

"Margie."

"... Marge here is Your witness, enter into the heart of Kathy Mist, who is ready to receive You." Padre paused again, opened his eyes and cued Kathy. She dropped her head to her chest, signalling submission or prayer, as he continued. "... so she might be Your servant, never to serve Evil again. Amen."

There it was again. The word, servant.

Kathy started to sob. I felt as though Padre and I had erased her history. She was now as pure as Padre believed himself to be, but it made me want to puke. This was Sylvan's tract, ass-backwards. Had Kathy gained her own soul in this interaction, this exorcism, or had we stripped it? Padre had clearly gained something; he stood holding out his arms, his face peacock proud, righteous. I couldn't stay silent.

"I think we're okay, all of us, just the way we are," I blurted. "We're, like, we get a choice to be better, with more love, right? Right?" I couldn't suppress the pitch of my voice, the intonation rising at the end. I felt I owed Kathy an explanation for whatever weirdness Padre had visited upon her. I was an accomplice, a collaborator in this bizarre religious transaction. But I didn't sound confident. I couldn't undo what had been done.

Padre ignored me and moved to embrace his newest convert, someone he seemed to now view as a white-washed saint of his Kingdom. Kallik really was Kathy now. In Padre's mind she had shaken off the Shaman's curse, and she was well and truly free in Jesus Christ, our Lord and Savior. Amen.

Except the final *amen* was held by Padre Bridges.

"These things you will do — casting out demons, healing the sick — you will do them in My Name. These things, and more." He was full of his own sense of power.

It was creepy. I felt tainted and complicit. I couldn't begin to imagine how Kathy felt. I couldn't wait to get away. And I left her there with him. I went home, rattled and sick to my stomach.

Kathy went to the Mission church for six, maybe eight weeks. At first, she stopped me in the hallways of Sir John to say hi, to let me know she remembered our covenant. After Christmas she stopped saying hi, and soon we both tried to avoid the other. Embarrassed by the exorcism, I did not ask about Lawrence, about life in the hostel. It wasn't long before I heard she stopped going to the Mission fellowship.

It was Suz Kout who told me Kathy Mist was pregnant. "I think she got knocked up by one of those holy rollers, you know, those kooky Mission people? You were one of them once, weren't you, Margie? I could have sworn ..." But I denied my association and prayed Kathy would go back to her settlement before the baby showed.

Like Jennifer predicted, the Bridges moved away after Padre's wife delivered her fifth child, a girl my mother told me they named Misty.

I thought Kathy had gone, too.

Will was giving me a driving lesson in the old Meteor, once through town until the pavement ended, and then once out on the gravel, *for practise*, to Prelude Lake, when we spotted a girl on the side of the road, outside the Giant Mine bunkhouses.

I pulled over as soon as I saw her, but I remembered to use my signal light so Will wouldn't fail me. "You're not supposed to pick up hitchhikers," he mumbled, as Kathy hauled open the passenger door. I didn't know she was hammered until she climbed into the backseat and the smell of drink permeated the car. Once in, she saw who was driving. "I'm still born again," she slurred. "I'm stillborn again." And then she laughed with such bitterness and contempt, I completely avoided the rear-view mirror.

Will and I dropped her off uptown near the Miners Mess. Just before she walked away, she put her head into the driver's-side window. "Thanks for the ride, Margie."

"You're welcome, Kallik."

"It's Kathy," she said, "You should know that. You, more than anyone." And she turned away from the car and was swallowed by the double doors of the Mess.

Foreign

In the social studies room, in the last few months of Grade Ten, our regular teacher suddenly disappeared. In her place was a small, bald man wearing a full three-piece suit. He stood stiffly in the front of the blackboard. He told us his name. Boris. Boris Dotsenko. Some of the kids laughed when he introduced himself.

"You will call me Doctor Dotsenko." Doctor, not Mister, or Miss, like all the other teachers.

"Before now, I taught in Kiev, at the University. I am a research scientist, a nuclear physicist." His accent was heavy. Physicist sounded like Vizz-a-cyst. The crown of his head was ringed with sweat.

"Are you Russian?" one of the back-row boys asked. "Isn't Kiev in Russia?" And we held our breath, waiting for the answer.

We'd learned about the Soviet space capsule Sputnik, and the evil Russians, racing to dominate space. They were communists who wanted the whole world to give up believing in God and believe in communism instead. Wasn't Hitler a communist? Or was he a fascist? I wasn't completely clear on the difference, but he must have been part communist to kill all those Jewish people, because how could anyone who believed in God kill anyone?

"Kiev is in the Soviet Union," our teacher said, shuffling foot to foot before mopping his shining head with a small, white hanky he pulled from his vest pocket. "I was there. Now, I am here." He looked around the classroom and I felt a wave of resignation in his statement. He asked us to turn to chapter six in our social studies textbook.

A boy at the back wouldn't be hushed. "Does that mean you're a communist?"

The new teacher removed his glasses, small, rimless orbs, and placed them on the desk beside him. He looked directly at the boy. "Turn to page ninety-six, please." He enunciated every word. "We will begin."

At break the talk on the school grounds was all Dr. Dotsenko.

"He's a spy. Don't tell him anything."

"He's with the KGB. They break your fingers, one at a time."

"He's here to get secrets about the bomb."

"He's just pretending to be a teacher."

I overheard Gregory Smith, a fellow Grade Ten, tell classmates about a dog. "The Russians sent a dog into orbit as a test to see if life could survive in zero gravity."

That afternoon, in social studies, I watched the back of Dr. Dotsenko as he drew a diagram illustrating the political spectrum. In my mind, I dared him to calculate the days and nights a dog could stay alive in a spacecraft sealed by Soviet cruelty. I imagined that little dog circling endlessly around the earth, first yelping, finally quiet, and eventually dust, while people like Dr. Dotsenko continued to spread their evil doctrine.

Within weeks of his arrival, he decided we needed to know about the resources beneath our feet. As part of our social studies, he organized a field trip to Giant, the huge gold mine north of town.

A Dene boy from the Hostel, someone named Jarvis, refused to go. "We can't go below the earth. Our Elders told us. Not into the sky, either. We should stay on the ground." He spoke softly but with conviction, and when the class laughed and three or four boys started scoffing and repeating the word Elder, he stopped talking and sat down. He never came back to class. I don't know where he went, dropped out or skipped, but I was embarrassed for him.

Dr. Dotsenko ordered a yellow bus to take us, fifteen kids, and we drove to a place we'd seen hundreds of times before. This time, knowing we were going below, the slag ponds looked more sinister, with dead trees, stripped of their bark, sticking out of the murky swamp-water runoff. The trees stood in pools of arsenic, the clumps of branches like the heads of horses, or like corpses on poles displayed on the out-skirts of a medieval walled city.

The bus was noisy, my classmates wild with anticipation of going underground. I thought of dropout Jarvis and his Elders. I saw the dead trees around the mine site sitting in the poison brew. Was I the only one slightly sick to my stomach with thoughts of journeying a mile below the surface of the earth?

A large wire fence surrounded the mine, and the gates were topped with barbed wire. The bus stopped at what appeared to be a small, covered building, and as soon as we entered, we were herded into a cage, a mesh elevator that dropped into a dark shaft. I imagined the bedrock, the split-open earth. Doesn't drilling into something weaken the structure? But there was no room for questions. I tamped down my anxiety. We were going below. A cage operator was with us. He didn't blink.

One of the girls from my class, I think it was Sandra Stonehouse, blanched, bent over, and began clutching at her stomach as the pulleys and hoists jarred and jangled, moving us lower and lower into the earth. Sandra crouched in the cage and began to mewl as the cage clattered down its endless descent. The cage operator motioned to Dr. Dotsenko: "Is she okay?"

Our teacher frowned. This was not anticipated.

Sandra started to pant like a dog. I thought about the Soviet experiment again, how the Elder said people weren't supposed to go into space, and I was relieved when Sandra was delivered to the surface. It was my opportunity to back out. But once up, I changed my mind. Sandra now had to wait all afternoon by herself on the bus. The wire-mesh door was pulled across my escape a second time, and, again, we descended.

It was dark, but Dr. Dotsenko pointed out the different stratified layers of stone and sediment. I felt Sandra had stolen all the air in the mine shaft, which made it hard to listen. I watched the boreholes become blurs as we fell, two hundred, three hundred, four hundred feet into the ground. Dr. Dotsenko was talking about ventilation shafts and rock bolts and engineering formulas designed to shore up tunnels and shafts.

I was dizzy and relieved when we stopped and unloaded into a horizontal tunnel. We followed the cage operator down a shaft covered in metal mesh, and instinctively each of us ducked our heads even though there was room to stand. It was so dark in the tunnel, and somewhere, not far away, I heard water dripping. Our headlamps were pitiful beacons in the stale, opaque, dusty air, and Dr. Dotsenko, who had likely never been underground before, finally stopped his teacher talk.

"Just think of what's on top of us," said one of the boys. "We're at least a mile, mile and a half down."

"Be quiet," said Jane Laidlaw, Sandra Stonehouse's best friend. "You can't think of that."

But it was too late. I felt the weight of the earth above, and the tunnel suddenly felt narrow and insubstantial. The air became tight and scarce, and I was slightly nauseous knowing there was only one way back.

On we marched, until, like a miracle, a room that seemed cavernous opened up in the earth. It felt bigger than our high-school gymnasium, but, after coming from the tunnels, my sense of scale was warped. There were Caterpillars and yellow backhoes working, but the space seemed so large and so bright after the darkness, they reminded me of Tonka toys, left in a backyard sandbox. The large working space full of machinery was dusty and lit with glaring florescent bulbs.

"I can't believe this," I whispered to Gregory Smith. "How did they get these huge machines down here?" I thought of the cage and the narrow opening that brought us below.

"They bring them down in parts," he said. "Piece by piece."

We both looked at the enormous trucks being loaded with blasted stone, the backhoes grinding and pushing, the iron ore dumped onto huge conveyor belts and moved to another area beyond our vision. So much of the mine was invisible.

From what he'd said, the machines never came out of the mine once they went down.

That dog. She was never meant to come back to earth. Her bones would always be in space, orbiting, the same way these machines would always be down here. Once they broke down and could no longer be repaired, they'd remain underground forever. How did the earth feel about having something foreign lodged inside it forever? And that Jarvis kid, who opted out of the field trip? What he said made sense to me.

Dr. Dotsenko made a sweeping motion with his hands, gathering us and herding us back toward the tunnel that would take us to the cage. The light reflected off his glasses and his eyes seemed frantic. As I clumped along, I pondered how out of place we were here, below earth. I thought about what belonged, what didn't, until the rattling cage drew us up and spat us out, blinking, beneath the wide, open sky.

It was the same question, asked many different ways. Did the horses belong? Did we belong underground? The equipment? Did the Akaitcho kids belong in Yellowknife and did white people belong here at all?

Those teenaged Royals, the Prince and Princess, swatting mosquitoes and trying to pretend it was okay to dance with hundreds of eyes measuring their every step, how painful. How wretched to be subjected to your subjects in that way. I thought of Carmel going door to door in the Old Town like that poor old Muskox man, as she tried to get Indians to come to the New Town carnival.

Dr. Dotsenko didn't belong, and even though he was brilliant, even though when he talked I had a feeling he was telling only a tiny part of what was going on in that big dome head of his, we made sure he knew he didn't belong. He taught one winter, a single semester, and in the spring, he was gone.

⌇

I quickly forgot about Dr. Dotsenko and all school routines as summer rolled in, the snow melted, the dog shit surfaced, and life became a wide-open adventure again.

One day, towards the end of June, I saw Maryanne sitting on one of the benches outside the post office. She had her bare feet tucked up underneath her and was perched, eating an orange, watching people.

"Hey."

"Hey." She seemed happy enough to see me but didn't ask about my school year at Sir John or my plans for the summer. "I gotta steal a few dogs. Want to help?"

It was like being pumped full of air, breathing laughing gas. Of course, I wanted to help. Maryanne made everything seem daring and fun.

"Steal dogs?"

"Yeah, well not steal, not exactly."

"From who?"

She jerked her head down the hill towards the water.

"When?"

"Now. Let's go," And I fell in beside her as if no time had passed, and even though I know it had, it didn't matter two cents. That's what summer was like. That's what being with Maryanne was like.

The dogs belonged to Maryanne's uncle's stepson, a twenty-two-year-old named Eli Crapeau.

"There's a shitload of Crapeaus here," she said, when I laughed at the name. "They were some of the first, so don't laugh." And then she laughed. "Copper People."

"Like police?"

"No. You don't know nothing."

That stung. "Tell me, then."

"Maybe later. When we camp."

That helped. "Where does Eli have the dog? And where will we take it?" We were heading to her house, and all I could think was how lucky it was Saturday. I had told my mother I was working on the McNiven Beach spring clean-up with the Girl Guides all afternoon. Rescuing a helpless dog from a cruel master was almost the same thing, but way more daring.

"Eli's starting his own team, but he's taken the pups too young. He's got them on an Island in Back Bay. I'm bringing them back to their mama. They need to stay with her the summer."

"What does he think?"

"He's like you, doesn't know nothing."

I was not going to take her Crap-ola. Maybe I'd help the Crapeau guy, secretly be on Eli's team. "You got a boat?"

Maryanne nodded. "My place. You been there before."

"Yeah, a couple, three years ago."

"Only birthday I ever had."

"Oh."

"Still got that rock pick. It's good."

Wow. "How many dogs?"

She stopped then, a few minutes from her yard. "You sure ask a lot of questions."

"Yeah, I want to know things."

"Then you got to listen. There's one too small, for sure. One, two, I don't know. The rest are weaned and ready. Eli can't know it's me. We're going to go across this afternoon, take fish for feed, bring back the runty one for sure, maybe the other, too. The bitch was howling, no pups, just like that." She snapped her finger. The thumbnail had chipped polish, purple; the fingernails, chewed, were crescent moons of grit. No running water in Willow Flats. I was having second thoughts.

Maryanne expected full participation. Near the shore, off the rocks, she had an old blue canoe with a flat stern and a gas tank, but no motor, tied to a clump of willows.

"Is this the one you paddle to the East Arm?" It seemed so small.

"Nah, this is just for fun. Besides, it leaks. That's your job, to bail. You stay here. I'll get the feed."

She came back with a burlap sack of frozen lumps and dumped it in the centre of the boat. "Go to the bow. I'll paddle."

As I scrambled over the sack, I saw there was only one paddle, splintered at the end. "Are you sure about this?" Maryanne didn't bother answering.

We followed the shore around to the Latham Island Causeway and slipped under the bridge. No one seemed to notice. I'd never been on Great Slave before when there wasn't ice, and I started to relax and enjoy this unexpected adventure. The island was an outcrop of rock, maybe eight hundred yards offshore. Sure enough, five small dogs sat pitifully at the waterline, waiting for us to draw the boat onto the bedrock. They were sad looking, with matted fur and shit stuck to their bums, and I could see from the boat, they would be wriggly. Did we really want them in the canoe?

"Get out. You got to get out first."

I crawled over the gunnels and the dogs leapt. Oversized poopy paws smeared my jacket and fishy breath fouled my face. I no longer wanted to rescue them.

"Get off." I pushed the grubby dogs away, throwing ineffectual punches at the pups, no longer small, no longer cute.

Maryanne scampered after me, and they must have smelled the food, because they followed her to the backside of the rocky outcrop. She dumped the fish and brought on a feeding frenzy.

"See that little one, the skinny dark one? They don't let him eat."

"Is that the one you want to kidnap? It looks like he might have worms. You can get them from raw fish."

"Nah. He's just a runt. That white and tan one looks okay. We'll just take the dark runt. Grab him." She handed me the sack, now empty of fish but for guts and slime on the burlap.

"In the sack?"

"He'll bite if you try to pick him up." She held out her hand and I saw a ragged wound, a week or so old.

"Did you get tetanus?"

"What?"

"A shot. Did you get a needle?"

"You a doctor?"

I took the bag, Yukon Gold stamped on the loose weave. A runt in a potato sack.

Maryanne came between the pup and the rest, fighting over the fish carcasses. She herded the dog towards me as I readied the bag. The puppy must have thought there was still food inside because he came to me, and I pulled the bag over his head and half his body and lifted. The hind legs kicked and a muffled yelp sounded from inside the churning sack. I got him.

Maryanne cheered. "Nice one." And she took the potato sack from me like she'd done it herself. "We'll let him out in the boat once we're out. Eli might think he drowned. Hope so." She smiled then. "The bitch will be glad. We done a good thing, Margie. Maybe you can paddle home, I'll calm the pup. He's going to live with me, see the summer out for sure."

"Won't he miss his brothers and sisters?"

"You miss yours?"

I had no answer.

I paddled, first on one side, then the other, concentrating on keeping the canoe straight. The puppy whined as the rocky island receded, and the dogs left on the island whined, too. They were crying for each other, aware of the water between them. Or maybe the ones still stuck out there were crying because they weren't rescued? As the chosen pup lurched between the gunnels, I decided my job was not to ask questions. My job was to get us back to shore. After that, we'd plan the camp-out and our dog — the one we'd rescued — would come with us.

The camping trip didn't happen right away, and later, when I saw her downtown again, Maryanne told me our daring rescue was for nothing; the mother rejected the runty husky pup. The bitch was done with pups, according to Maryanne.

Eli Crapeau found out about our escapade and came over to Maryanne's to reclaim what was his. There were words, apparently, and some things were *thrown around*. Eli not only took his dog, he absconded with a choke chain and a leather lead Maryanne had braided from hide. "He thought I owed him," said Maryanne, "but, don't worry, I'll get him back."

I wasn't worried. In my mind, she could do anything. She was the true Caribou Queen, a servant to the runtlings and vulnerable, the rejected and ill-used.

We chose a weekend to go camping and a meeting place. "Your job," said Maryanne, "is to bring everything."

Cracks

The tent was stupid hot inside and my body was soaked with tiny beads of sweat. Maryanne was lying next to me, still asleep. She was half out of her sleeping bag and her naked bum was showing, the tan line of her swimsuit making her dark skin ever darker.

As I reached to shake her awake, her mouth fell open and she sucked in the hot tent air with a moist shudder. All I wanted was out. I scrambled over my sleeping bag to the front of the tent. The zipper stuck for a second and then released and I pulled up, letting the morning air wash over me. It was Labour Day 1974, two days before school would start, but the autumn air was still weirdly warm.

Last week, after intense lobbying for a two-night camp-out, Maryanne and I were dropped off at Sammy's Beach by my father. We'd set up camp on the southern shore of the lake where the bedrock dipped its toe directly into the water. Maryanne and I had argued earlier about my choice of tent site, a reedy beach with a strip of foamy sand. She'd told me the shallows were thick with green bloodsuckers and black leeches.

"We'll be *by* the water, not *in* the water," I argued, but Maryanne refused to hear, declaring my site too exposed. My brothers and I had spent hours on the lakeshore when we were younger, digging pits, filling them with leeches and clapping and laughing as the water drained away and they curled up and died in the dry pits under the hot sun.

I liked Sammy's Beach. I'd never been allowed to camp this far from home, but my parents' permission was granted because my dad would be nearby. He was in a golf tournament across the highway.

Yellowknife Golf Course was the most northerly course in Canada. It hosted, perhaps still hosts, the Midnight Madness Classic, a tournament that began on the longest day of the year, June 21st, at the stroke of midnight. For us, it signalled the pinnacle of summer. It was on solstice eve that summer seemed unending. Without any night, a certain mania set in and everyone was energized and active. It was not uncommon to hear birdsong at two a.m. and sirens and shouting in hours normally reserved for sleeping.

Now, summer was waning. This final golf tournament was unofficially called the Labour of Love, because each golfer had to drag a great bristled mat across the oiled greens in order to erase both footprints and putting trails. The clubhouse had to be closed, winterized. That, and the fact mosquitoes were fierce and ravens were out to steal the golf balls, meant the Labour Day tournament was only for diehards.

For us, it was the second bell ringing after recess, the sound of summer's end. Yet today, with the heat, I was not convinced summer was over. Perhaps this year I could camp clean through October.

Last night I told Maryanne about the golf course, how we'd been hanging out there ever since I could remember. How, if we didn't build forts or kill leeches at Sammy's Beach, we'd go to the first tee-off where Dad would send Will and Ned and me under the wooden clubhouse to look for money in the sand.

"He probably did that to get you out of his hair, you know, so he could suck back another," Maryanne challenged. "I bet you hardly ever found money."

I didn't tell her we always did, because suddenly it sounded lame and childish, the three of us looking for coins in a crawl space that wouldn't allow standing. I saw Ned and Will and me crouched amid long needles of light slanting through the rude cracks of the plywood floor above. We would sift powder-soft sand peppered with cigarette butts and ash through our fingers, to mine nickels and pennies and sometimes the thin but coveted bluenose dime, with its promise of pirates and plunder. It was like discovering a secret fortune, as low voices and laughter drifted above.

I looked out to the lake, and then kicked at the ashes left inside the ring of our campfire stones. I wondered what was going on with Maryanne and Will. She wanted me to talk about him last night, but some strange loyalty to my family prevented me.

I secretly hoped Will wasn't dating her. It would be too complicated.

If my father purposely dropped coins through the floorboard cracks, or if, like Maryanne suggested, we picked up the fumbled change of guys drinking at the makeshift honour bar, so what? We were just kids back then. Even if they dropped the money on purpose, why did Maryanne have to spoil it?

I looked to the rocks and the sky, wishing she hadn't suggested he planted coins to buy more drinking time with his buddies. But she was practical like that. She didn't have time for imaginary things. She was too busy living.

Will and Ned would often become bored with the money mining and would leave me underneath the clubhouse while they played more dangerous games, rolling on oil drums behind the first hole or pawing through the bush for unbroken tees or even wading into sloughs to plunder the bottom sludge for lost balls.

I would sit in the soft shadows and sift the same handful of sand back and forth, back and forth, listening to stories of government people having crazy adventures in float planes and on dogsleds, while the comforting aroma of Erinmore pipe tobacco assured me my daddy was nearby.

But he wasn't nearby, not nearly enough, according to Maryanne.

"He sounds like he's always travelling," she'd said last night, as the campfire burned down. "It's like being from a broken home without the fighting. Face it, Margie, you got one of them absentee fathers."

"That's horseshit." Why should Maryanne have any opinion of my dad? "He travels, that's all. He has to do his job. Besides, he's almost always home on the weekends, except when school is in, up north."

She poked a stick in the fire, and held up the flaming end, pointing it across the highway in the direction of the golf course. "And where is he the weekends he's at home?"

I felt the burn. He did travel back and forth across the Arctic, and sometimes up the Mackenzie River Valley, but that was typical of so many of my friends' fathers. I used to make up stories about him taking me on the tours. I'd look at the maps and memorize the names of the places he visited — *Tuktoyaktuk, Aklavik, Igloolik, Arctic Red River, Paulatuk* — and repeat them under my breath like a mantra of his certain return.

I told Maryanne the names of those places last night, a sketchy defence, but it didn't shut her up.

"You know what I heard, Margie? You know what I heard about the guys who take government tours to those half-froze-over settlements?"

I shook my head, not sure if I wanted to hear. Maryanne's eyes shone yellow in the fire's glow.

"The Eskimo men give their daughters — kids our age, even younger, thirteen, fourteen — to the visiting big shots. They give them as gifts, so the government men will have someone to keep them warm at night. That's how the Eskimo men honour the white people, by giving their daughters. Can you imagine? The girls are supposed to keep them warm in the igloos, but I bet more than that goes on, right? Old, fat white men, poking little girls. It's gross."

Maryanne didn't say my father was a visiting big shot. She didn't need to. He was an absentee father. I was his fifteen-year-old daughter.

I knew what she said was crazy wrong, and I couldn't understand why she was throwing this in my face.

"You don't know anything about my dad," I countered. "How could you? Do you even have one?"

And instead of crumpling or fighting back, Maryanne spat

into the firepit. "Who needs them? I don't need no old man telling me what to do, where to go, when to be back."

But I was still pissed off. I conjured my dad's face and scowled across the flickering light at Maryanne's dark shape. "You can say what you want, Maryanne, but my dad is the best. Might be hard for you, but don't put me with kids whose dads are long gone. That's not how it is, anyhow. Who do you think drove us out here?"

And, perhaps knowing she'd gone too far, I heard the sizzle of more spit in the fire. "I guess. You're lucky."

In those two phrases I heard apology struggle with longing. I knew Maryanne's father had walked. "I'm going in the tent. You coming?"

She may have shaken her head, but she didn't move, just poked around in the embers some more. I knelt and pulled back the flap of the tent.

"Okay, good night." But she didn't respond, and I was too weary, and too perturbed to care.

⌒

The tent flap rustled, and Maryanne was beside me. She looked damp and puffy from too much sleep.

"Hot, eh?"

I was still irritated, remembering last night, so I didn't respond. Maryanne didn't even look at me, she just stretched and squinted into the morning sun. "What time is it, anyhow? How long you been up?"

She had put on her shorts, cut-offs with frayed hems, and the same t-shirt as yesterday, soot smudged from last night's fire.

"It's probably ten thirty or eleven. I just got up, too."

"Did you bring anything for breakfast?"

"We've got a can of beans. Or tuna fish. Which should we open?"

She grinned. "Let's have the beans. Otherwise, tomorrow's going to be both hot and stinky. Beans in the morning, and we got time to blow the farts out during the day."

Farts. Maryanne was encouraging me to swear. So far, I'd said *shit*, *ass*, and *Goddamn it*. Except for that one time at Caribou Carnival, I'd never said the word *fuck* out loud. The *Goddamn it* made me the most uncomfortable. God still felt connected to me, even after my complete and utter break with the Mission church.

We ate the beans out of the can, cold, with two spoons, sitting on the rocks so the lake breeze kept the bugs away. I was planning to ask about her and Will, and just when I figured now was as good a time as any, we saw people on the beach. They had to be strangers. No locals swam at Sammy's Beach.

Maryanne and I crouched in our camp and watched from the shore. We could both see and hear the people, but they were not speaking English. We knew they were French, not from our year and a half of Madame Mache's *Ou est la gare?*, but because of what they did. Right in front of each other and our spying eyes, the two men and the woman stripped down to their bare skin. Maryanne watched intently. I giggled nervously, my eyes widening and then sharpening so as to not miss a thing.

They looked old. The woman had baggy face skin and terrible sagging breasts, two weights that hung from her chest like the egg sacs of spiders. A thatch of patchy hair mercifully covered her private parts. The men seemed more naked somehow, stepping out of their long blue jeans like loose-limbed creatures shedding human form. Their thin chicken legs reflected the sun, drawing my eyes up to the dangle in their middles. I was riveted, fixed like a raven on roadkill.

"Look at those dinks," whispered Maryanne.

"Dinks," I echoed, as the three crept into the leech lake. Ankles, knees, thighs, and then the stick at the men's centre drew up like a bloodsucker after salt, as they flung themselves forward into the lake.

I was so busy watching them flounder in the icy water, I was unprepared for Maryanne's piercing whisper. "Let's steal their clothes."

Before I could say anything, she was off, darting across the rocks, crouching low like one of the guerrilla fighters on *The Rat Patrol*. I followed, not convinced naked, wet strangers — particularly strangers so free with themselves — were people we wanted to mess with. Surely those naked foreigners would spot us as they frolicked in the nippy lake, but Maryanne was an arrow, out on the sand, scooping up the ragged clothing and darting back into the bush before I could even shake my head.

We had the clothes, and except for a single sock, which fell, undetected, to the sand, we had them all. We skittered back lickety-split to our shelter at the top of the lake.

There was confusion when the three people emerged, mostly because hundreds of bloodsuckers had attached themselves to their flesh. They shouted and groaned, plucking leeches from each other like monkeys. Even when the last leech was pulled from their gooseflesh, the men continued to dance across the beach, dinks flapping and slapping their thighs as they leapt foot to foot to dry or warm themselves, or simply to keep the sandflies and no-see-ums off their exposed selves.

The search for their clothes brought more shouting, and we would have remained undiscovered if not for Maryanne's snorting guffaw. The strangers turned and made eye contact. A rapid string of French and, *un, deux, trois,* they were after us.

I did not want a confrontation with naked people, so with a nod from Maryanne, the two of us dropped the bundle of clothes and fled, jackrabbit fast, into the bush while the Frenchies reclaimed what was theirs.

Our campfire that night involved recounting the size, shape, and angles of their nakedness, details that threw both of us into fits of giggles.

"They were horny guys, eh?" said Maryanne. "I'll bet, if the lady wasn't there, it would have been different."

"You think? What do you mean? They were a lot older."

"Older men like young girls, don't you know?"

It made me think of Inuit girls and absentee dads, so I just shrugged in the dark. The constellations and blinking stars reminded me of the coins under the clubhouse, and they too were suddenly lost in a broil of resentment and confusion.

"If we hadn't run, imagine ..." but I couldn't, so I just laughed loudly, glad the fire had burned down and Maryanne couldn't see my eyes.

It was a seed Maryanne planted, old men liking young girls, and even though I'd defended him, I knew my own father could be implicated. What he did for his job, supporting teachers, educating people, filling the hostel with kids, might not be completely right. What did Maryanne care about Dick and Jane and Mother who wore an apron and Father who went to work carrying a briefcase? That worked for me, my father did carry a briefcase, but for her? It germinated inside my belly, that seed.

It also made me wonder about my own motives. I knew I loved camping with Maryanne. I found her daring, exhilarating. I loved her brash attitude, her seeming fearlessness, but I also knew in my dark heart that I didn't want other kids to know we camped together. Sammy's Beach was far enough away from town that no one saw us.

Maryanne was a perfect friend in the summer, when school was out and the harsh judgments of others didn't apply. After Labour Day, the school bell rang us back to the confines of appropriate friendships and Maryanne and I moved into a pattern of brief nods of acknowledgement in the hallways, but nothing more. I didn't claim her friendship, despite it being Maryanne and her cousin, Lawrence, who made me feel entirely and completely alive. She had a different way of being in the world, one I didn't consider compatible with my New Town life. She didn't talk on the phone, or hang around the drugstore, or go to the Capitol Theatre for Saturday matinees.

I recalled the mortification of the stranger's hand in my crotch at the movie theatre and my inability to speak and how shame prevented me from acknowledging my experience to the other girl, Annie.

But Maryanne had done nothing wrong. She just was, but the same feeling persisted, swirling around our association. It was not sexual shame, but something else, something more subtle and, now I know, much more sinister.

White

After I denied any association with the Mission church and Kathy Mist, Suz Kout and I made an uneasy truce. High school had taken some adjustment. There were hundreds of new faces, most of them from away. Suz wasn't my first choice of friend; Maryanne was, but Maryanne was now a year behind me. I hadn't forgotten her insinuation at our camp-fire either. Nor had I forgotten about her and my brother up on the rocks at McNiven Beach and, later, arm-in-arm at the Caribou Carnival.

I wondered if I should tell someone, but what? What did I really know? Will seemed completely happy, at last. He still didn't hang around home much, but when he did, he was cheerful and polite.

It was spring break, Grade Eleven. Suz's family travelled every few years back to Greece, the homeland, and she'd just come from there, so she needed the diversion of our house and potential engagement with my brothers to beat back the tedium of her own post-holiday home. Boredom was not exclusive to Suz. I felt it, too. We were both sixteen and the town had become too small for us. Winters were too long, people were too boring, parents were stupid, school was a waste of time, and spring was always, always too far away.

Edmonton, the nearest city, was just a dream. "It's almost fifteen hundred kilometres," said Suz, twisting a lock of hair around her index finger. The Greek sojourn over the Christmas holidays had Suz saying all distances in metric. "Where are your brothers?"

"Out." I didn't really care where Paul and Will and Ned were. I knew the main reason she came to our house was to attract their attention, but playboy Will had called her a piece of work and I knew how much he hated work.

I wanted to do something. I felt like we were hamsters in a cage, but the cage was everlasting sameness, that end-of-the-road feeling, combined with a powerlessness, a lassitude, and just plain old boredom. We couldn't enjoy spring break because spring was still so far away. Sometimes the weather broke in May, sometimes not until mid-June.

The bush was calling. "Hey, I know. Let's ski across Great Slave. Let's go to Dettah."

Suz wrinkled her nose. "Why?"

"For something to do. Will and Ned skied across a few weeks ago. You can wear Jennifer's skis and my mum's boots will probably fit. What size are you? A seven, seven and a half?"

"What's the temperature?"

I looked outside. The sun was bright. It was mid-morning, early March, two weeks before Carnival, but it was relatively

warm. "It's only nineteen below." The outdoor thermometer
hovered around twenty, but there was no wind. "Come on.
It will be fun."

"How far is it?"

"Five miles, maybe less." I was guessing.

"That's more than eight kilometres. That's far. Plus, we
have to ski back. Sixteen kilometres, round trip."

"You got a better plan?"

"Will did it?"

"Yeah, he and Ned. They said it was a blast."

"Okay, why not? Let's do it."

I was happily surprised. We now had something concrete to do, something different. Neither Suz nor I thought
of what, or who, we would find in Dettah. It was simply a
destination when destinations were hard to come by. We
didn't contemplate the fact that we were invading the space
of people — Tłı̨chǫ people — who had settled on the lakeshore thousands of years before and resisted moving into
Yellowknife.

"Do you think this outfit looks dumb?" asked Suz, as she
wrapped her flared pant legs into stovepipes and pulled a pair
of Ned's woolen socks over her calves before lacing up my
mother's ski boots. "I mean, we don't want to look like we're
retarded hobos, do we?"

I ignored her. Suz was all about looking smart. "Peanut
butter or tuna sandwiches?"

"The ones with the least calories," said Suz. "What's the
point of burning off all that fat, if we're just going to eat it
back on?" Suz was all about looking thin.

"So, you want tea instead of juice?" I was about to mix
some Tang.

"The thermos would be heavy. Let's just take tea bags and matches. We can make a fire, melt snow. You carry the kettle since this is all your idea."

Neither of us thought about wood or fuel for our fire, we just carried on like winter camping and ski trekking was an everyday event. We were aiming to leave before midday, but it was early afternoon by the time we headed onto the lake. The first few glides we were the Lone Ranger and Tonto, Franklin and Akaitcho, we were polar explorers, skiing into the unknown. For the first fresh half-hour or so we followed the ice road, broad at first, quickly dwindling as we got farther onto Great Slave. We were no longer polar explorers or even casual adventure seekers. An hour and a half into our ski, we had been reduced to two foolish youngsters, well beyond our safety zone, and woefully ill-prepared for a long ski.

"Nobody's driven across for a while," I called back to Suz as we struggled along a track with only two or three Ski-Doo treads, at least a few days old. Where was the good wide road? And what had happened to the sun and the bright blue sky? I stopped skiing and took in my surroundings. Except for Suz, huffing and panting behind me, everything was entirely without colour.

It was all white. Everything, white.

We had become snow blind by the uniformity of snow, by the absence of colour. The enormous expanse of ice in front of us was white, the afternoon sky around us, also white. There was no visible shoreline, no direction, no momentum. It was as though we were skiing inside a cloud and the sun, our compass, had completely disappeared.

"Let's go back," wheezed Suz. "This is bullshit. Do you even know if we're heading the right direction? Do you even know where we are, Margie?"

"We've got to be close. How long have we been skiing? Two? Two and a half hours? Dettah is closer than home. We have to press on, just so we can stop and rest for a while. We can't stop out here. There's no way we can stop." I was aware of the creeping cold, even as we paused to speak.

Suz nodded and suddenly that was scarier than her disagreeing. We both knew we were in trouble, serious trouble, but we had no choice but to keep moving. Somewhere ahead was warmth and shelter. The community of Dettah burned in our imaginations and forced our bodies forward.

Push, glide. Push, glide.

I was more frightened than I was cold, but I knew if we stopped, the cold would come upon us quickly and would take us. How long could you last, exposed on the ice like this? Half an hour? When would the false warmth descend? When would we start taking off our clothes out there on the lake, as our core body temperature dropped beyond recovery? Was Sylvan's fate about to be my own? Was that Suz sobbing behind me, or was it the wind in my ears?

I heard them before I saw them. Just as I was beginning to resign myself to death on the ice, I heard the faraway sound of barking dogs. Like a mirage, a qamutik emerged from the white. There was a man mushing a team of seven huskies towards us, calling out "Aye. Aye, Haye."

He stopped short of us, eyeballing us up and down; two scared white girls, sun-blistered, blinded, and blubbering, and with a curt nod, indicated we should take off our skis and climb into the canvas qamutik.

"Do you speak English?" Suz tried, but the man just thrust his chin towards the sled.

My hands could barely undo the bindings on my ski boots, and I collapsed into the qumutik, frozen and so very relieved.

The dogs surged forward, and because of the extra weight, the man ran alongside the team, calling out encouragement. It was only when the sled got up to speed that he leapt on the end, cracking a long whip over our heads, mushing the dogs toward the village that materialized on the near shore. It was just the edge of town, four or five small houses, all pumping woodsmoke from their chimneys, but it emerged from the white blanket of ice fog like a mirage. The village solidified the closer we got. The white lake receded. I could see an enormous wall of split firewood separating the houses from a cluster of sheds and lean-tos. Four Ski-Doos, and two trucks, one idling, were parked on the frozen road.

The lip of the lake was another heavy pull for the dogs, and the musher jumped off the qumutik again and, grabbing the steel runners, pushed it up and over the embankment with us in it, dead weight. The dogs seemed to know they were home and stopped just outside one of the smaller houses.

Suz and I sat, uncertain about what should happen next. The man gestured to us to come, and slowly we unfolded our stiffened limbs and stepped over the canvas wall of the sled onto the packed snow. I couldn't feel my feet at all, and it felt like I was walking on stilts from the knee down.

The driver of the dog team walked over to another man sitting in the idling pickup, said something, glanced over at us, and then handed the driver something I couldn't see. I didn't know what was going on, but I knew we had to get inside quickly. The cold was moving further up my legs and

I hobbled across the yard towards the door of the musher's house.

A tiny woman greeted us, her eyes downcast as we entered. A wood fire roared in a pot-bellied stove in the centre of the room and there was a daybed pulled close to it. The woman indicated we should sit and, again, without raising her eye, she offered us two steaming mugs of tea, sweetened with condensed milk. Suz started to cry, mostly, I thought, from relief.

"Thank you," I said to the woman. "Thank you." And she looked at me then, her eyes amused. She said something to her husband in Maryanne's language, and they both began to laugh. Because I didn't know what else to do, I laughed too.

Suz cried and I laughed, while the fire popped and hissed and our frozen clothes became damp and warm and the scalding tea slid down my throat, warming me from the inside out. My feet were tingling, coming back to life, little rocket shots of sensation, painful but beautifully so. I could wiggle my toes, feel the clunk of my toe mounds against the top of my ski boots. My cheeks still felt numb, and I raised my hands to my face, hoping it wouldn't be dead flesh that I touched. Some feeling was there. Not much, but some.

"We've got to get home," said Suz, sniffling.

"Look."

Out the window I could see the man from the pickup loading our skis into the back of his truck. "They're going to drive us."

"I can't get into a truck with those guys. You think I'm crazy, Margie? My mum would kill me."

I was shocked. "Look, Suz, we don't have a choice. It's getting dark. Honestly, they saved us, Suz. Your mum should be happy."

That shut her up.

The musher clapped his hands and stood. Suz and I followed him out to the frozen driveway. The truck was waiting and even though she was first, Suz made me get in so I was sitting next to the driver. The truck cab was warm. We were safe.

The younger man pushed in the clutch, put the truck in gear, and we lurched away from the lake, the village. It was at least forty-five minutes around the lake by road, but I think the ice road was too weak for vehicles. It was too late in the year. At the turnoff, one way to Prelude, the other to town, the man pointed his truck south. He was not kidnapping us. He did not want to hurt us. We were heading home.

"Get him to drop us off uptown," whispered Suz.

"Why?"

"My mum will kill me if she sees me with this guy."

I glanced at our driver. His face was impassive; he stared straight ahead at the winter road.

"We've got all the ski stuff. Just don't tell her." I was about to say something else when the man nodded.

"I'll take you where you need to go," he said. "The lake at night is dangerous. You should not travel at night."

I didn't think he could speak English.

"We didn't mean ..." started Suz, but I elbowed her in the ribs. I felt bad and I didn't want to make it worse. The man heard us. I didn't want Suz to speak again.

We rode the rest of the way in silence, and when we dropped Suz off, a block away from her house, as she insisted, neither of us mentioned plans to get together again. In fact, I knew I was done with Suz, and I felt lighter and almost happy as I thanked the driver and watched his red tail lights grow smaller and smaller in the dark night.

Hunt

I was in Grade Eleven remedial math that second semester of high school, having barely scraped through the academics, because of my inability to understand polynomials and trigonometry. Slowly over the course of the last term, as I fell farther and farther behind, I moved farther and farther towards the back of the classroom.

There was a slew of guys in the in the last row, a slump of boys, too big for their desks. Lawrence was among them. I'd noticed him right away, of course, but because we initially sat on opposite ends of the classroom, we did not speak. I moved towards him incrementally over the course of that winter, assured my inability to understand the concepts where the function of *y was equal to x* would make me invisible, like the rest of those bored boys.

The class was well into the coursework when I finally established myself in the second to last row. I took a seat hoping to go unnoticed and tried to focus on the board. That's when I felt a tap on my shoulder. I turned. A blurred boy, one of the five or six lounging, asked, "Do you mind if I share your textbook?"

It was Lawrence. I felt this queer shimmy and then a swoop in my chest, lightness, yet, impossibly, a feeling of falling too, a knot letting go, that moment when what is snarled and seized becomes fluid in your hands.

Our eyes met. I saw dark lakes, reflecting the night sky. I saw the underside of turned earth, shadows of water and soil at the same time. What was happening?

I'd seen him at a distance, cruising the halls of Sir John, head down, hugging the wall like most of the residential kids, but this time his eyes held mine in an embrace, as if there was no possibility of release and not even my nod — *yes, you can share my book* — loosened the pull.

He watched me, waiting with a small, half-smile softening his mouth. I wanted to urge it on, to have him really smile, but I was made instantly shy by simply thinking of his mouth.

Instead of answering, I opened the text, fumbled to the spot, kept the pages apart by placing the tiniest tip of my baby finger on the very farthest lower corner, the trembling edge of the page. The formulas swam, a school of char, and the only thing I could see was the anchor of his large hand on the opposite page, the line of elongated fingers, the mesmerizing hook of nails, blunt and trimmed, spinners below the surface. I was barely able to breathe, and love fell upon me as certain as snow in October, as surely as the after-school bell would buzz me back to reality.

I learned nothing that class. The voice of the teacher, a well-intentioned Mr. Mao whose accent blurred the already fractured formulas and equations, droned on until the time was up. Remedial math ended in the scrape of chairs and Lawrence's inevitable leaving.

He stood, nodded his head in thanks. "Margaret, right?" And my heart lurched in my chest, a husky hungry for the harness.

Then he was gone. He strolled from the classroom, turned towards Akaitcho with a clutch of other hostel kids, and was lost to sight before I could trust myself to stand. Had what happened to me, happened to him, too? I had no way of knowing.

But I did know it was real. That it could have happened so suddenly, and to me, and with him, seemed both impossible yet exactly right. I left that math class with new energy, with oxygenized blood rushing through every part of my body, with an insuppressible smile lifting me up, floating me above the crowded hallway of ordinary time. The normal crush of students and the grey rows of lockers seemed suddenly less oppressive. School danced and I danced with it.

It wasn't until I got back home that I revisited my experience. This was what they talked about in songs, in poetry. This was love, I knew that, but I also knew I had fallen in love with someone very different from myself. He was a Hostel kid, a boy from the bush. I was in love with a guy from Akaitcho, a residential kid.

How could that be? And yet, how could it be any other way? The feeling was so complete, yet it was nothing I was prepared for, or even believed existed. It was sudden, completely unexpected and forbidden. Surely forbidden. How would I see him again? Was he with someone else? How would I bring our worlds together when we had always been held apart?

That spring, just before Grade Eleven ended, our worlds did merge, ever so briefly.

~~

Two weeks after our shared textbook experience, as I was counting the days to our next math class meeting, Lawrence approached me outside the library.

"You want to go after birds this Saturday? Early. At five."

I gulped and nodded yes.

He ducked his head and moved immediately towards the machine shop. I had a date with the man of my dreams. The Caribou King. I was delighted, but as I looked through the library window to the rocks and trees, I was plagued by the eternal question *Seventeen* demanded of all first dates: What should I wear?

At home I found a plaid mackinaw Paul left in the basement and, with it, an old red hunting hat with earflaps, purchased by my father in the early days when he still believed white folk could live off the land.

Utilitarian and grungy, the outfit felt right as I tied the straps and cinched them down around my chin. It was still chilly, mid-May, and we were heading out in the dark, at five in the morning. It was cold. I was ready, but nervous. I recalled Paul killing the ptarmigan and my mother's intensely disturbing reaction. Hunting was not something we did, not something I'd ever tried. But, I reminded myself, neither was dating.

Sure enough, five a.m. Saturday morning, there was Lawrence, idling outside our house in a battered maroon Chev half-ton, a truck he'd borrowed from a different cousin, not Maryanne. He had a weekend pass from Akaitcho. I had told my parents I would be babysitting early and all day. Lawrence often got out all weekend because he had Maryanne's family, his auntie, in town.

I noticed the front fender of the truck was crumpled, but I stepped forward bravely to meet him. I imagined my footsteps across our frost-thick lawn as a trail, an indication of my leaving. The night before, instead of talking to Jennifer, I elected not to tell anyone of our plan. Our date was private. This relationship, like my friendship with Maryanne, was too important for public consumption.

Here, I have to pause and consider my motives. Why did I want my friendships with Indigenous kids to be clandestine and secret? Was I embarrassed or ashamed of that association? I don't think so. Perhaps the closest thing to the truth is simply that I was a teenager wanting to fulfill some presubscribed notion of the status quo. I wanted to blend in, win some sort of imagined approval in the society to which I was born.

I wish it were different. I wish I'd had the backbone to buck the system, stand out, extend a sincere offer of friendship to my Indigenous friends, but, alas, teenaged angst, my own inward nature, and all expectations of others, real and imagined, precluded any possibility of open honest, friendship.

Or maybe that is too easy. Maybe I am simply dancing around my own racism, the horrible part of myself I am loath to claim.

I remember the house was hushed as I slipped out the side door. I hurried to the Chev, as Lawrence leaned across the bench seat, pushing the passenger door open for me.

It was a heft, because the truck was high, but I clambered in, suddenly shier than ever in the hot, close cab.

It smelled like cigarettes and something else, something sharp and acrid, maybe the smell of gunpowder, certainly the smell of novelty, adventure. I was relieved and embarrassed to see our jackets matched. Lawrence's was purple checked, and mine, a slightly smaller pattern, was red, the colour of danger.

He put the truck in gear, and we headed out on the only highway south. One-way out, one-way back. For a moment I imagined us running away together, heading to Edmonton, beyond, before I realized how ridiculous that was.

The truck rounded Suicide Corner and I attempted conversation. "Have you ever done the Miles for Millions? You know, the walk-a-thons?"

Lawrence glanced over at me. He pushed in a cigarette lighter. "Why would I?"

"Oh, it was for money, to raise money for . . ." this was suddenly awkward, but I had to continue ". . . for poor people."

"Where?'

"What?'

"Where? Poor people where?"

"Oh." I really didn't know. "Africa?"

He looked at me then, and there was nothing to do but look away. Why would he walk for poor people? If Lawrence was going to walk, I thought, it would be for something real: for digging out a Ski-Doo stuck in a snowbank, for tracking a moose or going down the hill to visit his relations. He didn't even live here in the summers. It was a dumb question prompted by the guardrail at Suicide Corner where I had to rest because my blisters started to bleed.

Silence lapped at the shore of our strained conversation.

For someone who wanted exactly this — time together — I realized I really didn't have much to say.

Instead, I watched the landscape: the Bristol, where the horses were before they were abandoned, Long Lake where he showed me the head and asked me if I would be his girl. Was I his girl now?

We passed Sammy's Beach, where Maryanne and I camped, and across from it, the golf course. I thought of my father. Would he like the fact that I was hunting with a stranger? I thought he wouldn't mind, but he didn't know, so it didn't matter.

We continued driving, neither of us speaking. I thought about asking Lawrence what was next for him. I knew after Grade Twelve I was heading south. But I was afraid to ask him, perhaps afraid more of the answer. What were his aspirations? What did he want to be? Somehow those common questions seemed inadequate and inconsequential. Maybe he was going home after high school.

Sitting across from Lawrence in the truck, I realized I knew very little about him.

But, for reasons I can't explain, I felt I couldn't fill the cab with small talk.

There was still ice glinting in the ditches, fog on the road. We kept driving.

After a good half-hour, when the quiet between us had become almost comfortable, we pulled off the highway and stopped at the entrance to a gravel pit. Lawrence handed me a rifle, a .410. He was casual about it. "This is my auntie's. I didn't think you'd have one." A shotgun. I guess I hadn't thought through the details of *going after birds*. I'd never handled a shotgun before.

"Is it loaded?" I was holding the .410 away from my body, as though it could explode.

He reached across me, tapped a mechanism near my shoulder. "Sure," he said, "but keep the safety on. Follow me."

I followed. The bush was dense with black spruce and the occasional willow, but we followed the vestige of an old trail through the thick undergrowth. It was still dark. We walked a good quarter mile until we came to a bulrush blind, a sort of straw fort built with reeds and bulrushes pulled from the shores of a pothole lake it stood next to. My feet were cold in my rubber boots, my fingers numb in my gloves, and the cold of the heavy weapon was seeping up my arm.

"This is it," said Lawrence, flicking off the safety latch. *Click.*

Oh my God, the sound was exhilarating. I was alert, fully alive, all my senses heightened by that one small click, the warmth from Lawrence's hand near my face, the slightest whistle of the spruce boughs bending in the morning wind, the dark water lapping just beyond us, and the funky smell of runoff infused with soil, winter surrendering its stronghold.

"Is this legal?"

"Of course, it is."

"I thought hunting licences were only issued in the fall."

"I don't need a licence, besides snow geese are now."

I didn't know what he was talking about, but I hunkered down with him behind the blind. I was so aware of his body next to me, not quite touching, that when he leapt, I did too. The birds startled at our presence. They churned across the water, flapping and splashing, until, at last, they lifted off. Their wings cut the sharp air as they gained altitude. I felt their sense of panic, the flurry of escape. Like Lawrence, I first shouldered and then pointed my rifle to the sky, squinted and pulled the trigger. The double blast from our rifles reverberated across the slough. This was it. I was hunting.

A white bird fell from above, tumbled straight down, splashed into the lake less than a hundred yards in front of us.

Lawrence yelped triumphantly; the first time I'd seen him fully animated. He was jubilant, excited for me. "You got one."

I got one?

"Go get it," he said.

"How?" I asked. "It's way out there." Dawn was coming. The slough was brightening. The bird was floating farther away than I initially thought.

"Yeah," said Lawrence. "Go see."

"But it's cold. There's slime." I didn't like the sound of my own voice. Neither did my date. Lawrence scowled.

"It's yours," he said.

"You can have it." His eyes were flat and serious.

He looked at me, uttered my full name. "Margaret."

It stopped me cold. Except that one time in math class, I hadn't heard him say my name before. I didn't even know if he knew it. But he was attaching me to an action, an expectation, and it was something I did not want to do. I was out of my comfort zone. I had killed something, some living winged creature. This felt deeply wrong and yet, I'd done it. Almost by rote, I'd done it.

It was my bird.

I went to the edge of the slough and waded out. I'm not sure if I was trying to impress Lawrence or trying to overcome my own awkward realization that I'd acted entirely against my nature. For the first few steps the bottom felt frozen, firm, but a step further and I sunk into sludge. The bottom was spongy, uncertain. Cold water flooded my right gumboot. My jeans were wet and still the blob of floating feathers eluded me. I waded further into the duck-shit pond, to my knees, to my thighs, and as I was about to grab the stupid goose, it frothed and twitched, squawked and closed its bill around my arm. I screamed. My feet slipped from beneath me and I went down in the freezing sludge. I've never forgotten the momentary sensation of that beak, the dying bird, the gunk. Panic, utter panic.

Lawrence was beside me in the blink of an eye. He grabbed the bird, wrung its neck, and righted me at the same moment. I was soaking wet, covered in stinking algae, weeping with rage. The only good thing was my goose was now dead.

I hated the goose, I hated the lake, I hated hunting, I even hated Lawrence. Instead of offering comfort, he turned away from me and started the truck.

"Wait inside until you warm up."

So much for our date. I sat shivering in self-pity for half an hour, until he opened the door, indicated I should come out.

Grudgingly, I clambered down from the truck and immediately saw a small fire, a battered pot, something steaming. There were bones and pinfeathers nearby. Lawrence handed me a bowl of soup.

"You need something hot."

"You made this?"

"My mom taught me. It has oatmeal in it. I always keep some in the truck. It sticks." He smiled, embarrassed.

As I held the bowl to my mouth, the salt, the grease, the wild fowl flavour, and his care melted my anger. He had plucked and cooked that bird on the spot. My mind flitted back to the horse head, his pulling my hand into his pocket. I'd thought of it as a leash, a tether, but maybe it was like this, an act of steadying, an act of great care.

"It tastes good."

He nodded. "Warmed up?"

"Yup."

It was fully morning. The sun was bright. Nothing was hidden from the new spring light. The entrails of the goose were there, bloody and visible beneath slough muck hastily kicked over them. The fire was small and smoky. There was a charred pot, blackened on the outside, glommed with oats and grease on the inside. The site was entirely unappealing, yet strangely beautiful to me in its mean reality. I didn't transform it. I didn't change any of it. I just stood still and looked. I saw, and what I saw did not disappoint.

Lawrence doused the fire. A small hiss of steam rose and evaporated as another flock of birds flew overhead in perfect formation. The rising sun caught their wingtips. How magnificent they were, heading north in that imperfect vee.

"Where are they coming from?" I asked.

"South. They winter in Mexico, I think, but every year they come back."

I kept watching as vee after vee of geese surged north. I might never hunt again, but I understood I had witnessed something pure and rare and lovely, something that seemed to assure my return to this place.

The Territories was in me the same way Lawrence's soup was in my belly. He seemed to know it too, in his barely-there smile. I was covered in goose shit, standing by a beater Chev with broken bits of machinery and tools in the back, on the edge of a nameless lake with a boy I hardly knew. He didn't touch me. He just stood there, our shoulders even, looking up at the brief passage of birds.

I felt at home in a way I had never been before. I wanted that moment to go on and on and never be lost, but without a word to each other we climbed into his truck and headed back to town.

~

We had another strange encounter before summer. In Grade Eleven we were allowed to take semester-long optional courses. Coincidentally, Lawrence and I both chose drama. Beside math, a full year course, we were finally in another class together. Mr. Puce was our teacher. I have no recollection of ever performing a play or attempting a musical. Mr. Puce, however, acted out his own fantasies in that twice a week, two-hour time slot while the sun was gone from the sky.

We called him Mr. Puke. He had two leisure suits, which he alternated: the first a pastel blue and the second a festive Hawaiian print on a fabric that may have been gabardine. Both suits had flared bell-bottomed legs that swished across our faces as we lay on the floor in the drama room darkness, as Mr. Puce's hushed cigarette voice spoke of visualizing, fantasizing, and actualizing, the holy trinity of actors everywhere.

Our teacher did actualize on a day in late May, a few weeks after our hunting expedition, when the possibility of warmth was seeping through the cracks of the territorial high school, enticing skippers and smokers to abandon their books and head to the bush.

"I have after-school passes for any of you who would like to come to my home for a movie," said Puke. He was speaking to the whole class but aiming his invitation at the kids who lived in the Hall. They were always looking for passes.

Lawrence raised his hand. He did, so I did, too.

I tagged along, with three boys from Akaitcho. Puke had a two-bedroom apartment up in the rocks, between the only high-rise — named Fraser Arms but forever called The High Rise — and the radio station. The building was called Raven's Court, subsidized housing for temporary northerners.

His apartment was a kitchen and a living room combo. "This is it, little friends," said Mr. Puke in an affected British accent. "Not a mansion, by any means, but my personal studio is just down this way." He motioned us to follow down a short hallway to a bedroom. We stood at the door frame and gaped.

Mr. Puce had two queen-sized mattresses on the floor, squished together so the entire space was one large bed. On the wall opposite, the single curtained window held an enormous television, turned off, and on the other wall in specialized shelving, were racks and racks of VHS videotapes.

I glanced at our host. His plump face was often florid, but it seemed more flushed than usual. I noticed his perpetually pursed lips, a purple vein on his downturned lower lip, pulsating in its liquid bowl. He chuckled and his toad throat vibrated while we stood and gawked, and then, with a sweep of his hand, he propelled us inside the room.

Except, I ducked. I ducked under his arm.

"I have homework, too much, and chores, and yeah, I said I'd help a friend with her essay, so I've got to run. Sorry. Can't stay for the movie."

I backed down the hall, scrambled into my shoes, and shut the door as nervous laughter issued from inside the apartment. I left Lawrence and his friends with our drama teacher. I didn't know what else to do, or who to tell, so I just went home and pretended it hadn't happened.

I have thought often about Puce and some of the other teachers in Yellowknife in those early years. Some of them were likely recruited by my father, and some just presented themselves with seemingly fine qualifications. I later wondered if they were adequately vetted or if the positions were filled with whatever warm bodies seemed the most likely to stay.

What I do recognize now is many of those northern teachers were young, some just seven to ten years older than their students. Many education graduates gained useful experience in the North but sought urban posts once they had a year or two under their belts. Isolation, mental health challenges, addictions — the North can exacerbate these very human issues. Despite social and emotional tolls, many fine teachers fell in love with the North and its people and stayed to share their expertise. Conversely, other teachers, rejected in the South for reasons I cannot begin to speculate upon, came north for work and left an unbearable legacy of grief in their wake.

Alone

In June 1975, the kids from Akaitcho Hall went home, Lawrence among them. We never talked about the goose hunt or what happened, if anything, at Mr. Puce's apartment.

I lay in bed thinking about me and Lawrence as a unit, and my usual habit of world building and fantasy overcame reality. The gangly, slope-gaited, soft-spoken teenager transformed into a mysterious warrior imbued with spiritual powers. He didn't just take me hunting, he taught me the value of the natural world; he offered tobacco to the spirit of the goose soup; he semi-morphed into the Dettah man who drove us into town after we almost froze to death. No longer in town and not returning for at least two months, Lawrence went from a kid with a shy presence to a stealthy hunter, all necessary virtues bestowed by my own overactive imagination, which had galloped from everyday common happenstance into the realm of high romance.

I think, for me, even as a teenager, my imaginative world felt safer than the real world, steeped as it seemed to be in unknowable sexual and physical threat. I preferred my imaginative world, and it was there the flip side of racism, the noble savage, showed itself.

I thought of Lawrence constantly through July and August in the languid nights of midnight sun. Whatever had transpired between us suddenly felt fully sealed, destined. We'd waltzed around each other for years, from that moment in the back of the trading post, to Maryanne's birthday, to the dead horse, to our recent encounter in math class. Now we had hunted. True, I hadn't stayed to witness what transpired at the Puce apartment, but we would talk about that later. Things were different. Both of us were ready, and I decided when he returned our relationship should be lived out in the open. I thought I was in love, but I had no idea if he felt the same way. I couldn't wait for my final year of school, for his return.

Nights were particularly interminable. I flipped back the covers, figuring I could feign a headache and go talk to my sister, Jennifer. She was almost twenty-years-old and back north for the summer holidays, after two full years at the University of British Columbia. We were getting along well enough that I thought perhaps she could advise me in matters of the heart.

Rather than go to her, I paused, recalling Jennifer's Yellowknife departure after a gap year working in a sign shop. It had been a singularly unremarkable event. Like my eldest brother, the first sibling to leave the Territories, Jenny left mid-August on a huge blue-and-white Pacific Western airplane the summer after my only real academic success, the prize for the still mortifying "Pride of My People." It was the same summer Maryanne and I rescued the pup.

I think my parents assumed we would all eventually leave the North. Even though it was the only place my sister knew, she seemed so casual about leaving. I lay in bed remembering our farewell, the way Jennifer hugged my parents hard and then left, just left.

She looked so beautiful as she departed, beautiful and brave. The wind from the propellers whipped her navy pantsuit against her lean body, but her Jackie-O headband kept her hair from flying out of control. She was carrying a black leather briefcase, a parting gift from my parents, and she looked entirely grown-up. My sister was going to earn a degree in arts with an eye to law school, and I remember wondering as she waved goodbye if she even saw the pink rocks and the blue lakes and the gravel roads and the little clutch of people who loved her. Jennifer was single-minded. She let me in when, and only when, she wanted to.

For months before her departure, she had been poring over books about Vancouver. She had circled the patch of green that represented her university residence and had earmarked sites she planned to visit.

"This is Granville Island Market," she told me, pointing to a photograph of an Asian lady shaking a bunch of radishes at a man in a frayed apron.

"This is Gastown."

I squinted at an image of an old-fashioned lantern perched on a pole.

"Why is it called that? Don't they have electricity?"

Jennifer flipped the page, unwilling to admit her own ignorance. She had earmarked a scene of two people walking along a sidewalk by the ocean. "That will be me," she said. "The seawall, the seawall at Stanley Park. Yeah, maybe, if you visit, we'll stroll there."

"Stroll?"

"That's what you do in Vancouver. You stroll the seawall."

"Can't you just walk?"

I must have said that just to annoy her.

"Of course you can. Look at these two" — a couple of silhouettes, holding hands — "that's what they're doing."

Jennifer was anxious to leave and seemed ready. She looked so determined. And my parents looked determined to let her go, too. When she walked across the runway, she only looked back at us once, just before she mounted the stairs to the airplane. There on the tarmac, Jennifer gave a little queen wave, squared her shoulders, and left the North. It seemed completely natural and entirely easy.

Now she was back. Had she strolled the seawall? Had she held hands with a real flesh-and-blood male, not the mysterious silhouetted boy from the magazine? Would Lawrence and I hold hands when he came back? Would we kiss? Just thinking about Lawrence and my uncertainty around his true feelings gave me such a stab of pain, I didn't have to lie to my parents about the headache. I needed to confide in someone, and Jennifer seemed my best bet.

I moved towards my bedroom door and opened it carefully, quietly.

My parents were still up, a sign that something was amiss. I huddled at the bathroom door listening for Jennifer's voice. But no, she, too, had been sent to her basement room. Could

I get to her without them knowing? I barely breathed, and in the silence, I heard my parent's conversation, serious and low.

"You can't blame yourself, Norm. Some are made like that, hell bent on self-destruction."

Ice swirled in a glass. My father was not a drinking man, especially this late at night.

"I had no idea. What can we tell the staff? Come on, Ethel. Try to imagine."

"I won't pretend it's not difficult, but if he'd spoken out, if he'd seen a counsellor… You have people to deal with this sort of situation, don't you?"

"He didn't trust them. Obviously, he couldn't speak. It wasn't part of his cultural conditioning."

There came the ice sound again.

"Norm, no one put a rope around his neck. No one kicked away the chair. I won't have you implicated in this. People die. He might have been mentally unbalanced. You have to get a hold of yourself. This is an isolated incident. You must deal with it practically. It's not the first time. I'm sorry. There's no other way."

"Eth …" his voice was strangled. I rattled the bathroom doorknob on purpose, walked toward the living room.

"Margie?"

"I've got a headache and can't sleep. Where is Jen? What's going on?"

My questions shifted the energy in the room. My father sat back in his chair as my mother sprang into action. I was hastened back into the shadowed hallway to take a pill and have a pee. I asked for a back rub, too, in order to forestall more conversation between them. I was surprised when my mother agreed.

She sat on my bed, and I was ten again. As I felt her hand go round and round on my back, I knew she loved me and she loved my father, too. I knew she would protect him at all costs, and while I didn't know precisely what they were talking about, I knew something had altered.

Much later I learned that one of the custodians, a local man, had hanged himself in the boiler room of the school. It wasn't a kid, thank God, but my father blamed himself. Was he having doubts about the federal mandate to educate in English, regardless of the costs? I never asked him that question. I'm not even sure I could have formed it at the time.

I also never talked to Jennifer about my burgeoning romance. She left for her third year at UBC before we had a chance to connect.

⌇

A few weeks later, my father had a heart incident. It happened on his way to work. It was minor, two days in the hospital, a battery of tests. The mild heart attack was chalked up to stress and job pressures. A few days after the results were returned, I learned my father had been transferred to Ottawa, the capital of Canada. It was the place Trudeau lived with his child bride, Margaret, the Princess of Canada. I thought of my father's new placement at the Department of Indian and Northern Affairs as a calling up, maybe Trudeau himself surveying his company of civil servants and selecting some unlikely candidate to come to the palace and sit next to him on the throne. That he would choose my father didn't completely surprise me. He was the servant king, after all, the centre around which our family revolved. But that he would go, that my father would surrender his own cold kingdom for something unknown, puzzled me.

Their decision to leave had a lot to do with timing. Jennifer was well settled at UBC, and as a long-time resident of the Territories, she was eligible for grant money, enough to pay her tuition and give her a modest living allowance while in school. The funded education system encouraged Territorial students to return north following their post-secondary education, in order to bring much needed skills back to the towns and settlements. For every year a university graduate worked in the Territories, two years of debt was forgiven.

Paul was in the process of paying off a university debt. He'd finished his first degree at the University of Saskatchewan and, tired of school, was intent on making money. He was taking a gap year, working on Baffin Island building an airstrip.

Will had also just graduated. He'd saved enough money working summers in the mine to get a Eurail Pass and was determined to see the Europe of his social studies textbook. Ned would go with my parents.

I had one year left in high school. My fate was the slippery fish, the one that refused to be caught, and if caught, slithered from the shore back towards the lake. I couldn't imagine leaving.

"I don't want to be a new girl in Grade Twelve. I can't do it. Plus, there's Grade Thirteen out there. I'm almost finished here. I want to stay. Please, please, I'm almost seventeen. Men went to war at seventeen. Please!"

My mother: "Seventeen."

My father: "You are not a soldier." His eyes softened. "Besides Margie, you're sixteen, your birthday is four months away, and we have a responsibility to you. You'll like Ottawa. An adventure."

"I don't want an adventure. If I did, I'd choose an adventure like Will's, travelling on my own."

"On your own," my mother repeated, lemon juice in milk, curdling even as she spoke.

"But I'm not really on my own if I stay here. I mean, look, this is home. This is where I'm from. What can happen here? Nothing happens here. Ever. I finish Grade Twelve and then I can decide, right?" I paused, adding the kicker. "If I do all my schooling here, Grade One through Twelve, I'll get a full grant. I can go on. I can continue my education and it won't cost you guys a cent."

"There's that." My father seemed to be considering my pitch. "Where will you live?"

Before I thought, it came out. The place all unanchored children lived, the place Lawrence lived. The place I could see him more often. "Akaitcho Hall. The Hostel."

This seemed to please my dad, but had an instantly adverse effect on my mother.

"Akaitcho? Are you kidding, Margie? You have no idea what that would be like, living in those circumstances."

"Lots of kids go there," I countered. And then to appease her. "Lots of white kids, too."

"She's right, Ethel." My dad sucked on his pipe and tapped some of the embers out into the large amber ashtray reserved for serious after-supper conversations. They both knew RCMP kids and the children of Arctic teachers were sent to Yellowknife to get their high-school diplomas. My father was reflective. "I'm sure there would be others. And the system is set up so that anyone who needs to can attend. This is the twentieth century, 1975, and our girl can meet that square-shouldered."

He turned back to me. "Do you really want to stay, Margie? It would be a huge change. The house will go to the next Director of Education. There won't be any family around. Jennifer has almost got her grant paid off, so she may not return, and I suspect Will might eventually come to his senses and move south to get an education."

My mother started to clear the table, a sure sign our family discussion was over. She was not interested in my answer. She fussed, stacking plates and saucers noisily, gathering utensils that clattered across serving dishes.

"It's just wrong," she muttered, and then her voice rose. "This is not some sort of social experiment, Norm. Our daughter will not be a lab rat in one of your cross-cultural experiments. Margie will not be raised with a bunch of others who have been largely under-parented. How can you think that some government-appointed matron could do for our own daughter what we can? Be reasonable, Norm, for heaven's sake."

My father pushed back his chair. "So, what's good enough for them is not good enough for us? I think quite the opposite, Ethel. I think leaving Margie in the residence for her final year will speak loudly to the policy of equal education for all. It's what we've been working toward all along."

My mother was shaking, she was so angry. Her voice was constricted. "Our daughter is not here to get your name in the history books. She is not to be experimented upon. We have no idea what happens in that place, not really. Oh, I know you think institutions can be like second homes, but they can't be, Norm, they just can't. Trust me. There's no..." she floundered around, looking for a word. "... There's no commitment to the children."

"Sure, there is." I was thinking of living down the hall from Lawrence.

My mother glared at me and then turned to my father. "Help me in the kitchen."

⌇

I did get to stay in town my final year of high school, but I did not get to live in the Hostel. Instead, I was boarded with the Community Church minister and his wife, a couple who rented out two basement rooms in their modest bungalow.

"They're very nice," my mother explained, sitting me down in the kitchen, perching across, looking directing into my eyes. "They are friends of the Maples. You remember Ross and Diane Maple? You babysat for them all through junior high. Well, it's their pastor and his wife, the McKnights. Apparently, they take in boarders, but only a certain type of boarder. They have young kids, and Margie, they were thrilled, just thrilled, when we talked about an eight-month term."

It felt like my mother was trying to sell me something, when in fact, I believe she was trying to sell herself on the idea of leaving me in the North. I wasn't thrilled — who the hell were the McKnights? My religious encounter with Padre flashed through my brain, making me wince. My mother misunderstood, laid her hand on my shoulder. "It's just for a few months."

"Sure, Mom. Temporary. I get it." And I did. This was the only solution my parents could agree upon, some good Christian family looking for a teenage boarder/babysitter. It wasn't ideal, but at least I got to stay.

Packing boxes and crates with Allied Van Lines printed on their plain faces soon filled the house. Because it seemed impossible that my parents should leave this place we'd always known, I paid little mind to their actual leaving and was caught unaware when their departure date came.

Unlike my sister and brother before, my parents opted to drive out. They left at the end of the third week in August, on an overcast day. It was mid-morning, and they were getting a late start in what was anticipated to be an eight-day drive, down the Mackenzie Highway, across the prairies, and then the three-day journey traversing Ontario.

Ned, who would start Grade Ten in Ottawa, hugged me quickly as the car idled outside the McKnight's manse. "Visit soon," he said, folding his big-boy frame into a nest of blankets and comics in the back seat. "It's going to be weird without the rest of you guys."

My father had separated my two suitcases from the rest and set them outside on the lawn. The McKnights were out, giving our family privacy for this farewell.

My meeting with the McKnights two weeks earlier had been okay. My room was in the basement. There was a downstairs bathroom, mostly mine but shared with the other boarder, a person called Mike who worked "up north" and only returned one weekend out of four. The McKnights *were* nice, their kids polite and shy. They seemed happy enough to leave me alone. My parents wrote some cheques. That was it.

In the driveway Dad came up from behind and squeezed my shoulder, turning me towards him. "You can call us any-time, kiddo, and your mum and I will plan to fly you south at Christmas. Study hard, Margie. Make this year count." He embraced me in a quick bear hug and then stepped back, as my mother moved towards me.

She folded me into her chest and began to weep immediately. Tears filled my own eyes.

"You'll like it, Mummy. It's a city. More like the place you grew up," I comforted.

Why had I asked for this? It suddenly felt too painful, too impossible to manage.

My mother drew me back and cupped my face between her hands. She studied me, disregarding the tears that spilled down her own cheeks. Her eyes were intensely bright, and they darted back and forth, as though she was memorizing me.

"Don't let this get in your way. It is a temporary thing. You're still our girl and you've got friends in the community. The Johnstons will have you over every Sunday and the Lorimers and Mr. and Mrs. Patterson. Go to church, brush your teeth, don't forget to write. Your dad and I love you, Margie. We'll call you as soon as we arrive." She glanced at the McKnight house and turned back to me. Her hands tightened on my face and a terrible sob caught in her throat.

"Relax, Mum. It will be fine," I said, even though, at that moment, I was not entirely sure.

My dad leaned across and pushed open the passenger door of the Rambler, a new-to-them vehicle, tuned up for the long journey south. She stumbled into the car. Dad rolled down his window. "It's eight months, kid, eight short months. They've got it all set up for you inside." He nodded toward the house and then pushed in the clutch and found first. The car moved away slowly, and I made myself stay still, the impulse to run after them overwhelming.

I watched my parents pull around the gravel drive and turn towards Franklin Avenue. I imagined Airport Road,

Lakeview Cemetery where my mother always crossed herself even though we weren't Catholics. I imagined the turnoff to Long Lake. They were leaving it, and me, behind.

～

The first few weeks were odd, everything askew. I organized my small basement room, bought a box of granola bars to eat on the way to school in lieu of breakfast, and interacted as little as possible with the McKnights. I was attempting to be completely grown-up. This was the life I had asked for; this independence at the age of sixteen was what I wanted. Or so I thought.

It was twilight even though only four-thirty in the after-noon, and it was only the end of September. Instead of going back to my room in the basement of the McKnights, I headed towards our old house. Nothing had changed. The route I'd walked a thousand times still seemed like the way home. When I got to the street of our old house, I crossed to the other side and walked past it, slowly allowing myself to remember. An enormous sense of loneliness gathered as I gazed at the house so familiar and yet now foreign. I held the loneliness in on purpose, kept it there as long as I could stand, until it climbed my spine to prickle at my eyes, coughing and claw-ing its way out my throat.

It would have spilled, too, except there was a shadow man loping down the sidewalk towards me. I recognized his gait, the tiny list to the left, and I felt my heart rate speed, a throttle on a Ski-Doo. It was Lawrence.

"Hey." He was wearing a full-length beige overcoat, too big, and he pressed his arms into his side, shivering. "What are you doing out?"

"I used to live here."

He looked at the house.

"Nice place."

"It was."

He bent his head forward, looked into my face. I swallowed hard, trying not to let him see the double wave of emotion intersect in my eyes, the meeting of sorrow and excitement.

"It's hard." He stood beside me and we both looked up at the house. The living room light glowed orange behind a drawn curtain. "I've been coming to Yellowknife on and off all my life. I got polio when I was four." He said it casually like he caught a fish, or a bird.

"I spent lots of time in hospital here," Lawrence continued. "I thought I was done with that. Now I'm back, an inmate."

I couldn't talk, so I nodded. He continued to look at the lit window as he spoke.

"I should go back. I could walk you to your place first and then go. They're strict." He touched me lightly on the back, so I could barely feel the brief outline of his hand beneath my jacket, steering. We turned at the same time and walked together through the quiet streets towards my new home.

We didn't speak. Instead, we walked, in easy rhythm. I noticed his slight limp and the way he swung his arms. I also noticed something sad in his eyes, but the loneliness in him comforted and cancelled the loneliness in me.

Community

There were no dances or movies, no long conversations on the telephone, no physical intimacy beyond proximity. Lawrence and I just hung out. It may have had something to do with the absence of my parents. There was no one to judge my relationship, no one to question my choices, and in that was a certain reckless freedom.

Lawrence could get away for weekends. His mother's sister-aunt, Maryanne's mum, still lived in Willow Flats. She'd married a second time, a Quebecois pipefitter from the mine, and because of that union, her rights as a Tłįchǫ had been extinguished. I didn't quite understand it. She wasn't considered Indigenous anymore, but she wasn't white either. How could the law be that stupid?

With relatives in town, Lawrence had what the supervisors called an appropriate placement, giving him easy access to weekend passes and the freedom to shed the institutional routine and roam the town Friday night through Sunday afternoon, a free man, unshackled from the Hostel and its list of chores.

The boarding situation at the manse was quite straightforward. I had been given a key to the front door and told I could come and go as I pleased. The house was a split-level; the pastor and his wife and their two small children lived upstairs. I was welcome to join them for meals. I lived downstairs near the laundry room and furnace. By the time I turned seventeen in January 1976, I was, for all intents and purposes, living as an independent adult. The McKnights never questioned my whereabouts, and it was nothing to quietly slip out and make my way over the rocks to Maryanne's, where Lawrence and his friends hung out.

It didn't matter that Maryanne's mother's house was super small either, because on those weekends, the group of us slept wherever we found ourselves, at the Singing Swede's shack, or the Pott's place in the Woodlot, or down at One-eyed Tony's in Peace River Flats.

Lawrence knew everyone and he could always find a party, a crib game, or some smoky talk about hunting and guns, an event told and retold while a bottle of rye circulated among the gathered, along with laughter and lots of ribbing.

Most of the people I met were related to Lawrence's extended family in some second-cousin way, and the easy teasing never stopped, particularly when it became obvious that we were always together.

"You and him, you live together, yeah, in the Hall?" probed one of the older aunties at a Saturday night gathering. "You sneak into his dorm room, keep his bones warm at night?" And the group chuckled before I could explain that I didn't live there. They laughed as though this was the most natural thing in the world, not something shrouded in burning mystery.

We were only able to meet in town. He couldn't — or at least, didn't -- invite me to the Hostel and I couldn't invite him to the McKnights. Perhaps it was only in the company of others he felt comfortable admitting an association with me. I didn't know why, but he often alerted me to his weekend passes and implied I should try to meet him. It was an invitation for us to be together in the town that somehow had become more his than mine.

He knew people. I knew places. If we were to be alone, it was always outside. I showed him trails across the rocks that led to secret keyhole gullies, soft with moss and lichen in the summer, sheltered from the wind in the winter. I liked to find private places where we could rest and talk.

"You know your way around."

I blushed. It seemed the highest praise. "I was raised here, and I used to walk a lot. To get away." He didn't ask from what. Lawrence was never direct; he just left the space for me to tell more.

"I think that's the worst thing about being in Akaitcho," he said. "Not being able to go when I want. Not being able to walk."

I nodded in agreement. "I like being out." I looked off toward the trees and kept my eyes focused on the distance before I finished. "With you. I like being out with you."

He looked at me sideways, semi-smiling, and I felt compelled to continue. "You know lots of people and it's fun to be part of your circle."

"Yeah, it's open." And I didn't know if he meant it was open to anyone or if it was open just for me, but as I waited for an answer, I realized it didn't really matter. It was up to me to claim my own space.

The invitation to hang out meant I was welcomed into a series of warm houses, often with the generosity of shared food. We waited for the older people to eat first, and when they were finished, we would eat while they filled their pipes and began to tell stories, some which took so long in the telling, I'd lose track of who was who, and the original point of the story would become fuzzy. It didn't matter that I didn't understand. "The stories are part of something else. They are told over and over so you notice the smallest differences," said Lawrence. He pointed at his head. "Once they get in your thinking, they get into your doing." He pointed to his chest. "One of the lessons."

"Lessons?"

"You call them laws, like your ten shall-nots."

I looked at an old man, knowing he could easily be the man from the trading post, Archie. He was lit from the window where the moon reflected off snow on the lake, and the light animated his face. He seemed to pull each rumbling word from the shadows of the darkened room. He was talking about bad medicine, about a wolverine, or maybe it was about a woman who was like a wolverine, but everyone was hanging on his words. Or maybe, like me, they were trying to figure out what he meant.

"Why don't you live out?" I asked one night as Lawrence

and I nested together on an old sagging sofa in the basement of the Saunders'. "Living out would be way more fun."

"At home, they don't need someone else to feed every day," he explained. "At the Hall it doesn't cost nothing, and as long as I can come out on weekends, it works best. My auntie, she's already got four kids, and she's looking after two of my cousin's babies, granddaughters. At the Hall, someone else feeds you, gives you allowance, takes care of books and pencils and all the things they say we need, so why not?" And then he was quiet again.

He'd once said his original community was small, just one road and twenty-two buildings, less than three hundred people all together. "We get together in the summer," he'd said. I tried to imagine everyone being related to each other, a big summer camp, an eight-week family reunion.

Except, there was no highway. Few came in or out. What would happen if he brought me back? Not that he'd indicated any inclination to ask. I'd been to Dettah, but I couldn't imagine living in a place so small. I just couldn't.

～～

On a Saturday morning just before finals, I sat in the Miners Mess nursing a coffee. I was hoping to run into Lawrence. Meanwhile I was reading social studies notes on John Cabot and the New World.

That's where I was going, the New World. My parents had called, inviting me out to Ottawa. They were happily settled in the South, and although he was still relatively young in 1976, my dad was playing with the idea of an early retirement.

If Ottawa was the New World, what was this place? With Lawrence and his friends, it felt ancient. Or maybe this was the Old World if you were Indigenous, and I'd discovered it accidently. With home gone, Yellowknife felt like a place with no maps. Did John Cabot think his boat would fall off the edge of the world when he left England to sail to Canada? I imagine that edge, the Territorial border, the way Alexandra Falls dropped clean and frothing into the Hay River.

Louise Falls was further along the highway. They were large waterfalls, too, but not quite as dramatic. When I told Lawrence I'd been there, he said it was a sacred place and the twin falls were a Grandmother and Grandfather who guarded the river. Lawrence called the place *Hatto deh Naili*, yet according to my textbooks, Alexandra and Louise were daughters of an English King. Cabot made up new names for things he saw. I couldn't imagine the Grandmother and Grandfather spirit people liking that very much. *Who are you, that you should rename what is already named?*

I wondered about Carmel, what her name was before Eleanor Johnston named her. I thought about the Caribou Queen, the real woman, the one who butchered caribou on Back Bay long before she got caught in town troubles, long before the terrible incident that left Sophie Football dead in a snowbank. What was the Old World like, before us? What ever happened to the son, the boy in the black-and-white photograph? Did that woman bring him back? Would I ever know?

ᶜᵕᵕ

Lawrence and I were walking down Franklin on what was to be my last spring in Yellowknife when someone leaned out the window of a baby-blue half-ton and hollered, "Stick with your own kind, wagon burner."

The insult was a full body flame. I felt it sear us, like trout in a fry pan, the open fire licking and spitting all the greasy hatred of the world. We couldn't see the guy — it was a guy of course, a chick would do it privately, a mean whisper behind the back — but it didn't really matter because our briefly linked hands flew apart and the cold air between them was the difference again; after all the time building up the sameness, I felt the difference.

The truck was a clue. A white guy, an old classmate, probably drove it, maybe a cat skinner or slag hauler at the mines. Whoever he was, he was an asshole.

My hand, swinging empty for that crazy minute, felt like it was no longer attached to my body, so I pulled it into my pocket, giving myself a hug for comfort. Neither of us said anything. We just kept walking. When Lawrence nudged me up the hill between the rocks, I knew it was to get us off the main street and nearer the bush.

The road was not much more than a cutline blasted out of the rocks. It went past St. Pat's between Franklin and the Department of Public Works sheds where the town stored their graders and snowplows.

My brothers and I used to call the place Sand Valley because there were steep dunes behind the yard. When we were kids, we would launch ourselves off the top of the cliffs, crying out as the dirt near the edge crumbled underfoot. These were staged falls, a steep tumble into relative softness, the sand billowing applause. The possibility of hitting the gravel, of skidding off course, was what made the performances worthwhile. Gravel burns and scraped knees were badges of courage, battle scars. Now Sand Valley was the less travelled way back to the Hall, an overland shortcut between the plains of the New Town and the descent to the Old Town.

Lawrence turned to go back. After waiting all week, waiting for this chance to hang out, he was turning back before we got to spend any time together.

He didn't say anything. He normally talked about half as much as I did, but he was even quieter than normal. His face looked completely immobile. Anger was caught in my throat so my words couldn't get around.

"Don't go yet," I said, watching Lawrence's eyes. "We can go there, to the shed. My brothers and I used to hang out on the roof all the time."

Lawrence looked at the Public Works shed, with its one side open to the yard, the other built tight to the rocks. He could see the easy leap to the roof, but his eyes lingered on the high fence and the locked gate.

"We go around. I know a way. Come on." I urged.

He shrugged. "It's your town." He was right. And I was suddenly happy again. I knew my way around the bush, and I could find my way to the back of the compound where no fences had been built. The roof would be warm and private. Maybe we could talk.

I crashed recklessly through the bush, which was thick with brambles. A rosebush tore at my leg and I felt a thin line of blood rising to the surface of my shin, but still I pressed forward. If Lawrence continued behind me, if we could get to the roof, we could sit and rest in the sun and the whole Goddamn town could disappear.

He was still following, but more carefully, so there wasn't the throwback of branches, nor the give of rotten logs, the crunch of windfall underfoot. I was the one making all the noise, crashing through the bush pursued by the desperate knowledge that our relationship might end before it really began.

The leap to the roof was easy, the gap between the crumbling cliff edge and the solid asphalt shingles maybe three feet wide, but I paused at the edge, waited for Lawrence to stand beside me.

"If we stay on this side, no one can see us from the road."

He looked at me quizzically, a frown dancing between his eyebrows, as though not being seen hadn't crossed his mind. Still, he said nothing.

"You go first," I urged.

Why was I so keen to get to that safe place? The insult was still stinging. We needed to talk about what it meant, what to do. *Stick with your own kind.* I wanted us to be two beings, two humans, but somehow, someone else had decided we should not be together based on our race. Someone had shouted insults at Lawrence, at me, out the window of a moving vehicle, and yet there was no denying both of us had dropped our joined hands instantly, as though the driver were right.

Lawrence leapt the gap easily. He landed softly, bending ever so slightly at the waist. He was feline: all long muscles and fluid movements. It made me suddenly self-conscious. There wasn't a single catlike quality in my body. I was all dog, a Labrador retriever, like my dad, or some crossbred mutt because of my more refined Mother. I may embody the leaping loyalty of dogs, but not grace, not in the body. *Stick with your own kind.*

I looked down. There was a twelve-foot drop to the ground and in the valley between the building and the cliff edge, still patches of winter ice. The sun never got in there. I cleared the gap in one solid leap. I landed more heavily than Lawrence and held out both hands to break my fall, but he didn't notice, or if he did, didn't say anything. We were on the asphalt tiles, the warm, sunbaked roof.

I settled first and he folded himself down next to me.

"I don't know why I like it here. I just do. No wind, no other people, just the sun. My brothers and I used to jump from that cliff across the yard, over there. See who could have the most realistic falls. We pretended we were being filmed, our falls, like in a Western, and we'd, you know, be as dramatic as we could." I suddenly missed my brothers. Even though she rarely played with us, I suddenly missed my big sister, too. I think in some deep way I knew this was the season of endings.

There was silence.

Why did everything I say sound so pathetic? Lawrence's mouth moved. It could have been a smile, but if it was, I think he was remembering his younger self. He wasn't thinking of me at all.

I lay down then, near the top of the pitch, and spread my legs, winter white beneath my cut-offs. I'd like to see his legs, his beautiful skin, but he was in jeans, and as I thought about it, I realized I'd never seen him in anything else.

The warmed shingles smelled faintly of tar. Lawrence stood and strolled to the other side of the low-pitched roof, looking into the yard.

"My uncle drove one of those things." Was he looking at a grader? A backhoe?

"Did he work for the town?" At least we were having a conversation. At least he was trying.

"For a time."

"Cool." I guess it was cool.

He turned back towards me, and with a movement both graceful and shockingly efficient, he sat down again.

"When you opened the Hostel, it was all about heavy-duty equipment. Vocational school, perfect for Indians."

"I didn't open it."

He looked at me, and his face softened. "No. Your dad, I guess. Making mechanics. Everyone coming out of the bush to go to school here, hoping they'd get the one job back in their settlement, driving the water truck." He looked back out to the parked machinery, two large yellow Cats; two graders; one without a blade, a backhoe with a rusted bucket; and three pickup trucks with snowplows attached to their bumpers. "Funny place to want to come, a work yard."

The need to defend my choice rose, but instead I looked at him straight on. "You heard what that guy said to us, what he shouted from the truck?"

One of his shoulders twitched, almost imperceptible. His eyes gave nothing away. Still, I continued.

"I just thought, here, you know, it is private. We could talk."

"About?"

"What he said. About what's going to happen. Exams are in a few days. The break-up dance, the hostel will clear out. Everyone will go back."

"Yeah. So?"

"So what's going to happen then? To you? To me?"

Lawrence lay back against the roof, the centre of his head balanced on the ridgeline, hair flopping backwards. Was he going to pretend he didn't hear me? When he spoke, he looked straight up at the sky.

"I was going to go back north for the summer, but I haven't decided for sure. I'll go for a while, but I might come back here. There's more opportunity here." His head turned towards me. "You got to go on. It's your turn to leave, go south, see what's out there, more school, right?" He indicated the bush, trembling around us, and I felt tears again. He had stated something I'd known. That I would leave, that I was raised to leave.

"I've got a flight, a ticket, but I'm not ready. I like this. I like it here." A single tear escaped and landed on the warm asphalt shingle between us. "And so, this was nothing?"

He sat up then. He threw his long arm around my shoulders. "Hey. It was not nothing. It will never be nothing. It's always been for now."

"Not for later."

"I don't live in later."

We sat, something unsettled between us. The tears dried and the wind rose. Lawrence spoke again.

"You're right, it is nice here. Quiet."

"For now," I said, taking the initiative, feeling my anger. "Is it always that way for you, just for now? That guy in the truck, he's an idiot. So, some people think we shouldn't be together, so what, right? Or is that what you think, too? Is that why you don't want people in the Hall to know about me? You don't want people to know you've got a white girlfriend. Is that it? I'm an embarrassment to you?"

Lawrence closed his eyes. Was he blocking me out, or just digesting my words? And why had I said girlfriend? We'd never even kissed.

The sun low in the sky struck the broad plains of his face, and his body, stretched out long and open, instantly made me want to gather those words back inside my mouth. Maybe he didn't think of us that way, a unit, an item, something that could last. Maybe the drama was all inside my head, where it should have stayed. Maybe this relationship came out of my own longing. My loneliness.

A bird called above the sand cliffs and there was stirring in the bush, a hare or a fox perhaps, and still Lawrence lay still beside me, saying nothing, his face neutral.

"Look, I'm sorry. It's just that ..."

I was about to tell him I could go north with him for the summer, that we could stay together, when he pressed ever so slightly on my hand. There were two men down below us, walking around the yard. They had on government-issue coveralls, and they were inspecting one of the machines. They must have come from the shed because their appearance was sudden. Lawrence's hand still rested lightly on my wrist, and he smiled up at me.

We were immediately in cahoots, in perfect conspiratorial alignment. No one could see us lying on the sun-side of the roof in the late afternoon, and now silence was the only appropriate measure, because we were trespassers, trespassers together on government property.

I wrestled my hand from beneath his and turned it, palm up and held on. Our hands fit. His fingers were long and slender, the knuckles perfect joints, slightly bulbous, but they left me just enough room to weave my fingers between his, to slip in-between each finger, eliminating space. We remained still, breathing in unison, listening while the men moved between the machines, talking among themselves of delays and deliveries and the aggravations of getting adequate service in the North.

Nothing else matters but now, I thought. Nothing but this moment, and just as this realization was fully upon me, we were spotted.

"Hey," shouted the man below. "What the hell are you kids doing up there?"

And Lawrence was up on his feet and pulling me after him, so this time we leapt the gap together and plunged, laughing, into the bush, our future embodied in that simple getaway.

For Now

I've said there was no intimacy, but that night we conspired
to sleep side by side on the June-warmed rocks of Jolliffe
Island. Together Lawrence and I witnessed the entire sky
wrap around our eyes and very, very briefly a swaddling of ink
with the tiny typeface stars blinked their message of worlds
beyond. Both of us knew it was the last time.

   We placed our borrowed mummy bags next to each other,
mine nearest the circle of stones that held the fire we burned
down. We lay shoulder to shoulder on a bed of spruce boughs,
recently separated from their mother trunks. They smelled of
crushed resin and rosemary, but not quite that. Those boughs
smelled like life, like Lawrence, and the sap from the boughs
spilled stickiness on my bag but I didn't care, because with
our faces to the sky and only the glowing coals to light our

camp, the semi-transparent curtain of night came upon us softly, like no night at all. In the trailing twilight of sunset was a perfect sunrise. The two could not be separated. I lay breathless and astonished, watching the deepening colours of dusk, burnt umber and pink, ghostly green edging into sombre shades of purple, becoming usurped by the yellows and oranges of dawn.

I felt Lawrence's body against mine, sleeping bags between us, and it was enough to be there and to watch the movement of smoke and swirl amid the smells of spring, while all around the dome of sky held the light and refused to let it go.

Silently and together, we watched the day end and begin again.

Something about that last camp and that simultaneous sunset and sunrise made me know how puny we were, humans who lived mostly in great darkness. I saw the brevity of the light flares, their momentary joining, and like the two of us below, entranced, I thought about the blacker latitudes of space where nothing could be known except what was left behind.

Lawrence and I shared that night on Jolliffe Island, but we did not speak about what we had seen. Sleeping rough with the midnight sun as our night light, we closed our mouths, opened our eyes and absorbed both dusk and dawn before sleep came, because it would, and it did.

In the morning the sky was sky again, a dull pewter. Lawrence was not there. His sleeping bag looked like an opened shell, split, something shed and forgotten.

I was cramped and cold and the meltwater around our firepit had frozen, stitching my bag to the icy earth, freezing me in place.

He was gone. It was Sunday morning. There was nothing to do but go back to the basement of the empty manse. I left the sleeping bags as they were, not even sure who he borrowed them from or if he would retrieve them.

⌣⌣

We wrote our exams that week, and the kids from Akaitcho started to leave. Once, twice, sometimes three times a day, the Akaitcho van headed to the airport. Lawrence was one of those students in the van. We never said goodbye properly. He was just there and then not; really there, then really not there.

I headed to the Old Town. What mattered so much to me hadn't mattered to him at all. Or if it mattered, it was only for the moment. He made that clear. At least he was honest. My heart didn't hurt less. The ache was chronic and constant, like someone had dug into my chest with a blunt instrument, a spoon or an ice cream scoop, and pried out my insides, left my heart all connected and still intact, but beating on the surface of my skin. It called out for Lawrence. My heart never stopped calling out for him. But I also knew our relationship was over.

My parents had booked my flight south for the next day. I was packed. I'd said goodbye to the nice McKnights. My term at Sir John had finished.

I wandered through Willow Flats, down Ragged Ass Road to the Pott's place. But it was silent. I crossed Franklin to the other side, cruised through the Woodlot and Peace River Flats. I didn't know what I was looking for or what I needed or even how to comfort myself. Lawrence was back in his community, hundreds of kilometres north on the muddy banks of the Mackenzie River. I was going to Ottawa, and after that, travel, university, something that was not this town, the only place I had known.

I couldn't imagine two more polarized worlds, his and mine, and the space between our futures felt impossible to breach.

Mrs. Anderson's shack was still there, although no one had lived in it for years. The house had been condemned, the sign reading *Not Fit for Human Habitation*. Her wood-pile was depleted, but the chopping block was still there. I wondered briefly why my brothers and I resented that old woman so much.

As I was about to turn and head back up the hill, I heard music playing just beyond the Anderson place. It was coming from a house near the shore, a home Lawrence took me to once back in the winter, one of his aunties, maybe?

I suddenly knew. I wanted to see Maryanne.

I knocked but the door swung ajar. I stepped into the house alone. The tiny kitchen was familiar, and the auntie's name came back. Catholique. Auntie Caty to Lawrence. Through the doorway into the living room, I saw the press of many bodies. I edged forward, made brave by the number of people gathered.

There was a woman in the kitchen, laughing, holding court. It was Carmel Johnston, my childhood playmate. I went to her, stood nearby, almost, but not quite, touching her sleeve. She sensed me and shifted away from the group.

"Oh. You. Still think I should be dead?"

I was staggered, not that she would remember, but that she would confront me so bluntly. The past, my past, was a hot tide rising up my neck. "I ... I ... need to apologize," I stammered. "When your brother died, that day of the funeral, it was wrong, what I thought."

Carmel nodded. She was not going to let it go. She was waiting for me to say more.

"I thought it was you who should have died, instead of him. And I'm sorry. I might have thought it at the time, but it was not true. It has never been true. I don't think that way now."

Carmel met my eyes. "So, what do you think now?"

"I didn't know anything then. I still don't. I only know what I thought was wrong, and I'm sorry. I've started to notice things. Different things."

"Yeah?" she challenged. "What have you noticed?"

What had I noticed? That ever since I was little, I saw people through a lens of colour? That I thought myself better, a superior human for being white? How could I speak these things? In this place? How could I not?

"I met a guy, a Dene guy. He showed me stuff."

"Showed you what?"

"How to be. He showed me how to be."

Carmel nodded. And smiled just a little. "I guess you been hanging out with Indians."

It was a joke, but my heart was so full, I struggled for any response. I wanted to talk to her, really talk.

"I was ... I was ... always wanting to be you, not you, but who you are, the Caribou Queen. I know it sounds pathetic, but that competition, it was something I didn't understand, that I couldn't ... couldn't ... you know, be her ... be you."

She narrowed her eyes "Funny, I had to stop trying to be you to become myself."

"Trying to be me?"

"To be white. It's not a competition. It never was. That's what you guys think, eh? It's always a competition for you. It's not like that. For me, it took a long, long time to know who I was, because of my stepbrothers, Sylvan's death, being brought up in that family."

"What do you mean, competition?"

Carmel leaned closer and the years peeled back. "After Sylvan passed, I had to find my own way, because it couldn't work anymore, them wanting me to be him, and me wanting to be you, and all that shit."

"You wanted to be me?"

She snorted, a halfway laugh, but cruel, too. "You're right. I'm not sure why anyone would want to walk around, nose in the air all the time. Pretty hard to see." She paused, leaned in. "No, not you exactly, but like you."

I struggled to find words, and the only thing that came was a croaking apology. I had caused the division. I had kept us separate. I had to own it. "I'm sorry."

She seemed to consider this, and then nodded slightly.

I looked into Carmel's eyes and then beyond to the movement of the room. There were people, women, men, so many people. Some I knew from hanging with Lawrence, most I didn't know at all, but they were talking and drinking, some dancing, all of them leaning in, interested, engaged. "Maybe I could become a servant, learn stuff. Listen," I said.

Carmel looked puzzled for a moment. "Fuck that. It isn't about that, see? Sure, there are some people you could learn from, I 'spose, but think about caribou. There are lots of them. It's a herd." And then she really did laugh, fully, out loud.

It dawned on me Carmel was talking about community. The people she loved.

In that same moment, I felt my notion of the Caribou Queen lift and float just above my shoulders. She was not the romantic Indigenous princess I fantasized. She wasn't the alcohol-addled prostitute, either. She wasn't the door-to-door ticket seller, or the pageant winner, or the woman on the ice who butchered animals with quick and studied cuts.

I thought about the way the sunset coincided with the sunrise, the long winters of darkness and brief summers of light. The Caribou Queen held both those seasons in perfect balance. It felt like she was there, in the room.

Carmel elbowed me in the ribs. "It's up to you to make it right." She thrust her chin to the people dancing and laughing. "Want to join? Come on."

I was being invited. You had to be invited.

I was being offered the option to begin again. Despite myself. It wasn't forever. I knew I still had lots of work to do. But it was now. For now.

We moved together into the crowd, and just like that, I was there, exactly where I needed to be.

ACKNOWLEDGEMENTS

An earlier version of "Makeover" was published in *Alberta Views Magazine* in 2009.

The careful ministrations of many people over more than a decade have resulted in this book. Its arrival has been tumultuous. It was written, put aside, re-worked in a different genre, abandoned again, revised, and finally rewritten after much re-thinking and unlearning.

To Patrick Lane, who enticed me back to childhood.

To Linda Goyette, who told me the bones were good.

To Laurel Sproule and Katherine Koller, who witnessed and helped shape my clumsy re-construction of memory.

To Writers in Residence, Katherena Vermette and Richard Van Camp who both told me to forge ahead.

To first readers Sharon Kootenay, John Richardson, Lana Whiskeyjack, Elizabeth Haynes, Annelies Pool and Amanda Sokol who parced language and intention and led with gentle direction.

To friend and poet Kathy Fisher who whispered the word memoir long before I could hold that word in my mouth.

To fellow Edmonton writers including Jannie Edwards and the CNF community who coached by their very being.

To those who have encouraged, listened, empathized, commiserated, criticized and cajoled, you know who you are.

To my original family, everyday angels, always at the ready who gracefully gifted me the sharing of their stories.

For financial help over many years my gratitude goes to the Alberta Foundation for the Arts and the Edmonton Arts Council. Both institutions allowed me the tutelage of Sage Hill and the Vancouver Manuscript Intensive.

To Carol Rose GoldenEagle and Rhonda Kronyk and the Indigenous Editors Association for sensitivity reading and for granting space for this story.

Thank you to NeWest Press for taking a chance and to Jennifer Delisle for championing this book.

Thank you to Sinda Abbott for technical savvy.

To Mark and our children, who love despite and because.

And finally, thank you to Creator without whom I would have neither form nor substance.

Raised in Yellowknife (now Denendeh) NWT, Margaret quickly got an education in the real world, traveling extensively in Europe, Australia, and Central America before settling into an English Lit undergraduate degree in the early 80's at the University of New Brunswick, Fredericton. Margaret wrote for periodicals and magazines (as well as being sole employee of a Halifax volunteer-run leftist bookstore) during her eight years in Atlantic Canada before venturing to Bermuda as a full-time reporter.

Returning to Canada in 1992, Margaret embarked on a Master of Fine Arts in Creative Writing from UBC and completed the program as a visiting grad student at Edmonton's U of A. She published a few contract non-fiction books as well as a biography of firebrand Nellie McClung called *Voice for the Voiceless* in the early 2000's but it was the publication of her short story collection *Perilous Departures* that launched her career. Her first novel *Released* followed in 2009 and in 2011 her second novel *Body Trade* won the DeBeers NorthWords Prize for Fiction.

Meanwhile, Margaret acted as a fiction editor of *Other Voices* literary journal, became a driving force in the Alberta Branch of the Canadian Authors Association and was elected the Alberta/NWT Rep for The Writer's Union of Canada. Margaret formed an extraordinary network of creatives during two plus decades in Edmonton, living with her partner and three (occasionally four) children during her middle years she worked as a Writer-in-Residence for the Edmonton Public Library and mentored writers though the Writers Guild of Alberta.

She paints, travels, laughs long and often, and continues to explore and record the mystical communion of living things. Margaret has recently moved to Deep River in northern Ontario to begin her third act with her partner of countless wonderful years.